Introduction to Jazz Piano
A Deep Dive

60 Workouts with Classic Recordings for Building a Strong Foundation

by Jeb Patton

Cover & Book Design, Attila Nagy

©2020 Sher Music Co., P.O. Box 445, Petaluma, CA 94953
SherMusic.com. No part of this book or audio CD may be reproduced
in any form without written permission from the publisher.
All Rights Reserved. International Copyright Secured.
ISBN 978-0-9976617-5-03

*This book is dedicated to the memory of Jimmy Heath,
whose guidance and inspiration will last 100 lifetimes.*

ACKNOWLEDGEMENTS

Special thanks to all of the jazz masters from the recordings referenced within; Jimmy and Mona Heath, and Tootie and Beverly Heath for their love and encouragement; David Wong (bass), Pete Van Nostrand (drums), and Dmitry Baevsky (alto) for their beautiful playing on the play-along mp3s; Tom Tedesco and Tedesco Studios; Chuck Sher and the publishing staff; Attila Nagy for the cover & book design; Antonio Hart, Mike Mossman, David Berkman, and Dennis Mackrel, and all of the professors at Queens College; all of my students from Queens College, NJPAC, Five Towns College, and City College who helped assess what works and what does not; and of course, to my wife Kazue Patton and my loving and supportive family.

Table of Contents

Introduction 1

Chapter 1: Triads, Basic Seventh Chords, and the Blues 3
- A. Triads, I–IV motion in Folk Songs 4
- B. Intro to Dominant and Diminished Seventh Chords 12
- C. Groove, The Mixolydian Scale, Triad Pairs, and the Blues Form 18
- D. Blues Phrasing, Intro to Blues Language: Pentatonic and Blues Scales 28

Chapter 2: Basic Harmonic Connections 34
- A. The Guide Tones of Sixth and Seventh Chords 35
- B. Basic Comping Strategies 44
- C. Basic LH Voicings 51
- D. Guide Tone Voicings with Doubled Notes 56

Chapter 3: Closed Position Chords 65
- A. 3-note Voicings 66
- B. 4-note Close 78
- C. Connecting Sixth and Diminished Seventh Chords 85
- D. The Sixth-Diminished Concept: Playing Scales of Chords 93
- E. Comping Games 97

Chapter 4: Open Position Chords 101
- A. Simple Open Position 102
- B. Upper Structure Triad Voicings 110
- C. Spread Voicings 117
- D. Drop-2 Voicings 122
- E. 4th-Like Voicings 126
- F. Comping Rhythm Transcription 128

Chapter 5: Practicing Scales 131
- A. Major 132
- B. Tonic Minor 143
- C. Harmonic Minor 151
- D. Diminished 160
- E. Whole Tone 168

Chapter 6: Melodic Building Blocks for Soloing 174
- A. 5-note Scale Fragments 175
- B. Arpeggio-Patterns 183
- C. Approach Tones and Enclosures 190
- D. Bebop Scales and Triplets 197
- E. Intro to Transcribing and Assimilating Solos 206

Appendix
- A. List of Workouts with Corresponding Discography 214
- B. List of Duets 219
- C. 2-handed Warm Up Exercises for Building Technique 220

Play/Comp Along CD Information 225

INTRODUCTION

Introduction to Jazz Piano, A Deep Dive is a fully immersive course designed to shed light on the inner workings of jazz piano, and to help you attain skills necessary for basic comping (accompanying/playing chords in rhythm) and soloing. The 60 workouts found inside put you in the middle of the action. They are to be done while playing along with specific tracks from classic recordings. You'll be given the tools necessary to improvise, groove, and interact with the masters of this music.

This book is for pianists and non-pianists alike. Some basic theory and reading skills will be necessary before diving in, but overall, the point of this course is to start from the very beginning and build a strong foundation of rhythm, harmony, and melody. It is suggested that young students have at least 3-4 years of traditional piano lessons before starting.

In my opinion, the most effective way to learn jazz piano is through listening to and playing with the great jazz records of the past. Every question you can possibly think of can be answered definitively by simply listening to records from the jazz canon. The problem comes in deciphering these records, especially from a pianistic point of view, since the piano is often in the background. Instead of trying to transcribe every detail of the piano part, this course offers the fundamental building blocks, so that you can interact with your favorite records on a basic level.

In the end, you want to have a deep relationship with jazz records. These are the albums that you've listened to over 100 times; not the ones that you might have listened to once or twice on YouTube. You should be able to sing along with all of the solos, know the harmony of the tunes, know the sound of each member of the band, know how the record fits into the entire lineage, and most importantly, be able to play along with it in some way, in real time at the piano.

As you might know, there are hundreds of play-along records where the rhythm section is separated and there's a lot of empty space in which to improvise. Unfortunately, on a typical play along recording, the joyous feeling so central to jazz records is often also removed. This feeling of joyousness and jubilation is what you want to be soaking up, not merely scales and chords. You want to key into the sound of the piano on the recording, the touch, the rhythmic feel, the way the eighth notes are played, etc.

You may be asking, "But if there's already piano, how do I play along." That's probably the most valuable lesson you can learn from doing this: how to fit in with any ensemble. Pretend you've been called for the gig. Wynton Kelly is already playing the piano, but he's agreed to let you sit in on a second piano. By comping and soloing while listening to Wynton Kelly comp and solo at the same time, you pick up a lot of subtleties. It's about getting inside of the music.

In the appendix, there is a complete list of workouts. Each one corresponds to a track from a classic jazz recording that I've enjoyed playing along with over the years. All of the records listed would be considered must-haves by any serious jazz record collector. For this jazz course to work, you must first have access to these vital jazz recordings.

Introduction

To make it easy, 99% of the musical examples referenced in the book can be found on YouTube and slowed down to 50 or 75% as needed. If possible, you should purchase the music to have in your own jazz record collection. Not only is the sound quality much better, but you can then access the iconic artwork and informative liner notes from the original recording. Common places to purchase jazz recordings include: iTunes, Amazon, Apple Music, eBay, CD internet sites like Arkivjazz.com or CDconnection.com, bookstores like Barnes and Noble, or even other big retail stores such as Best Buy or Walmart. Alternatively, you can visit your local used record/CD store and take a look. Many towns and cities all over the U.S. still have mom-and-pop record shops. There is no replacement for getting your hands a little dirty, browsing through stacks of records. Jazz record stores still open in New York City, for example, include "Academy Records and CDs" and "Jazz Record Center."

In addition, downloadable **DL** tracks are available at www.shermusic.com with selected demonstration and play-along tracks at accessible tempos played by top NY musicians. Note: no count offs are given on these tracks. Since most classic jazz recordings do not include count offs, it is a good idea not to have to depend on them.

Jazz piano is less about patterns and muscle memory, and more about thinking on your feet, and playing what you hear in the moment. The aim is to participate with the musicians around you in real time, and to create something new every time you sit down at the piano.

Studying the history of this music is also very important. For each new musician cited, look up and listen to their most famous recordings. Then, write down the names of the sidemen and research their most important recordings. This is how you increase your knowledge of this music and its history. As Dizzy Gillespie said, "Always have one foot in the future, and one foot in the past." After getting familiar with these classic recordings, explore your own favorite recordings. Many of the same play-along strategies outlined here can be applied to other jazz recordings.

This book takes you through triads, guide tone voicings, as well as closed and open position chords with special emphasis on how to connect them so that you can effectively navigate through blues, standards, and rhythm changes. Comping strategies and authentic comping guides based on real comping transcriptions are provided.

How to practice scales and chord scale theory are also discussed, along with how to build a repertoire of melodic material for soloing. The transcription process is introduced with ideas about assimilation. Also, in the appendix, several two-handed exercises are given addressing technical issues. Along the way, duets are suggested for use in a group piano setting, playing with another instrumentalist or vocalist, or with a private instructor.

After completing the course, you should be able to confidently comp and solo along with many iconic jazz recordings, and be well on your way to becoming a contributing member of your band, ensemble, or combo.

Chapter 1
Triads, Basic Seventh Chords, and the Blues

Jazz is deeply connected to all American music. Before diving into the jazz voicings and scale theory we need to develop a foundation. The feeling of jazz is inseparable from the feeling of African American Folk Music and all of its tributaries. To understand the concept of swing, we need to understand the concept of the blues, not only the technical side, (scales and structure etc.), but the sound and the feeling.

Many of the most famous jazz pioneers of jazz got their start in the church, steeped in blues, or in early rhythm and blues. Being exposed to this history is important in our quest in becoming accomplished jazz pianists.

In this first chapter we'll go over triads in a fresh new way, and introduce dominant and diminished seventh chords. We'll take a peek at some of the basic secret moves employed by pros to help inject harmonic movement into our playing.

Next, we'll work on our groove. By playing along with some of the greatest jazz masters with the widest grooves, we'll be well on our way. At the same time, we'll incorporate the mixolydian scale, as well as learn about the blues form.

Finally, we'll tackle blues phrasing and some of the most useful scales to use when improvising the blues. In the end, we'll be jamming with Joe Williams and Count Basie.

Triads, I-IV motion in Folk Songs

Here's a very brief review of some basic theory. Triads are simple three-note chords made up of root, third, and fifth. In FIG 1 the four types of root position triads are illustrated. Major triads have a M3 (major third) between the root and third and a m3 (minor third) between the third and fifth; minor root triads have a m3 between the root and third and M3 between the third and fifth; augmented triads have a M3 between both the root and third, and third and fifth; and diminished triads have a m3 between both the root and third, and third and fifth.

FIG. 1

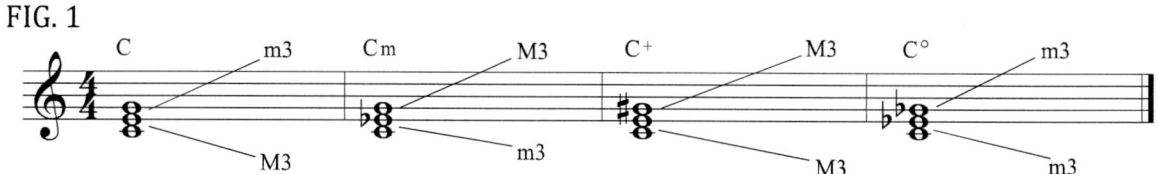

The following section is meant to aid you in inverting the triads in a fresh, non-traditional way while working on your groove. Inverting simply means playing the triad in a different order: R (root)–3–5 or 3–5–R or 5–R–3. Keep in mind, when you invert root position triads, the intervals change between the root, third, and fifth.

We will be using a Roman numeral system of identification to make transposing easier. Triads can be built on each step of the major scale to find all the diatonic triads (triads that are in the scale). When you do this, you find that some triads are major, some are minor, and one is actually diminished. Each triad is labeled in terms of scale step (I for the triad built on the root or tonic; ii for the triad built on the 2nd scale step etc.). Also, note that the Roman numeral is capitalized for major triads and in lower case for minor triads. The diminished triad that occurs on the 7th scale step is labeled with a lowercase Roman numeral and a small circle to the right (viio). Major scales do not contain augmented triads, but other scales do. In that case the triad would be labeled with a capital Roman numeral and a small + to the right of the symbol. Below are all of the triads found in the C major scale.

FIG. 2

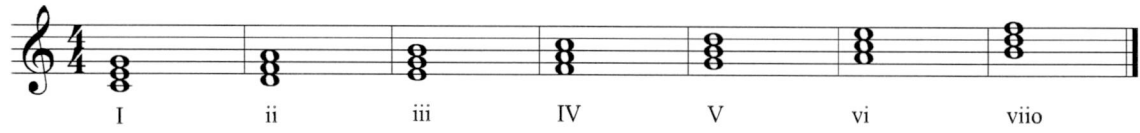

At this point, we'll be concentrating only on the I chord (known as the tonic), the V chord (known as the dominant), the IV chord (known as the subdominant), and the ii chord (often used in place of a IV chord and functions like a subdominant chord).

In Western Classical music, the motion between V and I is all-important. The magnetic pull between V and I is undeniable. The feeling of resolution is strong.
Practice V–I in many keys. When moving find the closest inversion. Starting in the key of C, resolve the leading tone (B) to the tonic (C). Also experiment resolving to minor (V–i).

FIG. 3

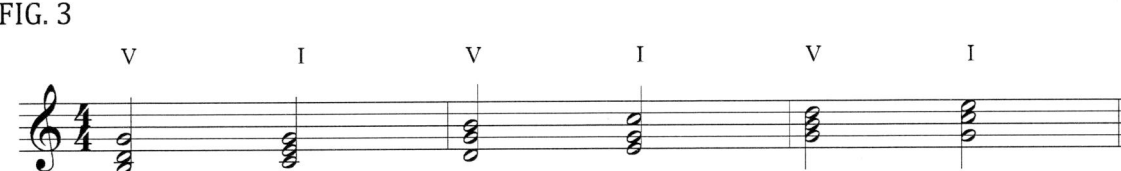

In a lot of blues and folk music the harmony moves back and forth between the tonic and subdominant. In church music, the motion from IV to I is sometimes called the "Amen" cadence. The feeling is more down home, and is not as severe as the V–I cadence. The feeling of resolution or returning home is not quite as strong.

To play blues and folk music, which make up the roots of jazz, one has to get familiar with the motion between IV and I. Practice moving back and forth between IV and I in all inversions as you move up or down the major scale. Like this:

FIG. 4

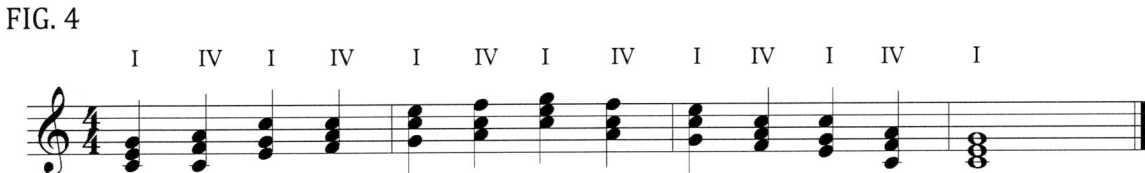

Practice the above pattern (IV–I) in 12 keys. Don't worry too much about fingering. Keep your right hand loose and supple. Use the right pedal to help connect the triads. Also experiment resolving iv minor to I (iv–I).

In many cases the ii chord is used instead of the IV chord. It functions like a subdominant chord, but actually creates a smoother scale of chords. Practice (ii–I) up and down the major scale like this:

FIG. 5

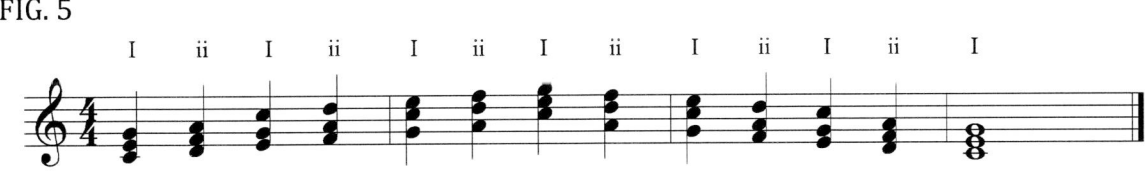

Jazz piano players are always moving chords around effortlessly. When I was younger, I often wondered what were all the passing chords that the pros put in when improvising. Often players insert a subdominant chord (IV or ii) not originally written in the chord changes to bridge between the written chord change and another inversion.

This helps in making the music smoother, and gives the pianist a whole series of chords to play, even if the lead sheet only indicates a single chord. This can be illustrated with the following familiar folk song. Below is a simple lead sheet to "When the Saints Go Marching In."

First play the melody with the simple half note bass line. It is important not to add any syncopation to the LH (left hand) when first starting out. Only play the root or fifth of each chord in half notes. The LH is your bass player, and it needs to be as steady as a rock. The interplay between the steady on-the-beat bass line with the syncopated RH (right-hand) melody will give the illusion of more than one person playing the piano.

FIG. 6

Now play the bass line with the simple chord changes while singing the melody.
As a jazz player, it's important to know the basic road map of the tune. In this tune, the first six measures stay in tonic. Then, in bars 7 and 8 the tune moves to dominant to end the first half of the form. Bar 9 returns to tonic, only to move to sub dominant in bar 11. The minor subdominant in bar 12 pulls you back to tonic in the next bar. Measures 13 and 14 contain a turnaround (I–vi–ii–V) that establishes the tonic again and provides a feeling of resolution. A tonic triad in the RH handles C and Am7 in bar 13; a subdominant triad handles Dm7 to G7sus in next bar. It's ok if some of the chord symbols are unfamiliar (we'll get to it later). The point is the last four bars basically stay in tonic. The big picture can help you memorize many tunes and to be able to play them in any key.

FIG. 7

Next insert subdominant chords related to the chord of the moment to add motion. In other words, on beat 3 add the subdominant of the chord that you are going to in the following measure. This is especially effective when the harmony changes.

The first four measures stay in C so place an F triad on beat 3 of measures where you want to add motion. In measure 7, the song moves to G momentarily. So, on beat 3 of measure 6 insert a C triad. On beat 3 of measure 8 insert an F to take you back to C in measure 9. In measure 10 use a Gm triad (the ii of F) to take you to F in measure 11. Use a Bb triad to take you to Fm in measure 12. Then you can use Fm again on beat 3 to take you back to C. In other words, play a whole measure of Fm (two inversions). IV may be replaced by iv to pass to I as a variation.

The last four bars follow a slightly different pattern. Notice how you are basically in C for the entire four bars. This means the RH is either going to play tonic or subdominant of C major. In measures 13, the RH plays I of C major while the LH plays I–vi. Measure 14 is unique because of how the RH alternates IV–I–ii in quarter notes starting on beat 2. This harmonic walk down is very common and contributes to the sense of resolution. This all happens over the LH ii–V. In measure 15 the half note alternation in the RH between I and IV returns.

The chart that follows shows the basic changes of the tune written with traditional chord symbols. Between the main chord symbols there is roman numeral notation showing the passing subdominant chords. Slashes are used to show where the subdominant chord leads when the chord of the moment is different than tonic (I).

FIG. 8

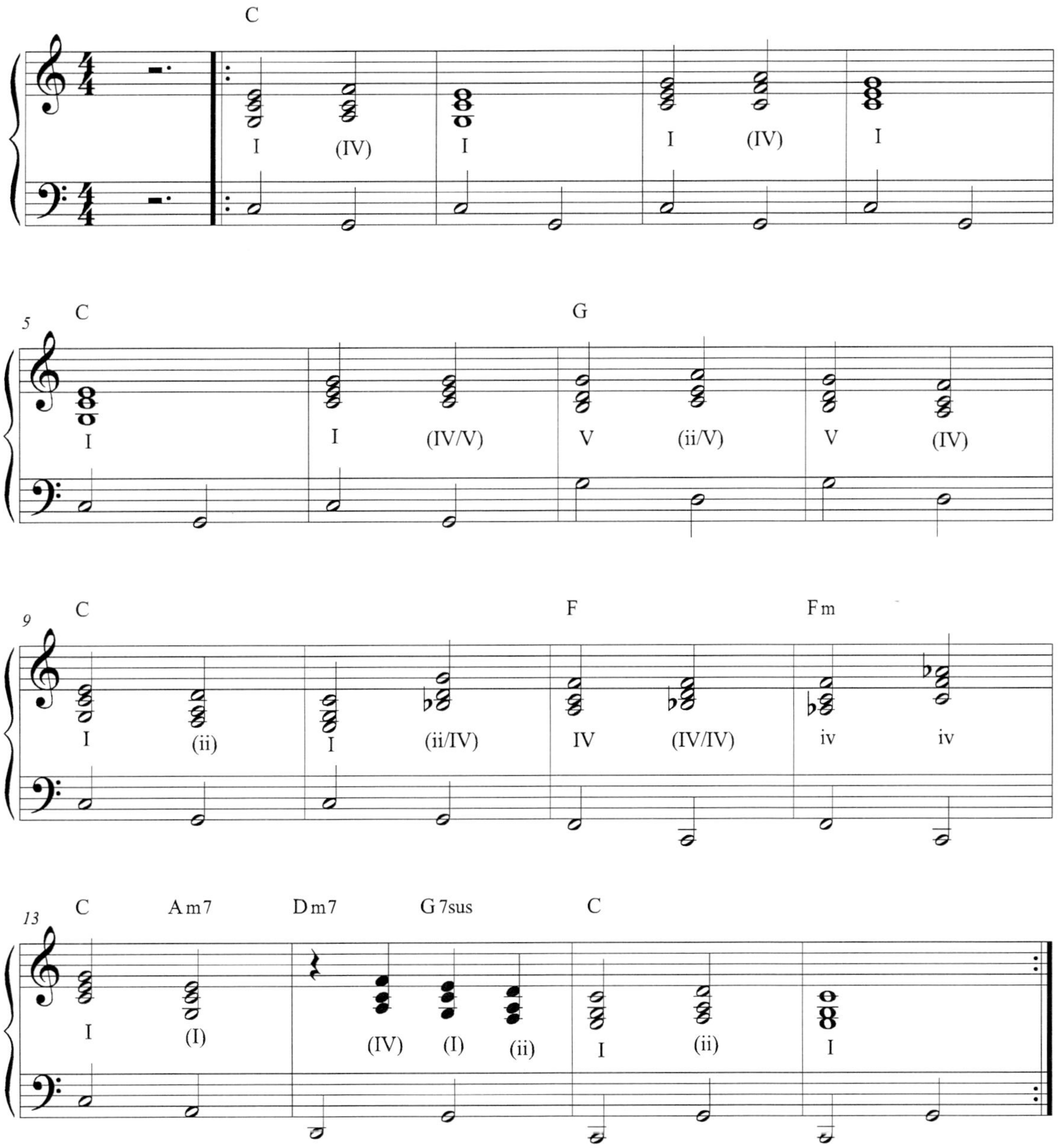

After getting comfortable with this back and forth between the chord of the moment and its subdominant, experiment with adding syncopation in the RH. Try to make the syncopations smooth and relaxed. It helps to think in triplets i.e. instead of playing chords on the upbeat, play them as if they were written on the third triplet of the beat. For example, a chord notated on the "and of 2" would be played later, on the 3rd triplet of beat 2. In doing so, you layback automatically, and improve your jazz swing feeling. Here is one possible accompaniment chart to When the Saints written in normal notation. Practice laying back when playing upbeats. Play chords in rhythm like this is known as **"comping."**

FIG. 9

Below is a different comping pattern transposed to G. Some different inversions of triads were used to keep the RH in a good range around middle C. Also, since this is usually an uptempo song, some of the busier rhythms in the RH are taken out. The idea here is that eventually you can improvise your own comping pattern.

Workout 1: Comping with Triads on the changes to "When the Saint Go Marching In" as played by Louis Armstrong. When you are ready, swing along with Louis Armstrong from *Louis Armstrong–Classics: New Orleans to New York (1950)*. Not all of the harmonies will be identical on the recording since we are only using RH triads, but you can accompany Louis just fine following the guidelines above. Feel free to use an application to slow down the recording if necessary. Refer to **DL TRK 1-2** for a demo and play-along track.

FIG. 10

Intro to Dominant and Diminished Seventh Chords

Dominant and diminished seventh chords are indispensable in all types of music, especially in jazz. They take you places, they're transitional, and they add a lot of beautiful movement to a song.

A seventh chord is a 4-note structure built by stacking an additional 3rd on top of a triad. It's more sophisticated than a triad, and is prevalent in jazz as a basic structure. Jazz players usually add colorful notes on top of seventh chords to create jazz voicings. Before going further, it's important to understand the seventh chord structure itself. Let's return to the major scale and build seventh chords on each scale step, like we did with triads in the last section.

FIG. 1

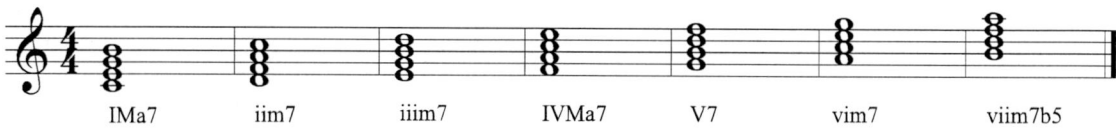

In Chapter 2 we will spend more time with all types of seventh chords; for now, we will concentrate on the dominant and diminished seventh chord.

DOMINANT SEVENTH CHORD

The seventh chord built on the 5th scale degree is called a dominant seventh, as it possesses a very strong magnetic pull back toward the tonic chord. The 7th of the G7 wants to move to the 3rd of the C tonic triad; and similarly the 3rd of G7, also known as the leading tone of the C major scale, wants to move up to the root of the C tonic triad.

FIG. 2

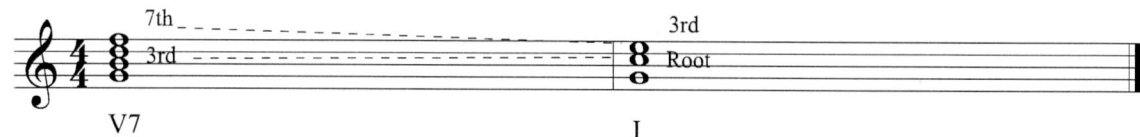

A dominant seventh (usually notated by placing a "7" next to a letter, for example, G7) consists of 4 notes: Root–3–5–b7. In other words, it's a major triad with a minor 3rd on top. In Western Music the V7 is the primary dominant and pulls you to I or i. G7 (built on the fifth of C major or minor) strongly pulls you to C major or minor.

Resolve dominant seventh chords (V7) to tonic major or minor chords (I or i) using different inversions. Make sure to move the leading tone (3rd of V7) up to the root and the 7th of V7 to the 3rd of the tonic chord.

FIG. 3

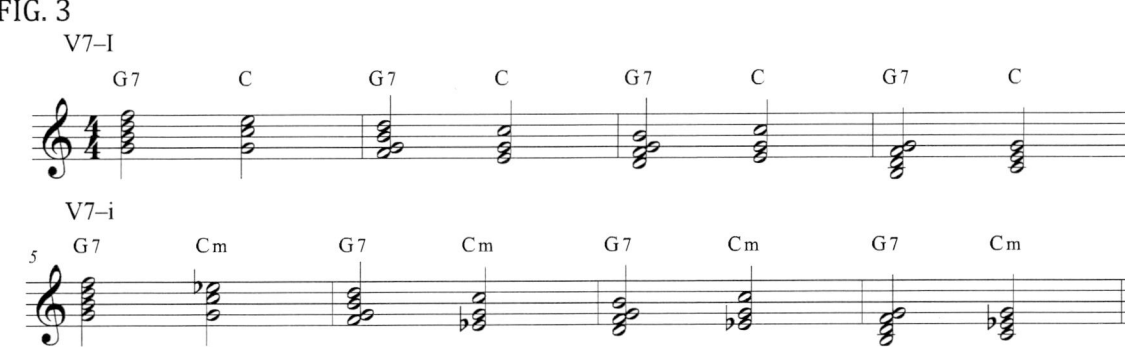

A dominant seventh chord that brings you to a chord other than tonic major or minor is called a secondary dominant. By building dominant seventh chords on other scale degrees you create secondary dominants that pull you to a major or minor chord a perfect fourth above. In many cases secondary dominants take you away from the tonic key. At the very least, they take you to another diatonic chord in a chromatically rich way. For example, in the key of C, E7 can take you to Am, the relative minor of C major. The G# is not in C major, but adds to the magnetic pull as you progress to A minor.

Practice the following progression: tonic to secondary dominant of relative minor, to relative minor, to secondary dominant of IV, to IV, to primary dominant (V7), back to I. In roman numeral notation it would be I–V7/vi–vi–V7/IV–IV–V7–I. In the key of C: C–E7–Am–C7–F–G7–C. Below, these chords are played in the RH in different inversions to ensure good voice leading. The LH plays the root of the RH chord. Transpose to 4 different keys.

FIG. 4

Chapter 1 • B

DIMINISHED SEVENTH CHORD

The seventh chord built on the 7th degree is called a half-diminished seventh, and is constructed by adding a M3 on top of a diminished triad. The formula for m7b5 AKA half-diminished seventh is R–b3–b5–b7. By lowering the seventh another half step, a half-diminished seventh becomes a diminished seventh. The formula for o7 AKA diminished seventh is R–b3–b5–bb7.

The diminished seventh built on the 7th degree (or leading tone) of the major scale has a similar strong pull toward tonic major or minor. By inverting diminished seventh you can find some very compelling movements between a diminished seventh chord and the major or minor triad a half step above.

Inverting diminished seventh chords is relatively easy. Since the chord consists only of stacked m3's, its structure is symmetrical. Each inversion has the exact same intervallic make up. Bo7=Do7=Fo7=Abo7. Note how all of these related diminished seventh chords are all a minor third apart. Therefore, if you successfully learn Bo7, Co7, and Dbo7 in all of their inversions you will have learned all diminished seventh chords in 12 keys. There are only three unique diminished seventh chords in the chromatic scale. In upcoming chapters, we'll delve deeper into the diminished seventh chord and the diminished scale. For now, practice moving between inversions of viio7 and I or i.

FIG. 5

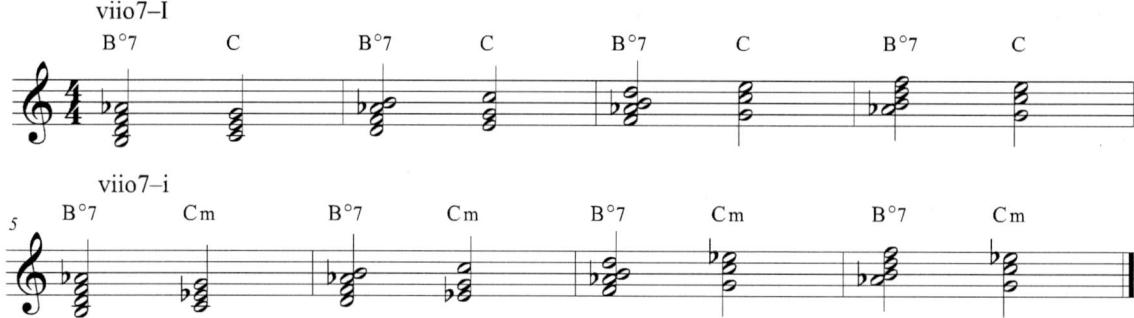

As an alternative, you can build a diminished seventh on the #4 degree of the major scale and resolve to the tonic. Practice moving from #ivo7 to I.

Tip:

1. Play any o7 in your RH
2. Pick any chord tone and play it in the LH
3. Resolve the LH up a half step to the V
4. Move to the closest inversion of a RH major triad that is a P4 higher than the new LH note. Doubling the top note of the major triad an octave down is ok when voice leading calls for it.

FIG. 6

Before starting the next workout, try the following three comping rhythms. Feel free to mix and match these rhythms or simply play a dotted half note on beat 1 as you comp an F major triad in 3/4 time.

FIG. 7

Workout 2: Comping with Triads and Basic Seventh Chords on the changes to Grant Green's "Sunday Morning." Groove along with Grant Green as you play through his gospel-inspired composition. Slowing down the recording may be necessary. Note the I–IV triad motion, the secondary dominant chords, and the diminished seventh chords built on the #4 that lead back to I. Listen to the way Kenny Drew comps on this track.

Employ rhythms from above as you play along. Here is one possible solution. If the second half of the tune is too difficult, feel free to simplify the rhythms. Refer to **DL TRK 3-4** for a demo and play-along track at a more accessible tempo. For the first chorus of the demo, the comping rhythm is simplified.

Chapter 1 • B

FIG. 8

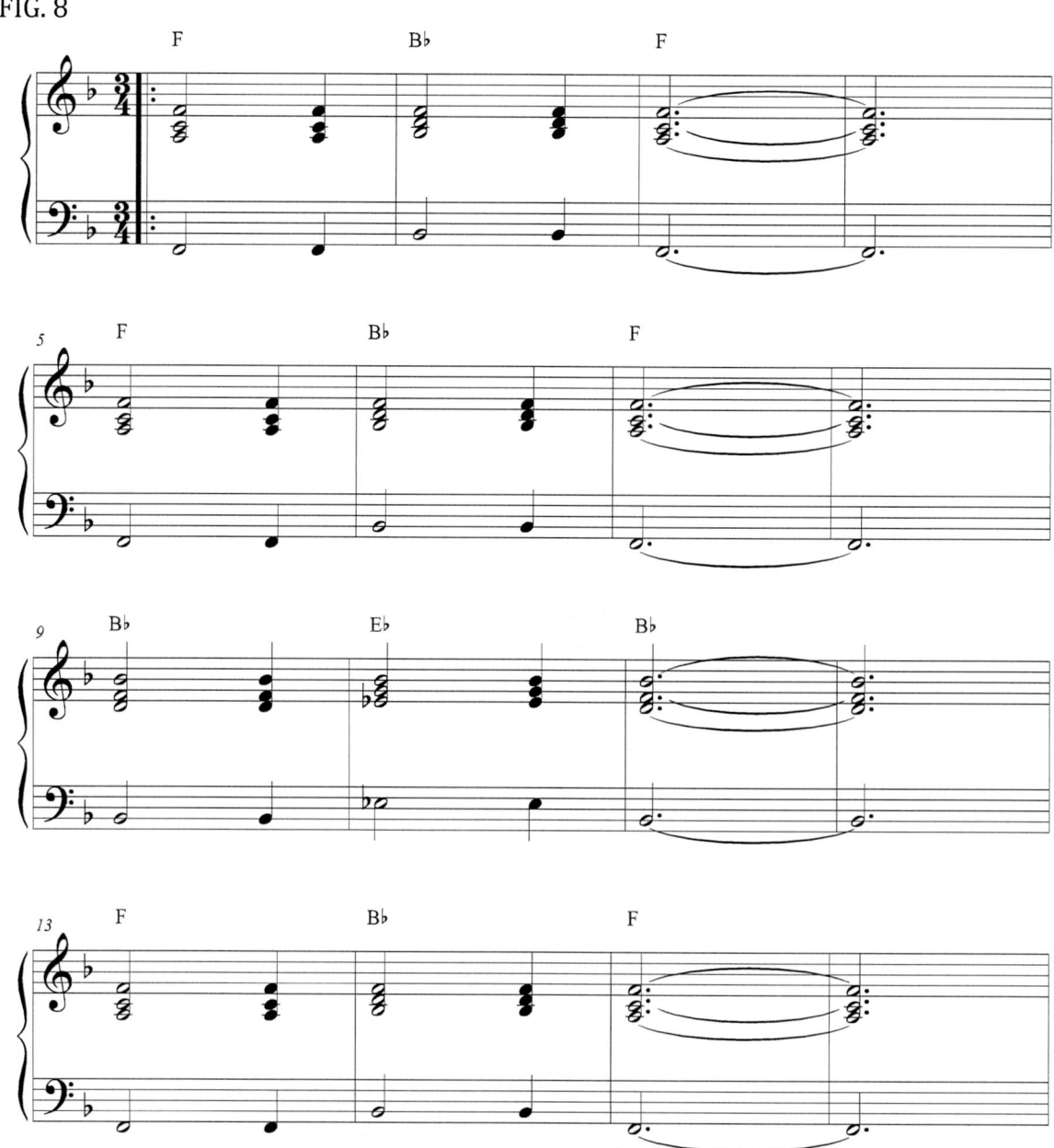

In measure 27-28, IV–I motion is employed in the RH over the ii–V in the LH. The chord symbols are merely implied. This movement is very similar to the harmonic walk down in m. 14 of "When the Saints Go Marching In."

Groove, The Mixolydian Scale, Triad Pairs and the Blues

Let's explore this idea of triplets. Play the bass figure below. A repeated figure like this is called a vamp.

FIG. 1

The triplet is at the heart of the feel, and it's very important to internalize this rhythm. Imagine a locomotive churning; imagine a wheel rolling. The circular nature of the feel is what is at the core. Swing and groove emanate from this round, ever-turning rhythmic feel. Feel the triplets especially during the time that you are holding the long note.

The mixing of the m3 and M3 in the bass line gives the groove a bluesy sound. In order to add some harmony, we need to switch scales. Remember, C7 consists of C-E-G-Bb. If we find notes in between the chord tones we can create a chord scale that describes C7. One of the most common chord scales to describe C7 is called the dominant seventh scale or mixolydian scale. It is constructed by flatting the seventh degree of the major scale. By its nature, it has a much more bluesy sound than the major scale.

FIG. 2

Looking at the scale we can see the chord tones: C, E, G, and Bb (1, 3, 5, and b7) embedded inside. Like before, we can build triads on each scale step. Playing the triads derived from the C mixolydian scale in succession gives the flavor of C7.

FIG. 3

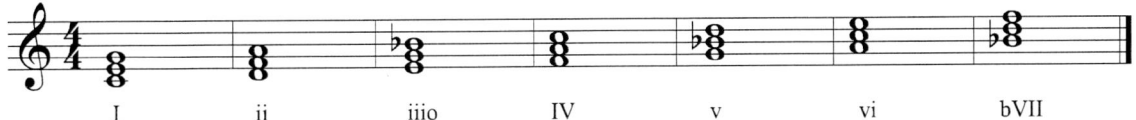

Using a metronome, play second inversion triads extracted from the mixolydian scale with the bass line from FIG. 1. Notice how the second triad of each pair contains at least two of the C7 chord tones. After getting comfortable in the key of C, transpose to several other keys.

FIG. 4

The 12-bar blues is one of the central pillars of basic jazz piano. Jazz has many roots in this country's blues tradition. Understanding a bit about the blues is very important. Below is a basic variation of the 12-bar blues progression.

FIG. 5

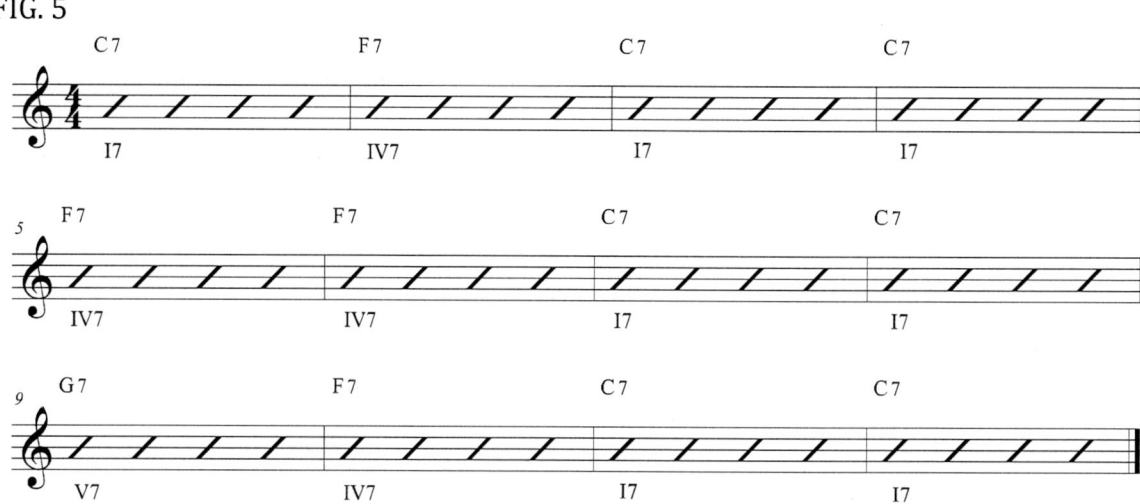

Now apply the second inversion mixolydian triads to the blues in C. You can use the same rhythm and bass line found in FIG. 5. Find triads extracted from the mixolydian scale corresponding to the chord of the moment. In other words, bar 1 is marked, C7, meaning find triads from the C mixolydian scale; bar 2 is marked F7, meaning find triads from the F mixolydian scale etc.

Workout 3: Comping with Triads on the changes to Ray Bryant's "Slow Freight."
Groove along with Ray Bryant from his recording, *Slow Freight.* A bass line is provided with a sample RH accompaniment (different than the melody) made up of second inversion mixolydian triads.

FIG. 6

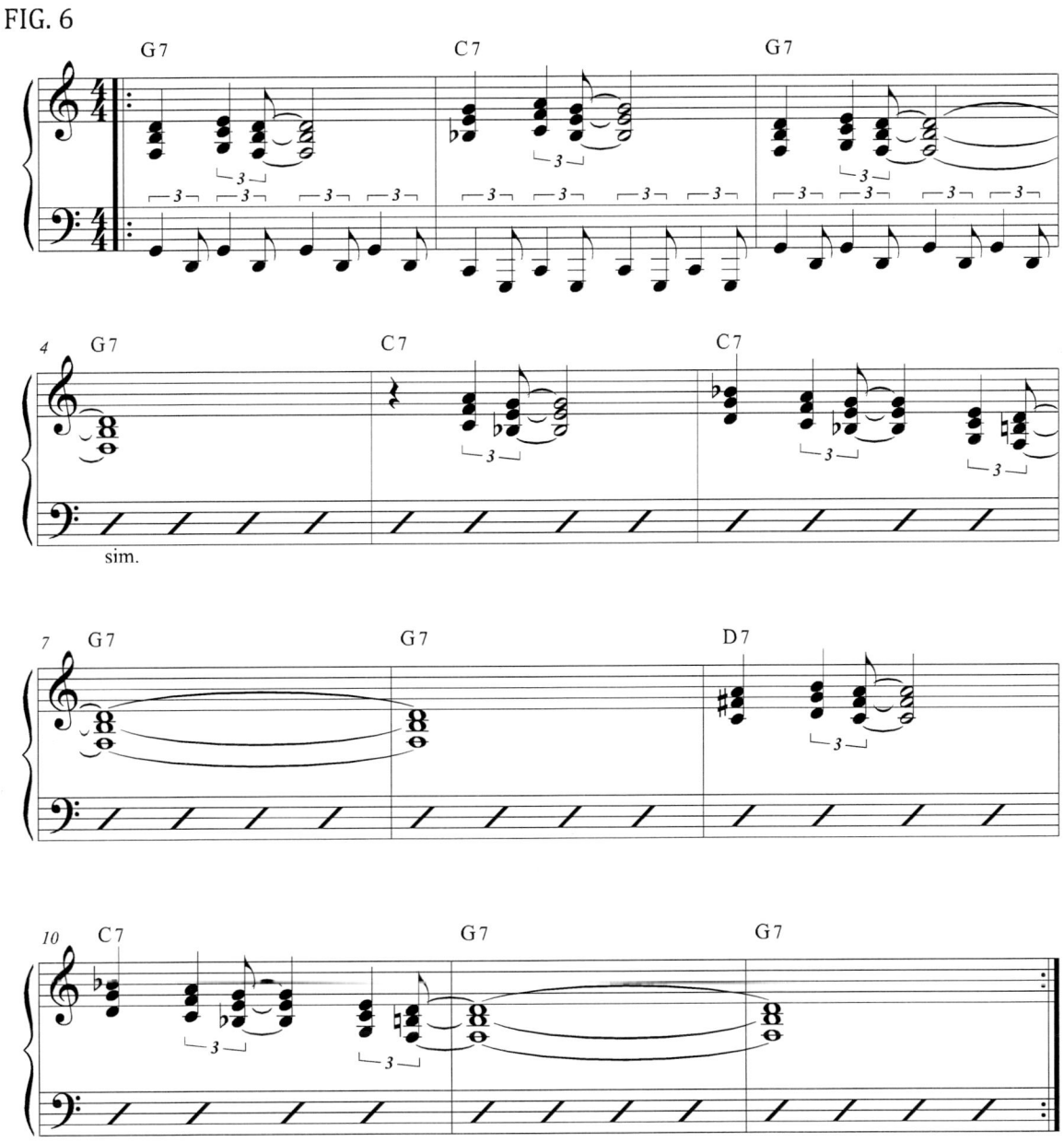

The boogaloo, originally a dance craze of the 1960's, mixes elements of rock and roll with funky swing, and is an important part of the jazz language. For the next workout we turn to tenor saxophonist, Hank Mobley.

Workout 4: Comping with Triads on the changes to Hank Mobley's "A Caddy For Daddy." Get funky as you play along with McCoy Tyner on the title track from Hank Mobley's, *A Caddy For Daddy.* A sample bass line is provided along with a RH rhythmic guide. Apply mixolydian triads to the RH rhythmic notation. For measures 9-13 you can use diminished triads built off the third degree of the mixolydian scale and then inverted to 2nd inversion. As we will see later, this three-note voicing is quite effective especially when playing the blues.

See if you can figure out the original comping pattern played by McCoy Tyner. Also, note that this is an example of a 16 bar blues (not 12).

FIG. 7

Below is a menu containing several possible triad pairs corresponding to each chord of the blues progression (I7, IV7, and V7). **The Roman numerals refer to the mixolydian scale associated with the chord of the moment**. For example, in the key of C: "ii–I" under the I7 column refers to Dm–C; "ii–I" under IV7 refers to Gm–F; and" ii–I" under V7 refers to Am–G. Feel free to mix and match. For example, you could choose "ii–I" or "IV–I" for I7; "vi–v" for IV7 and V7. In fact, by mixing it up you can achieve better voice leading. Also, experiment with changing the order of the triad pair, i.e. you can use "ii–I" or "I–ii."

TRIAD PAIR MENU

I7	IV7	V7
ii–I	ii–I	ii–I
IV–I	IV–I	IV–I
vi–v	vi–v	vi–v

Workout 5: Comping with Triads on the changes to "I Wonder Who" as performed by Ray Charles: play along with Ray Charles on a shuffle blues from *The Genius Sings The Blues*. Mix and match different triad pairs from the menu above to play over the bass line below. The triad pairs refer to the mixolydian scale associated with the chord symbol of the moment. Keep in mind, the part below is different than what Ray Charles is playing. It is not meant to be a transcription. Instead, it is a simple accompaniment. Your job is to offer support and contribute to the groove. Refer to **DL TRK 5-6** for a demo and play-along track.

FIG. 8

For the final blues of the section, we turn to an icon in blues music. Otis Spann played with Muddy Waters, Lightning Hopkins, among many others, and is famous for his captivating blues feeling. Even though we are now venturing outside of jazz, it's important to at least have a little understanding of the real down-home blues and what it sounds like.

For the next workout we will add a few more authentic blues moves. Instead of only playing a triad pair, we can move up and down the mixolydian scale to imply the dominant seventh chord like this (starting from the first inversion triad):

FIG. 9

Blues pianists are also famous for being able to give the impression of bending notes. This is done by playing crush notes, adding dissonant half steps in the chord voicing, or by mixing and matching minor and major. The b3 in a major tonality is known as a blue note, and is meant to mimic the expressive style of the voice central to blues music.

Let's concentrate on the latter technique. Before playing a major triad (in first inversion), play a minor triad and then bend into the major, like this:

FIG. 10

Workout 6: Comping with the Triads on the changes to Otis Spann's "Good Morning Mr. Blues." Groove along with Otis Spann, as he plays his slow, down home, "Good Morning Mr. Blues" from the album by the same name. Instead of trying to catch all of his bluesy fills, play a simple accompaniment made up of triad pairs, the bluesy moves outlined in FIG. 9 and 10 and second inversion mixolydian triads. A sample accompaniment is provided below. Note that the triad pairs often refer to the mixolydian scale associated with the chord symbol of the following measure (see mm. 1, 2, 4, 6 and 7). In this way, the harmony of the next measure is anticipated.

FIG. 11

A traditional blues would not be complete without a standard blues turnaround. It is used at the end of a traditional blues to give a sense of resolution. A blues turnaround signals the conclusion of the blues form and can either loop back to the top or serve as a final cadence to the song.

A standard blues turnaround occurs during the last two bars of the blues form (m. 11-12). The chord progression moves in quarter notes, moving from tonic through the subdominant, to the tonic with the V in the bass, to a V7 chord. Since the chords move quickly, typically this progression is used for a slow blues.

Otis Spann's blues uses a simplified version of this standard blues turnaround: I–IV–I–V. If we add a bass line (I–III–IV–#IV–V) we can add some more harmonic motion. By assigning chords to the bass line we can create the standard blues ending:

I–I7–IV–#ivo7–I–V7
And in the key of C: C–C7/E–F–F#o7–C/G–G7

FIG. 12

Standard Blues Turnaround

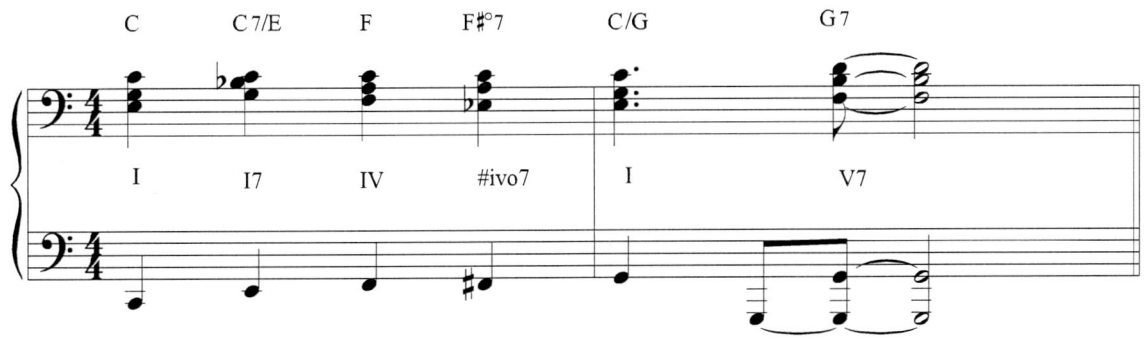

The standard blues ending is on one hand incredibly basic and simple, but on the other, somewhat complex harmonically. It's made up of both triads and seventh chords, with an added complication of a bass note that is not always the root. At this point, it's important when voicing a seventh chord, avoid doubling the bass note in the RH chord unless it's in the melody. Notice that there is no "E" in the RH voicing for C7/E; also there is no "F#" in the RH voicing for F#o7. This way the RH is always playing a unique, three-note shape, making the progression more uniform.

For now, try to memorize the standard blues ending in several keys. Also try to apply the standard blues ending to "I Wonder Who" and "Good Morning, Mr. Blues."

Intro to Blues Phrasing

Too often blues is offered to jazz piano students as an abstract 12-bar song form. Instead of trying to internalize the sound of blues, students often set out to memorize the 12-bar blues progression in FIG. 5 of Chapter 1B or one of several variations.

After playing along with Ray Bryant, Ray Charles, Hank Mobley, and Otis Spann it's clear that the blues is more than just an abstract 12-bar chord progression. Blues is a feeling; it's a sound; it's a language complete with its own unique, expressive grammar and syntax.

The blues has phrasing that is important to internalize. In many cases it's extremely simple. You can create a blues containing three identical 4-bar phrases. This type of composition is sometimes called a "riff blues" since it can be created with one riff (or short phrase) and easily learned by ear. There are several blues compositions that follow this format.

Stop now, and listen to the following songs: "Bag's Groove" by Milt Jackson from Miles Davis' recording *Bag's Groove*; "Sonnymoon for Two" by Sonny Rollins from Live at the Village Vanguard; and "Centerpiece" by Harry "Sweets" Edison from the classic recording, *Sweetenings*. Listen to the phrasing of the head (melody of the song).

Workout 7: Playing a Single Line Melody on the Changes to "Bag's Groove" as played by Miles Davis. See if you can figure out the melody to "Bag's Groove" by ear and play it with Miles Davis' recording, *Bag's Groove*. For now, just use your RH and play a single line. The chord sheet is provided below. Notice how the V7–IV7 blues and rock-based turnaround in m. 9-10 is now replaced with the more jazz-friendly ii7–V7. Write in the melody.

FIG. 1

We will be working with three basic scales to create our blues improvisations and compositions: the minor pentatonic scale, the blues scale (sometimes known as the minor blues scale), and the major blues scale.

The minor pentatonic is constructed: 1–b3–4–5–b7. It is derived from the ancient pentatonic scale: 1–2–3–5–6. But instead of starting with 1, you begin with 6: 6–1–2–3–5. When compared to the parallel major scale this new configuration creates the minor pentatonic formula listed above.

For example, in the key of C: C pentatonic is C–D–E–G–A, the related minor pentatonic scale is: A–C–D–E–G which is also known as A minor pentatonic. If you compare this new configuration to A major, you get the formula: 1–b3–4–5–b7. Therefore, to get C minor pentatonic you need to start with the Eb pentatonic scale.

The blues scale (minor blues scale) also has a melancholy sound, but has more emotional impact because it contains an added blues note (b5). The blues scale therefore consists of six notes: 1–b3–4–b5–5–b7.

Learn the pentatonic, minor pentatonic, and minor blues scale in several keys.

FIG. 2

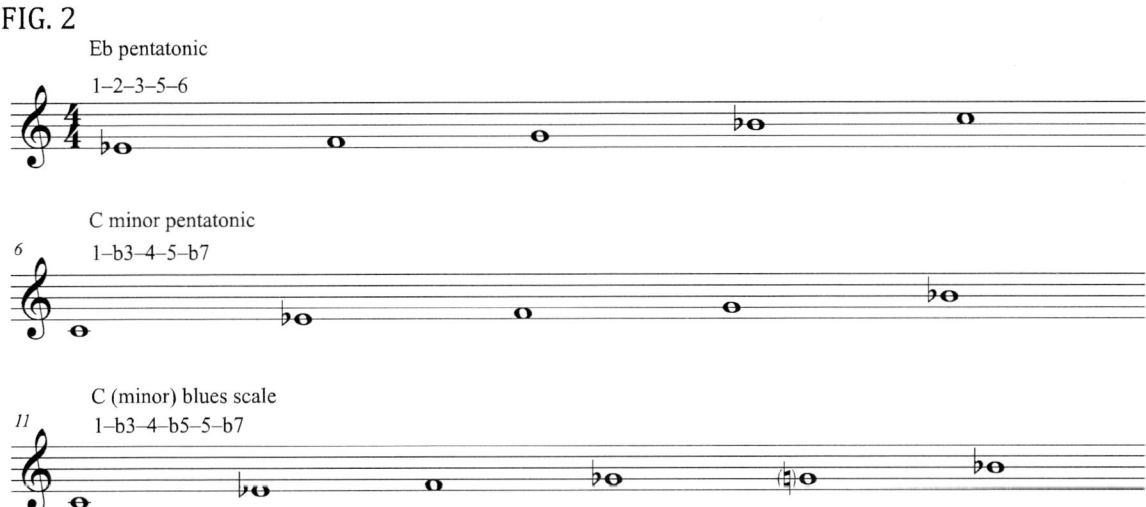

Bag's Groove consists entirely of notes from the F minor pentatonic scale: F–Ab–Bb–C–Eb. Notice how they are organized as part of the melody, and listen to the space between each phrase. Thinking in terms of complete phrases instead of merely a collection of pitches is key to successful improvisation or composition.

As you listen to Miles' solo see if you can come up with background riffs behind his solo. Come up with three repeated simple phrases, each four measures long, consisting of notes of the F minor pentatonic scale or F minor blues scale. Continue on during Milt Jackson's solo, and notice how Thelonious Monk makes his entrance with thoughtful

Chapter 1 • D

interjections. For now, come up with hip background riffs that don't get in the way. Here's one to get you started. Be conscious of dissonant notes–like playing the 4th on a dominant seventh chord. As long as you move off of them and/or play them on a weak beat, they can be quite effective.

FIG. 3

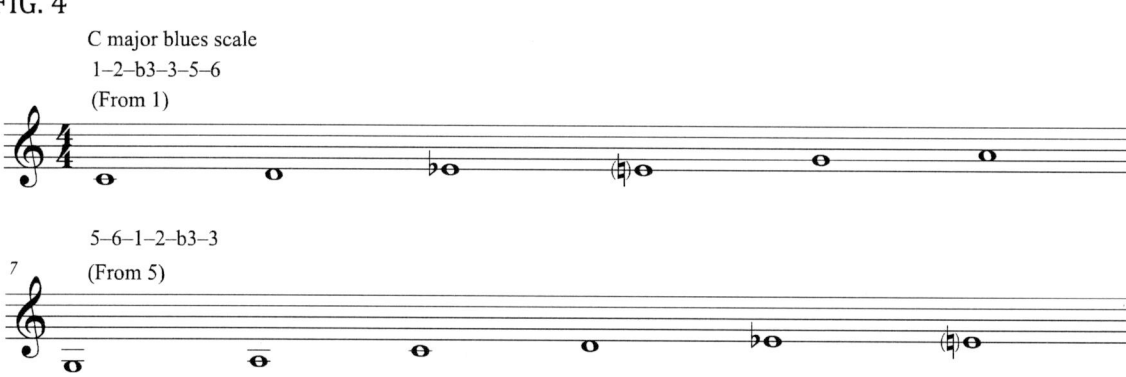

The major blues scale (1–2–b3–3–5–6) is a close cousin to the major pentatonic scale (1–2–3–5–6). When improvising using the major blues scale, it's common to start from the fifth (5–6–1–2–b3–3). Learn the major blues scale in several keys.

FIG. 4

Workout 8: Playing a Riff Blues on the changes to Harry "Sweets" Edison's "Centerpiece." This riff blues is derived from the Ab major blues scale and is featured on Harry "Sweets" Edison's classic album, *Sweetenings*. Learn it by ear, and then write it out in the space provided. Note that on some recordings the rhythm of the melody may be different. Play along with "Sweets."

FIG. 5

Interact with Harry "Sweets" Edison using the major blues scale to create background riffs on his classic blues composition. Notice the standard blues turnaround in m. 11-12. Here is a sample riff to get you off the ground.

FIG. 6

Blues with lyrics usually consist of three 4-measure phrases, often with the last four measures being different. Listen to the words and sing along with Count Basie and Joe Williams' "Every day, everyday I have the blues." This phrase fills the first four measures. For measures 5-8, Joe Williams sings the same words, "Every day, everyday I have the blues." The punch line, or resolution occurs in the last four measures, "Well you see me worried, baby because it's you I'd hate to lose."

Workout 9: Playing a Riff Blues on the changes to "Ev'ry Day I Have the Blues" as sung by Joe Williams. This seminal track is from Count Basie and Joe William's album, "Ev'ry Day I Have the Blues." Listen to this track enough times so that you can hum or sing along with Joe Williams. Pretend you're singing three 4-bar phrases just like Joe Williams. Create a riff blues with three phrases. Make sure to alter the third phrase to create the punch line.

Use the major or minor blues scale when composing your blues. When it comes to phrasing, use a set of lyrics from the song to help you. Simply pair the lyrics with notes from the given scale. Following the lyrics will give you the right pacing.

As you play along with the recording, make sure to start when Joe Williams comes in. For now, just improvise with your RH. Below is an example of a 3-phrase blues with a punch line that you can use as a guide. Keep in mind this is not a transcription of what is being played on the recording.

FIG. 7

Get your left hand involved. As you play with the recording, play a bass line "in two." In other words, play two half notes per measure. Take some time to analyze the bass line below as you get it under your fingers. Compared to bass lines from the last section, it's more linear. On closer inspection you can see that a chord tone (R, 3, or 5) is played on the downbeat of each measure. This gives the music its foundation. In fact, the root is always used at the crucial points within the structure of the blues: the downbeat of m. 1, m. 5, m. 9, and m. 11. The note on beat 3 can be a chord tone, passing tone, i.e. a diatonic step above or chromatic step below the next downbeat, or the V of the next downbeat. ii-V's are added in m.6 and m. 12 to make the voice leading smoother.

Practice hands alone and then put your blues composition together with the bass line "in two."

FIG. 8

Duet 1: Accompanying a Riff Blues with a Triadic Comping Pattern. If you are presently part of a group piano class or if you can find a friend that wants to jam, you can combine blues phrasing with the bluesy comping workouts from the last section. Learning to play with another individual is great training, not to mention extremely fun.

Have Player 1 play a riff blues with their RH only (without the bass line) on a separate piano or in the upper register of the same piano while Player 2 plays one of the triadic comping patterns on the blues from Chapter 1C.

Chapter 2
Basic Harmonic Connections

Jazz piano is all about connections. Chords connect to each other, a melodic idea connects to another, rhythms flow and move ahead, a thought connects to the next, etc. It's a good idea to think about learning jazz in this way so that you can start to hear the connections and then play them in the moment. Of course, the better you become at this the more personal connections you will end up making in the music world.

In this next chapter we'll convert sixth and seventh chords to guide tone voicings and shells that we can connect to each other in interesting ways while navigating through songs. By adding some rhythm we'll be able to interact with a rhythm section. We'll experiment also with adding chromatic movements to slow ballads to get us thinking horizontally.

The Guide Tones of Sixth and Seventh Chords

Triads, although useful in many ways, are not the basic building block of jazz voicings. Jazz chords are often seventh chords with added 9ths, 11ths, and 13ths. This is what gives them their sophisticated sound. Most jazz chords are voiced, meaning the notes are rearranged to create an open or closed sound that's clear and resonant. Before learning jazz voicings, we must be able to easily play through the three basic kinds of root position seventh chords in every key:

Major 7th	(maj7)	Contains a 3 and 7
Minor 7th	(m7)	Contains a ♭3 and ♭7
Dominant 7th	(7)	Contains a 3 and ♭7

To get these chords under your fingers, practice each type of seventh chord in the following way:

In half steps up and down

FIG. 1

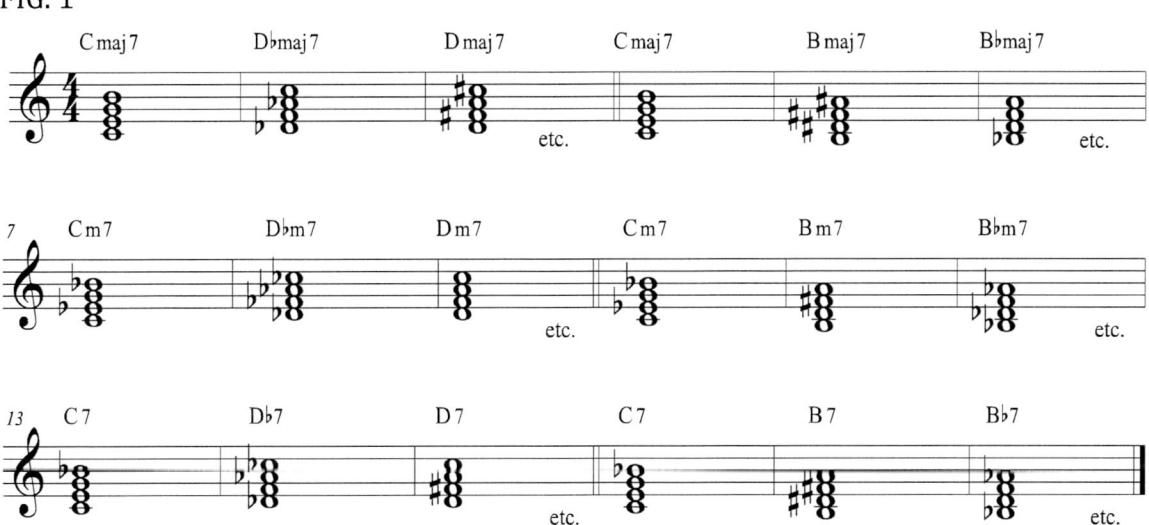

Chapter 2 • A

In whole steps up and down

FIG. 2

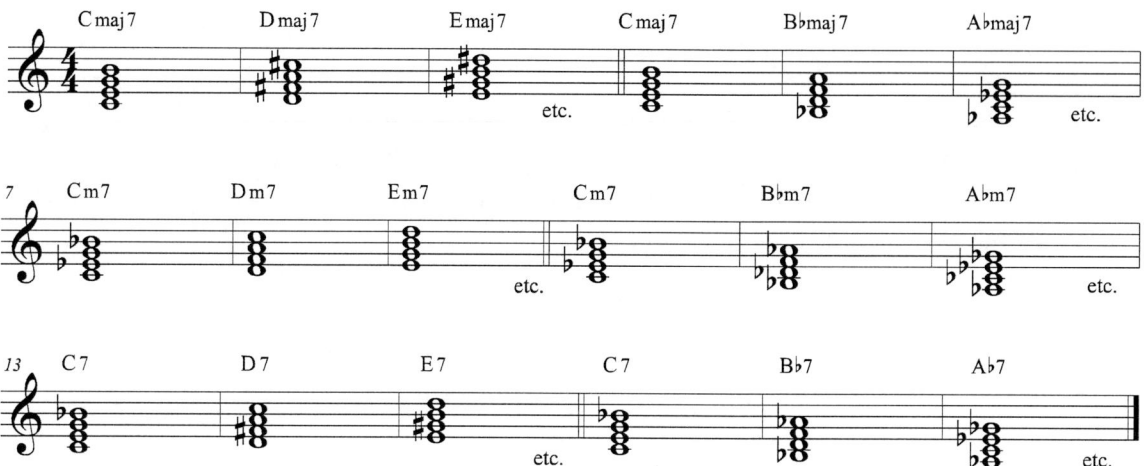

In minor 3rds up and down

FIG. 3

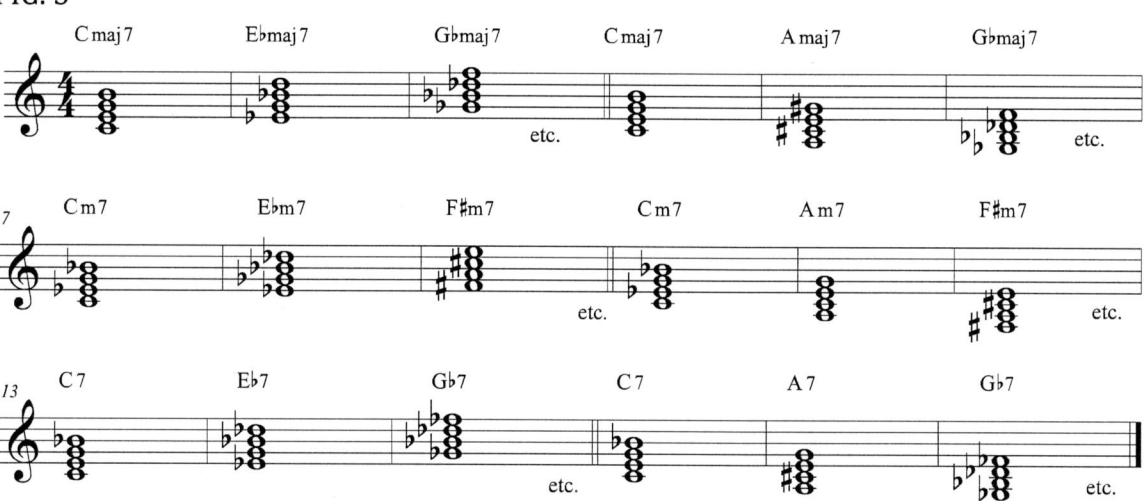

Root position seventh chords tend to be boxy and dull. To begin creating a more effective jazz voicing we will be concentrating only on the 3rd or 7th of the chord in the RH over a LH root. The 3rd and 7th hold the vital information about a chord, its identity, whether the chord is major or minor, whether it contains a major 7th (M7) or minor 7th (m7). It helps to guide us harmonically. For that reason, the 3rd and 7th of the chord are called *guide tones.*

When playing guide tones you can immediately start to find connections between chords. Moving from 7 to 3 or from 3 to 7 is a very fundamental harmonic connection in jazz. Understanding and hearing these connections will improve your jazz piano playing immensely.

To illustrate this, play through the circle of 4ths with your LH in half notes. Keep the range within one octave. This means you'll have to get creative in either ascending a 4th or descending a 5th.

FIG. 4

With your RH, begin with the 3rd of C and move to the b7 of F creating a descending chromatic scale. This progression implies dominant seventh chords moving through the circle of 4ths simply by alternating between the 3rd and 7th of each chord. The same thing happens if you begin with the b7 of C and move to the 3rd of F and so on through the circle of 4ths.

FIG. 5

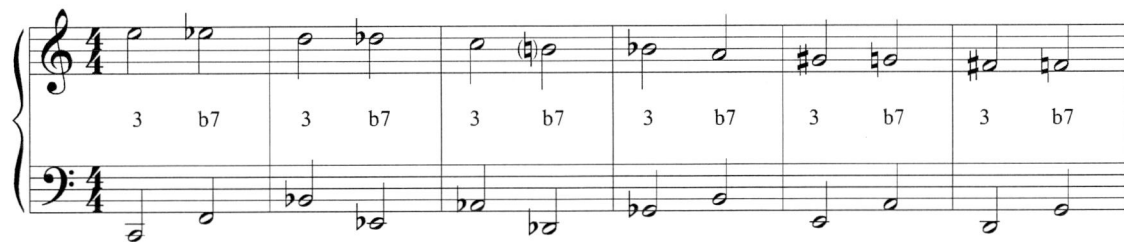

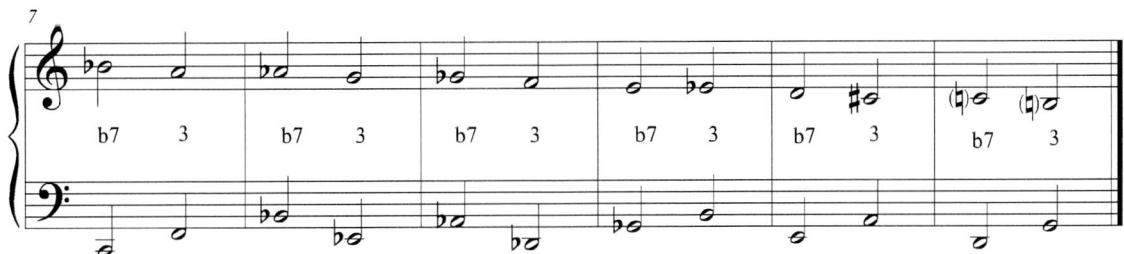

Returning to the three types of seventh chords, we see them expressed below with guide tones (GTs) over the root (R) in two inversions:

Position 1: 3rd in the right thumb
Position 2: 7th in the right thumb

FIG. 6

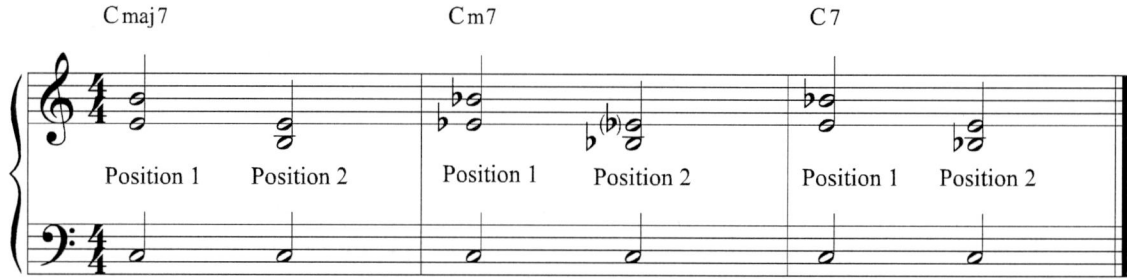

These shapes are economical and compact. They can be moved around easily, and still convey a lot of harmonic information.

To get these guide tone voicings under your fingers, practice in the following way:

1. Position 1 (3rd in the right thumb), up and down in half steps; up and down in whole steps; up and down in m3s/M3s; up a P4/down a P5
2. Position 2 (7th in the right thumb), up and down in half steps; up and down in whole steps; up and down in m3s/M3s; up a P4/down a P5

The magic of having two inversions to choose from for each guide tone voicing has to do with the way the chords can connect. This is especially apparent when the bass moves in 4ths. Practice each type of seventh chord going around the circle of fourths. Dominant sevenths are demonstrated below. Observe the smooth voice leading. To keep the voicing from becoming too muddy or too thin, keep the bottom guide tone around middle C (within a fifth above or below).

FIG. 7

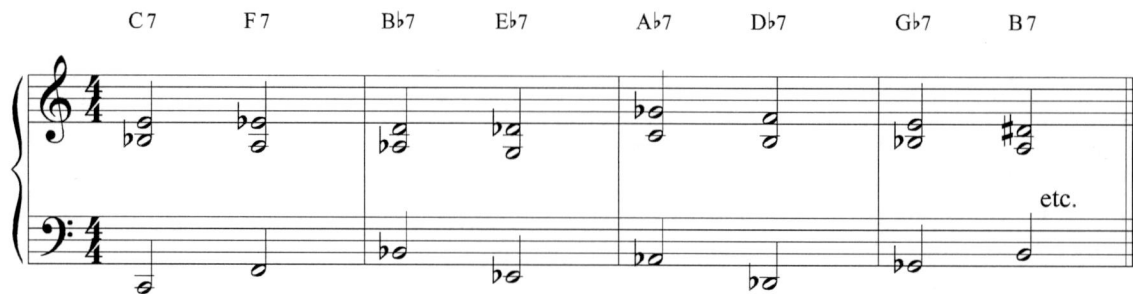

Below is the well-worn progression ii7–V7–Imaj7. If you haven't practiced this one, it's very important to get this one under your fingers. Notice how the progression moves in half steps down the piano.

FIG. 8

Imaj7–vi7–ii7–V7 is an important cadence found in countless standard songs. In early days this progression was used as repeated vamp to get acts on and off the stage. It really is just a loop or turnaround in a key that is static harmonically but provides some motion between chords. Below, this progression is combined with its more sophisticated cousin, iii7–VI7–ii7–V7. Practice with guide tones over roots in all 12 keys. Mix up Position 1 and Position 2 to find connections.

FIG. 9

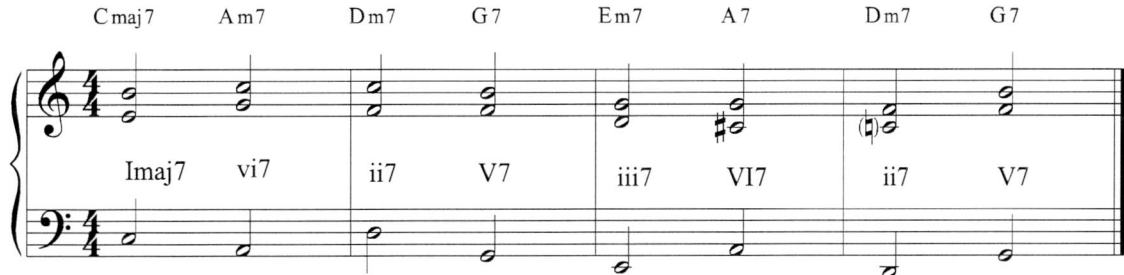

Let's apply these guide tone voicings to a standard. Below, Duke Ellington's Perdido is given as a chord sheet. The first four bars are expressed using guide tone voicings. Simply continue through the whole song reading through the changes while humming or singing the melody. Strive for smooth voice leading by inverting the guide tones. Keep the bottom guide tone within a fifth of middle C.

FIG. 10

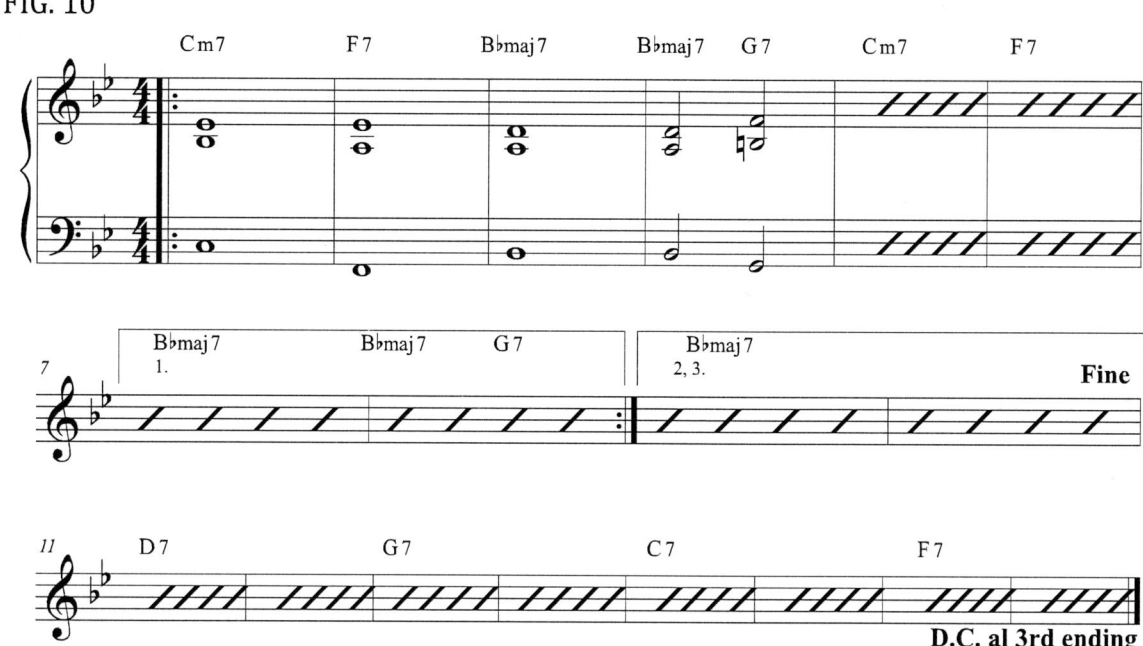

Workout 10: Comping with Guide Tones on the changes to Duke Ellington's "Perdido." Experience the timeless, incredibly deep groove of Ellington's orchestra as you play along to his masterpiece, Perdido from Duke Ellington's album, *The Best of the Centennial Edition*. For now play only whole notes and half notes. Playing beat one is always a swinging place to start.

Play through the chords of five simple standards using guide tone voicings while you sing or hum the melody. For now, select ones that contain mostly major, minor, and dominant seventh chords. Possible tunes include: Blue Moon, I Wish I Knew, Tune Up, Misty, September In the Rain, Beautiful Friendship, and Broadway. Play along with your favorite recording of one of these tunes.

Reading through tunes in this manner gives you an idea of some of the inner lines (or guide tone lines) that exist in the classic jazz standards. These beautiful, hidden, chromatic, lines exist everywhere in jazz, and they give a jazz standard its deep harmonic beauty. The harmony of a great song is more than a series of unrelated chords; it's all about the lines that exist underneath a beautiful melody.

At this point, let's add major sixth, minor sixth, half-diminished, and diminished chords to our vocabulary. In later chapters we will deal with the entire chords and all of their inversions; for now, we will be focusing on the 3rd and 7th (6th) of each chord. To start let's review all of these chords in root position. Sixth chords are constructed by adding the sixth to either a major or minor triad. Half-diminished seventh chords are constructed by lowering the third, fifth and seventh by a half step. Fully diminished (aka diminished) seventh chords are made by lowering the third and fifth by a half step; and the seventh by a whole step.

Major 6th	(maj6)	Contains a 3 and 6
Minor 6th	(m6)	Contains a ♭3 and 6
Half-Diminished 7th	(m7♭5)	Contains a ♭3, ♭5, ♭7
Diminished 7th	(o7)	Contains a ♭3, ♭5, ♭♭7

FIG. 11

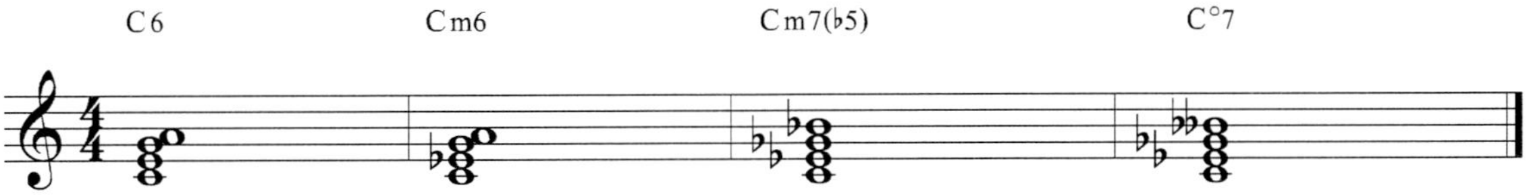

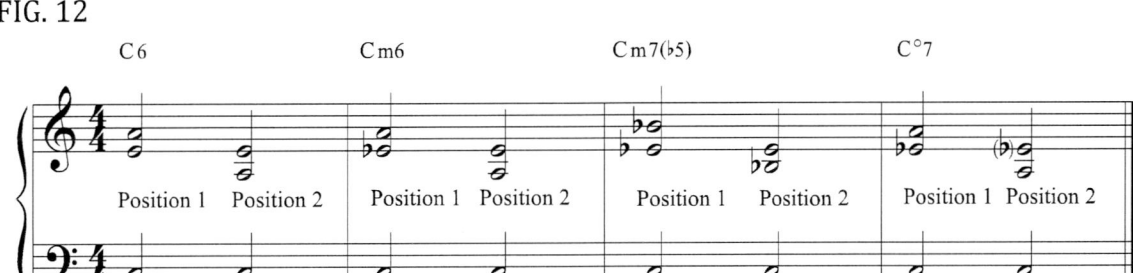

Practice transposing them using different intervallic relationships as you did with the dom7, maj7, and m7 chords. You should instantly be able to play a maj6, m6, m7(♭5), and o7 chord in root position in any key all over the keyboard.

Below we see the new chords expressed with guide tones (GTs) over the root (R) in two inversions:

Position 1: 3rd in the right thumb
Position 2: 7th (6th) in the right thumb

FIG. 12

To get these guide tone voicings under your fingers, practice both positions in different intervallic relationships as listed under FIG. 6. Notice how the guide tones for m7♭5 and m7 chords as well as m6 and o7 are identical since the fifth is missing from the voicing.

In later chapters, we will deal with the complete chord sound so that we can distinguish between these sounds. For now, it's important to be able to quickly find, be able to play, and hear the guide tones for major seventh, major sixth, minor seventh, minor sixth, dominant seventh, half diminished seventh, and diminished seventh.

Connect the guide tones as you play through the following cadence: I6–#io7–ii7–#iio7–iii7–♭iiio7–ii7–V7. This is a more chromatic variation of FIG. 9. When we study rhythm changes we will dive in deeper into these two important progressions. They both establish a tonality, and can be used with a few other elements to create intros for singers. Learn in all keys.

FIG. 13

Since we aren't including the fifth in our voicings, we can practice minor ii–V–Is in the following way: bVI6–V7–i6. bVI6 is very similar to ii7b5. In fact, bVI6 can be thought of as ii7b5 with the b5 in the bass. Learn in all keys.

FIG. 14

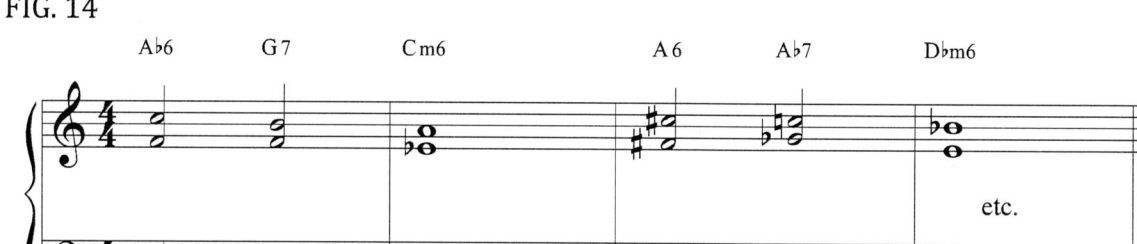

Apply these new guide tone voicings to the following classics, "All of Me," "There will Never Be Another You," "Autumn Leaves," "There is no Greater Love," and "It Could Happen to You."

Workout 11: Comping with Guide Tones on the changes to "All of Me" as sung by Sarah Vaughn. Swing together with the great Sarah Vaughan from her album, *Swingin' Easy*. A chord sheet of "All of Me" is given transposed to G with the first six bars written out with guide tones over a bass note. Since the melody starts on the tonic, G6 is a better choice avoiding a half-step clash between melody and the Gmaj7 chord voicing. In m. 2 Gmaj7 is used for variety.

As with all jazz versions of standards, it is important to research the original melody from other sources. The following version is free-wheeling and does not stick to the original melody. Keep that in mind as you enjoy comping with truly inspired singing. Also, listen carefully to the great piano accompanying by Jimmy Jones.

FIG. 15

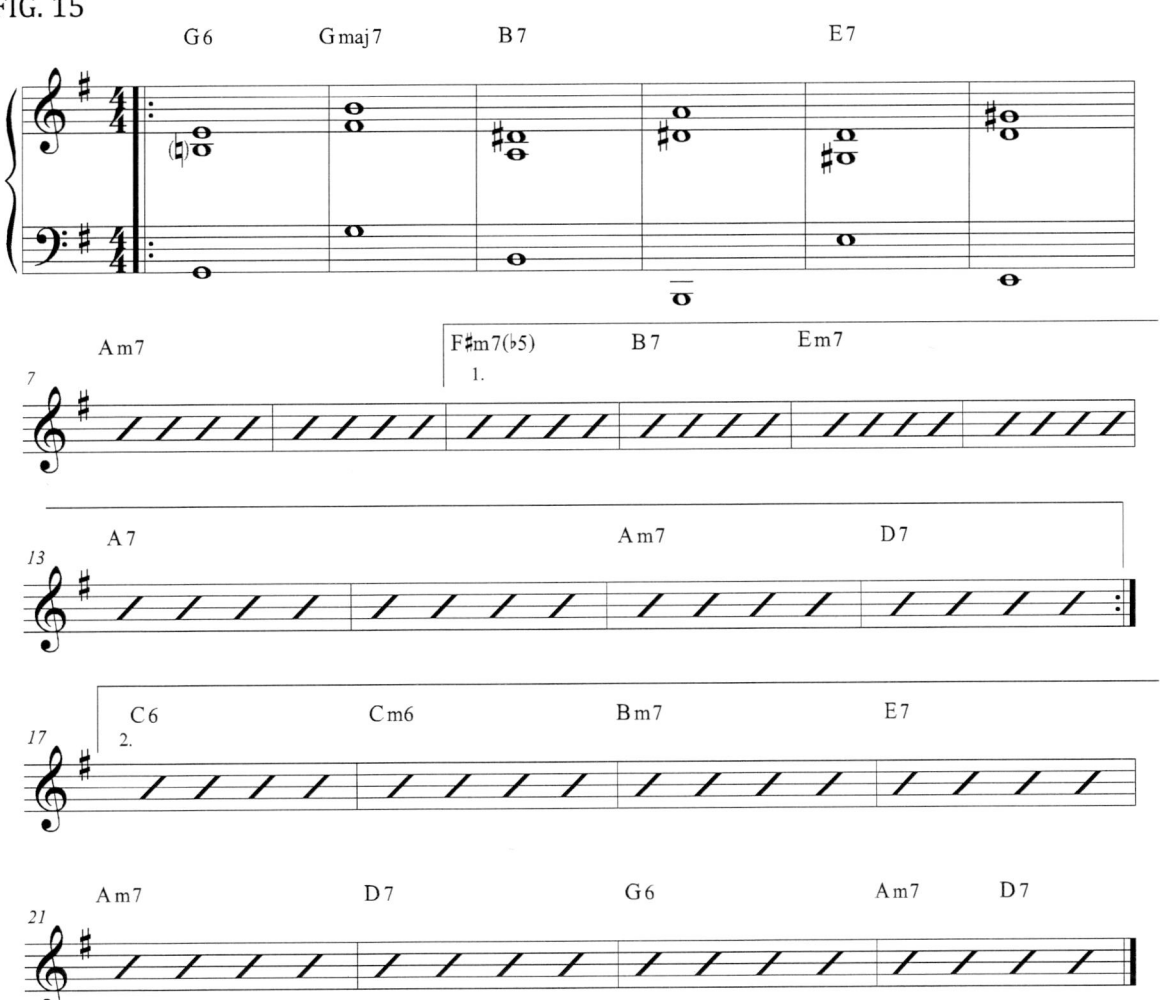

Basic Comping Strategies

"Comping" is a term jazz players use to describe accompanying. At its core, comping is simply playing chords in rhythm to inspire the rhythm section and support the soloist. Comping should also have forward motion, it should have a deep groove, it should be joyful, it should be hip and tasteful, it should drive the rhythm section, and should interact with everyone on the bandstand simultaneously. It's a tall order to say the least. That's why comping is an elusive art form, and its best practitioners have always been the most revered and most employable jazz pianists in history. It's something to pay attention to from the very beginning. Being a good comping pianist has much to do with an attitude of selflessness, and a desire to make everyone else comfortable and grooving.

The first step is to gain control of your comping so you *can* be supportive and selfless. It's a bit like driving a car. If we play off the beat the music tends to push forward; if we play on the beat the music tends to settle. Much like the gas pedal in a car, varying downbeats and upbeats can be an effective way to take control and add another dimension to your comping.

Playing an upbeat or offbeat (in 4/4 time that would be the "and" of 1, "and" of 2, "and" of 3, or the "and" of 4), requires some practice. This is especially true if you come from a classical background. In jazz the "and" comes a bit later than in classical music. It's closer to the third triplet of the beat. The exact placement is a personal thing, and is not meant to be measured mathematically.

Up until this point, you have been approximating the upbeat by "laying back." Now it's time to drill down on the concept of "laying back," and practice the third triplet of each beat. Begin by subdividing each beat into triplets so that you begin to internalize the triplet rhythm.

Workout 12: Practicing Upbeats on the changes to Sonny Red's "Bluesville." Practice the following rhythms on a blues. Loop each one-measure upbeat rhythm for several choruses, applying the appropriate guide tone voicing as you play along with Sonny Red. "Bluesville" is a C blues with a V-IV turnaround in m. 9 and 10.

FIG. 1

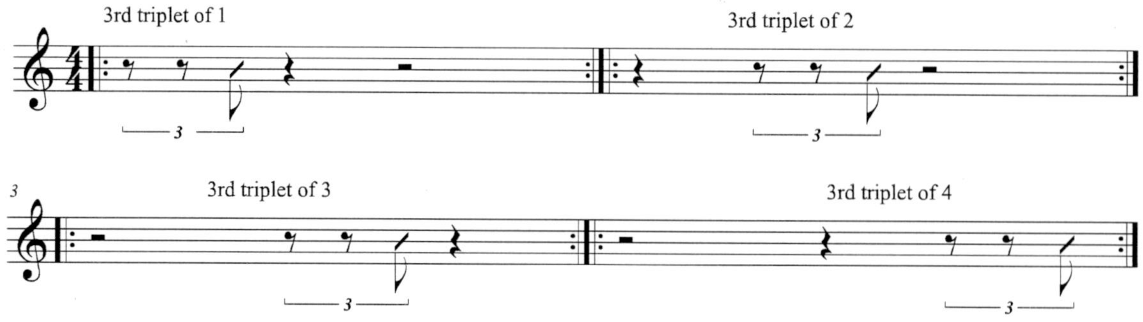

Now that you have an idea about how to place upbeats rhythmically, let's return to the gas pedal analogy, and explore what it feels like to pump the brakes or put your foot on the gas, musically. Keep in mind this type of slowing down and acceleration corresponds to a raising or lowering of musical intensity, rather than a change in tempo.

To get started, comp through the first eight bars of "Perdido."

1. Play a chord on beat 1 and/or beat 3 wherever there is chord symbol written. For now, keep it relatively short, but not staccato. This has a settling effect, as if your pumping the brakes in the rhythm section (without slowing down the tempo).

FIG. 2

2. Anticipate each rhythmic hit from FIG. 2. Either play on the "and of 4" or the "and of 2." This is one way to raise the intensity in the rhythm section (without speeding up the tempo). Remember to place the upbeats closer to the third triplet of the beat as you practiced in FIG. 1.

FIG. 3

3. Play after each rhythmic hit from FIG. 2. Either play on the "and of 1" or the "and of 3." This is another way to raise the intensity.

FIG. 4

4. Using FIG. 2 as a comping framework, decide whether to play on the beat, before the beat, or after the beat. Listen to the melody, and comp in a way that serves the melody. Remember, playing off the beat pushes the music forward; playing on the beat settles the music. Below is comping pattern that fits "Perdido." Keep in mind there is more than one correct answer here, it comes down to personal

taste and knowledge of the style. More on this a bit later. For now, notice how FIG. 5 contains the same rhythmic hits as in FIG. 2, only some have been moved back or forward an eighth note.

FIG. 5

5. Add some variety by varying the length of the chords. For non-ballads it's a good idea not to use too many long, sustained chords because they tend to cover up the groove of the bass and drums. But occasionally, a longer chord can add a dramatic effect. Also note the use of Bb6 as an alternative to Bbmaj7.

FIG. 6

6. Before we mentioned "knowledge of style." One way to increase your knowledge of the Ellington style is to check out some elements of the big band arrangement. For example, in "Perdido," the last chorus consists of a sax soli with an interesting brass background. These often contain valuable information about how to comp, as they usually contain very hip rhythms. The idea of having a hit on the "and of 4" in m. 1, 3, and 5 as well as hits on 1 and "and of 2" in m. 8 came from this background. Comp along with the Ellington band from 2:06 using the comping guide below modeled after the brass background.

FIG. 7

Workout 13: Basic Comping Rhythms on the changes to Duke Ellington's "Perdido." Comp along with the Duke Ellington band as you employ the above strategies. You can reference the chord sheet in FIG. 10, Chapter 2A. In the "A" sections you can sometimes substitute Bb6 for Bbmaj7 for variety. Refer to **DL TRK 7-8** for a demo and play-along. The demo track contains: 1st chorus: comping on the beat; 2nd chorus: comping before or after the beat; and 3rd chorus: comping rhythms and variations from FIG. 7 above.

Workout 14: Basic Comping Rhythms on the changes to "It Could Happen to You" as played by Miles Davis. Employ the comping strategies from above as you groove along with Philly Joe Jones, Paul Chambers, and Red Garland on Miles' landmark album, *Relaxin' with the Miles Davis Quintet.* Since the tempo and faster, use more downbeats. Below is a sample comping framework consisting of half notes and whole notes with chord symbols that are compatible with the recording. Apply RH guide tones over LH bass notes and play along with the recording. In mm. 5 and 21 play Ebmaj7 guide tones with a Bb in the LH.

FIG. 8

Chapter 2 • B

Adjust the framework backwards or forwards to create a balance between downbeats and upbeats. Have a nice mix of long and short chords. Keep the rhythm sizzling and feeling good. Notice how Paul Chambers stays in a "two feel" for the entire track. Below is an adjusted framework loosely based on Red Garland's comping.

FIG. 9

Basic LH Voicings

It's important to build a repertoire of LH voicings that you can use when you play RH melodies. Of course, the rootless "A" and "B" voicings that are so popular in jazz piano curriculums are effective, and in later chapters we will explore them in detail. For now, we need more basic structures that can serve simple melodies and not overpower your RH.

Two important LH voicings to learn that can immediately be applied to your playing are the shell voicing and LH guide tones. Both are simple two-note structures that imply a larger chord.

Shells contain 2 chord tones and come in different varieties. We'll be concentrating on 1-7, 1-3, 1-5, and 5-3. Because they are so compact yet carry a lot of harmonic information, they are effective when comping with the LH. Bud Powell and Thelonious Monk made famous use of these voicings and inspired countless pianists of today. Because they contain no tension notes, they work well contrasting complicated and chromatic bebop melodies in the RH.

Shells often contain the root, creating a sound reminiscent of stride piano. But unlike the larger shapes used in stride piano, shells are small enough so that they can be played by most pianists.

For best results the shell should be approximately between middle C and the C2 (two octaves below). More dissonant intervals 1-3 and 1-7 should be played in the upper range; 5-3 and 1-5 shells can be played lower since the intervals are more consonant. Pianists like Horace Silver experimented with playing shells much lower as part of his unique funky sound, but in general careful of making your shells sound too muddy.

Here is an overview of possible shells:

Maj7	Maj6	Dom7	m7	m6	m7b5	o7
1-7	1-6	1-b7	1-b7	1-6	1-b7	1-6
1-3	1-3	1-3	1-b3	1-b3	1-b3	1-b3
5-3	5-3	5-3		5-b3	b5-b3	b5-b3
1-5	1-5			1-5		

The 5-3 shell is not as common, and should not be overused.

Try ii7-V7-I starting with 1-7, moving to 1-3, back to 1-7 in all 12 keys. Do it again starting with 1-3, moving to 1-7, back to 1-3. The pattern below moves down in whole steps. After making it back to C major, start again a half step higher.

FIG. 1

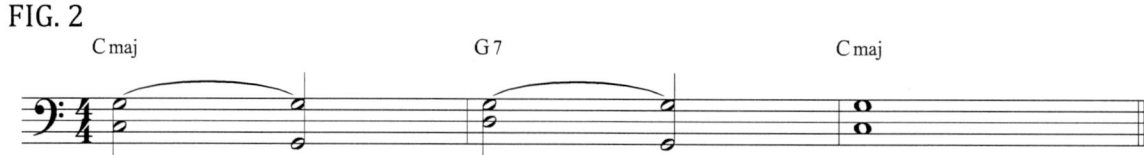

Another related progression that's incredibly important to practice is I–V–I. Here it is using the 1–5 shell and its inverse, 5–1. In m. 1, tonic is expressed using 1–5 moving to V in the bass. In m. 2, V is expressed with 5–1 (of V) moving to V in the bass. This drone effect was popular in the bebop era. Transpose through the keys.

FIG. 2

Finally, here is a fragment of the standard blues ending using shells: IV7–#ivo7–I. Notice how the 5–3 shell is used for the I chord. Transpose through the keys.

FIG. 3

Now apply shells to a tune. First practice shells on downbeats. By playing the V of the chord of the moment on beat 3, you can create a two feel. Strive for good voice leading in your shell pattern. If your hand is big enough, you can hold over the top note of the shell as you play the V with your pinky. For 5–3 shells on beat one play the tonic on beat 3 instead. The idea is to create a rocking motion back and forth between I and the V of the chord of the moment. By including the 5, even if it's on beat 3, we are now able to hear more of the chord. This is especially vivid on m7b5 and o7 in which shells alone don't adequately give the entire chord sound.

Play the melody to "All of Me" over a steady LH pattern alternating between shells and V pedals on beats 1 and 3. The first half of the tune is given below. Keep your ears open for the m7b5 chord. Your RH can be syncopated, creating contrast to the rock-solid 1 and 3 LH, and therefore forming the basis of your solo jazz piano sound.

FIG. 4

When playing with a band, playing less is a good idea. First, you don't have to play the V pedal on beat 3. Playing the V pedal now and then, however, can be quite effective. Second, you don't have to make a big deal about the root on beat 1. Instead, you can play the shell, but then immediately let go of the root while holding the 7th or 3rd. This way, you can get the complete shell sound without getting in the way of the bass player. If the chord is the same for 2 measures, you don't have to play the shell again in the second measure on beat 1. You can either play it on beat 3 or not play it at all. Even with less shell activity you can add forward momentum to the LH by anticipating some of the shells.

Workout 15: Playing the Melody over Shells on the changes to "All of Me" as sung by Sarah Vaughan. Freely play the melody over the following rhythm section-friendly shell pattern along with Sarah Vaughan. The first half of the tune is given below. Notice how you lift the root while still holding the 7th or 3rd.

FIG. 5

The benefit of this workout is that by playing the melody over and over in different ways with a simple shell pattern, you can zero in on the feel of the pianist, bassist and drummer. Try the same exercise with a different rhythm section.

Workout 16: Playing the Melody over Shells on the changes to "Autumn Leaves" as played by Cannonball Adderley. Experience one of the premier rhythm sections of all time as you play the melody along with Hank Jones, Sam Jones, and Art Blakey. The shell pattern for the first 8 bars of the tune is given below. This track is from *Somethin' Else*, recorded by Cannonball Adderley on Blue Note in 1958. This is an excellent record to access the music. Explore other recordings by the members on the record. Also, explore other records from the Blue Note catalogue during this period. Refer to **DL TRK 9-10** for a demo and play-along track. For the 1st chorus, LH shells are played under a RH solo/embellished melody.

FIG. 6

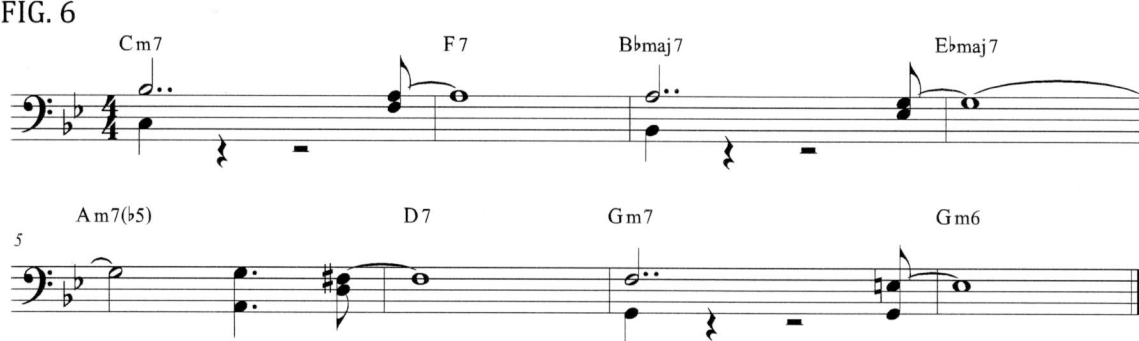

LH guide tones also contain 2 chord tones, but by definition never contain the root. Since they are 3–7(6) or 7(6)–3, they form an interval of a 4th and have a sleek modern sound.

They form the basis of closed position chords and should be practiced in both hands. Pianists from the bebop generation through the present day make good use of these beautiful rootless voicings.

Workout 17: Jammin' with Sonny Clark on the changes to "Blues Blue." Interact with Sonny Clark on his G blues, Blues Blue from the 1960 album, *Sonny Clark Trio* with drummer Max Roach and bassist George Duvivier (not to be confused with the Blue Note album by the same title).

First, just play along with the left hand. A simple LH comping framework is given consisting of LH guide tones and shells in whole notes and half notes. Feel free to add some syncopation, but keep it simple. Listen to the rhythms played by Sonny Clark. Playing mostly whole notes and half notes is perfectly appropriate in this situation. After you feel comfortable playing the LH alone, add some bluesy interjections in the RH.

A few new harmonic movements show up in this 12-bar G blues. Notice the iii7–VI7 in m. 8 taking you to the ii7 in m. 9. Also, be aware of the I–VI7–II7–V7 turnaround in m. 11-12.

FIG. 7

As stated in the beginning of the chapter, harmonic connections are paramount. Both shell voicings and LH guide tone voicings can be connected to create smooth harmonic progressions: 1–7 shells can jump to other 1–7 shells, but ideally move to 1–3 shells; LH guide tones 3–7 smoothly move to 7–3 and so on. No matter what structure you ultimately choose for your LH voicing, keep the harmonic connections in mind.

Guide Tone Voicings with Doubled Notes

Playing hip jazz voicings with lots of tension can be exciting, but if you are accompanying someone, if you are trying to establish a basic tonality, or if you are trying to play a chord that is welcoming and mild, then creating a full sounding voicing without tension is key. To do this, we need to double certain notes. Usually the notes of the chord to double are the guide tones (3rd and 7th).

Guide tone voicings with doubled notes are voicings consisting only of 3rds and 7ths (6ths) over a root with guide tones doubled in some way. Later we can move the 7th and/or the 3rd to create inner movement.

Common guide tone voicings with doubled notes include:

RH	3–7–3	7–3–7	7–3	3–7	7–3–7	3–7–3
LH	1	1	1–3	1–7	1–3	1–7

For Cmaj7:

FIG. 1

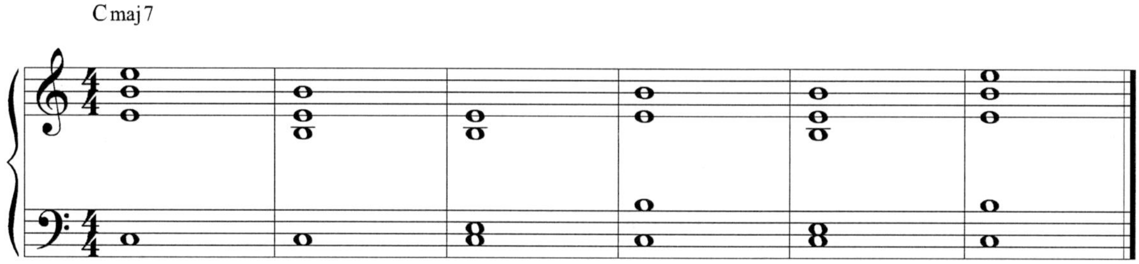

The fact that these voicings contain 4th and 5th intervals while still not containing any tensions, makes them transparent, open, mild, and incredibly useful for navigating through tunes with lots of bebop changes, or comping on ballads.

By changing the 3 to b3 and/or the 7 to b7 or 6 we can create guide tone voicings with doubled notes for every type of seventh and sixth chord discussed so far. Go back to FIG. 9 from Chapter 2A and play the pattern in all 12 keys using these new voicings. Here it is in C using an assortment of guide tone voicings with doubled notes.

FIG. 2

Workout 18: Guide Tone Voicings with Doubled Notes on the changes to "Sippin' At Bells" as played by Sonny Clark. Navigate through this F blues with bebop changes from Sonny Clark's seminal recording, *Cool Struttin'* using guide tone voicings with doubled notes. Listen to how Sonny Clark doesn't play the entire voicing every half note. Instead he finds connections between chords so that he can move just one note to imply the next chord. For example, for ii–V, Sonny Clark moves the 7th of the ii7 to the 3rd of the V7 while holding the other voices.

Even though the harmonic rhythm moves every half note, and consists of ii–Vs in many keys, the important signposts in the blues structure are preserved albeit disguised a bit.

Below is a comping framework for "Sippin' At Bells." Note that these changes are played only for the melody and the first chorus of each soloist. Like you did before with "It Could Happen To Me" and "Perdido," adjust the framework to add syncopation to the comping. Listen carefully to Sonny Clark. His rhythms are clear and perfectly compliment the melody. Play with the recording.

FIG. 3

By moving the 7th chromatically like in Sonny Clark's comping, we can create inner motion. Using LH 1–7; RH 3–7, practice tonic major (I) by moving through maj7, 7, 6, majb6, maj and back up again. Then practice tonic minor in the same way. This inner chord movement is sometimes known as a line cliché. Because the 7th moves up and down these voicings still have the feel of guide tone voicings even though at certain points no 7th exists in the chord.

FIG. 4

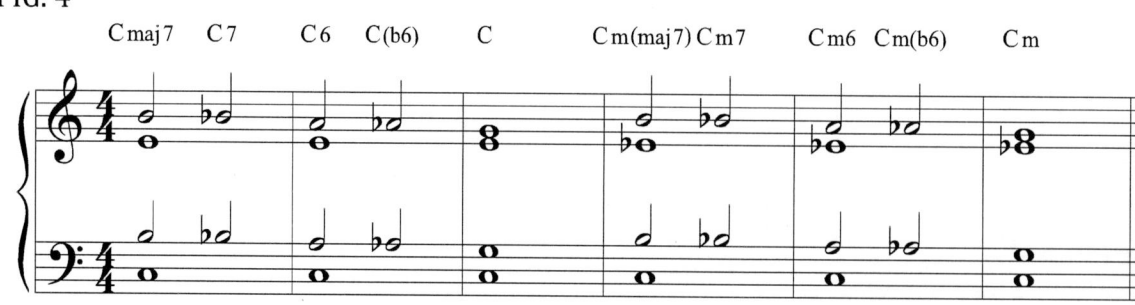

Workout 19: Guide Tone Voicings with Doubled Notes on the changes to "For Heaven's Sake" as played by Kenny Barron. Check out Kenny Barron's version of standard, "For Heaven's Sake" from his trio album, *Minor Blues,* or watch his trio concert from the 2015 Nice Jazz Festival on Youtube. Below is a chord sheet showing the harmonic progression. Practice this progression using guide tone voicings with doubled notes with Kenny Barron's recording. When you come to the second half of the bridge use the 4-note voicings with the movable 7th from FIG. 4 above. For half diminished chords (m7b5) include the b5 in the RH. Hold it over to create a b9 tension for the following dominant 7th chord. There will be more on tensions in later chapters. Sing or hum the melody. Selected bars are done for you.

FIG. 5

To internalize the movable 7th idea, apply the voicing to the major scale. On each scale step play LH 1–7; RH 3–7 and move the 7 to 6 (or b6) in both hands. Try in all 12 keys.

FIG. 6

Workout 20: Guide Tone Voicings with Doubled Notes on the changes to "Bye Bye Blackbird" as played by Miles Davis. Play relaxed, rich guide tone voicings with doubled notes as you comp along with Miles Davis from his classic album, *Round About Midnight.*

The first half of the song is voiced in this style and illustrated below. Notice how much of the comping pattern is just portions of the major scale pattern from FIG. 6 transposed to F, with the 3rd doubled in the melody to create richer 5-note voicings.

For the first four bars of the melody, stay on Fmaj7 or F6. On the solos you can play Gm–C7 in measures 2 and 4, and Abm7–Db7 in measure 6. Observe the moving 7ths starting in m. 9 to show m7 to m(maj7). Again, to create the half-diminished chord (m7b5) in the bridge, add the b5 in the RH. In general, keep the voicings very simple. It doesn't take much to provide a hip, supportive, cushion on top of which the soloist can shine. Finish voicing the second half of the tune notated below with chord symbols.

FIG. 7

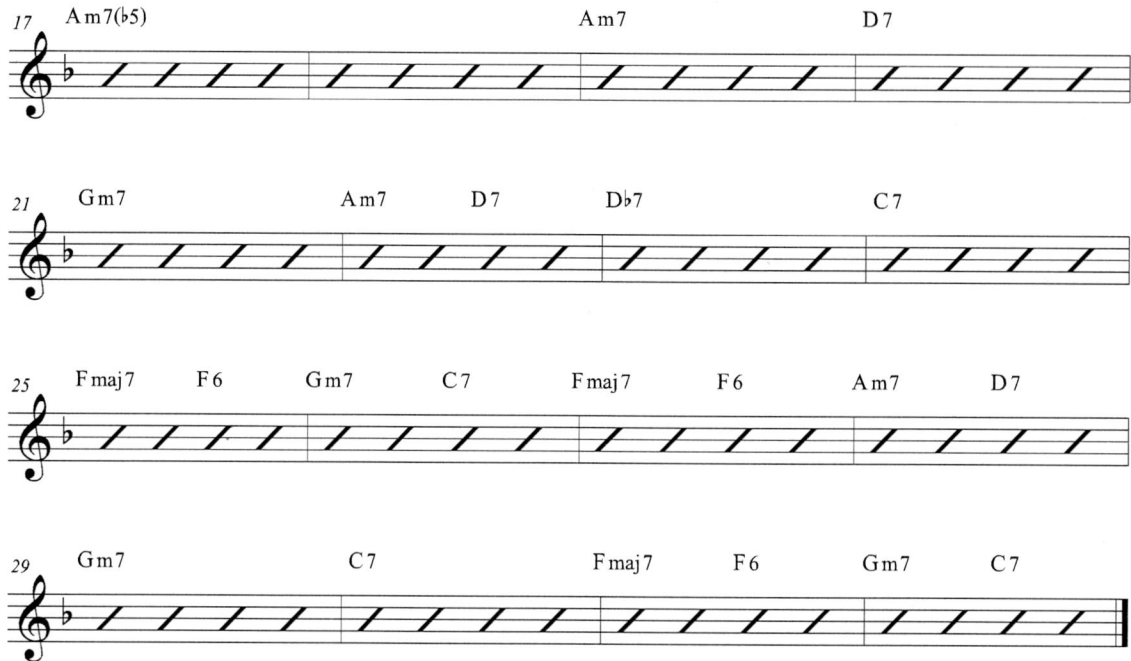

For more advanced students try the same exercise as in FIG. 6 but add a chromatic approach tone a half step below the 6 or b6. At times #5 is a more appropriate symbol to express the direction of movement.

FIG. 8

If we expand our chromatic inner movement to include moving the 3rd up and down chromatically, we can find a treasure trove of interesting harmonic connections while using these somewhat simple voicings.

Let's take the following guide tone voicings with doubled notes: LH 1–7; RH 3–7 and LH 1–3; RH 7–3. For each voicing you are allowed to move the doubled note up or down chromatically as you navigate through a standard. Rather than giving a laundry list of rules to follow, use your ears to find interesting chromatic connections. Below is an example of this style of voicing applied to "Autumn Leaves."

Naturally, if too much chromatic movement is added, it can get in the way of the melody. For the beginner, just add simple movements on maj7 (maj7 to 6) and for ii–V7 move the m7 to 6. Note that the added chromatic movements are not reflected in the chord symbol.

FIG. 9

Workout 21: Movable Guide Tone Voicings with Doubled Notes on the changes to "Autumn Leaves" as played by Cannonball Adderley. Comp for Miles Davis' solo. Following the example above, create a progression of guide tone voicings with doubled notes with movable 7ths and 3rds. Think about rolling out a luxurious carpet on which Miles Davis can effortlessly tell his story. Play mostly half notes and explore chromatic connections. Refer to **DL TRK 9-10** for a demo and play-along track. For the 2nd chorus of the demo, movable guide tone voicings with doubled notes are used. Try this same exercise on a medium/slow tune of your choice from your favorite album.

FIG. 10

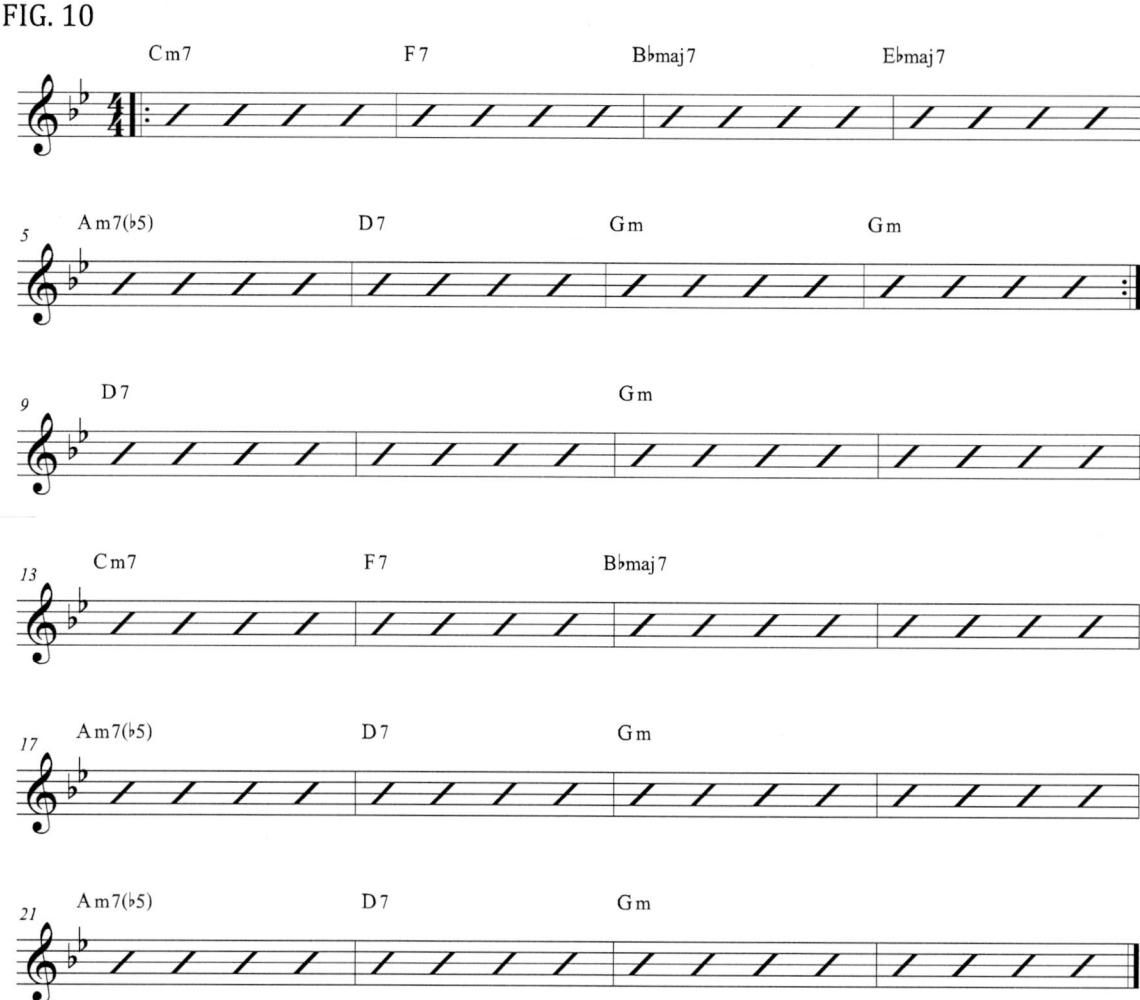

Duet 2: Accompanying a Melody using Guide Tone Voicings. ***Variation 1***: Player 1 plays a melody to a jazz standard in octaves; Player 2 accompanies using guide tone voicings with doubled notes with a moveable 7th. ***Variation 2***: Player 2 plays a melody in the RH over LH shells. Player 1 accompanies using guide tone voicings.

Chapter 3
Closed Position Chords

To understand chord construction, it's important to start with chords that are in closed position, or at least contain all of their notes within an octave. By building these compact structures that have all necessary harmonic information, you can quickly have access to voicings that can be moved around easily as you navigate through various chord changes. By playing these structures over roots you can get the complete chord sound so crucial when trying to learn the harmony of a song.

Closed position means all of the chord tones are played next to each other within an octave. 4-note closed position or 4-note close is the most common example of this kind of structure since all of the chord tones are included. Therefore, examples of 4-note close are all four inversions of sixth or seventh chords: 1–3–5–7(6), 3–5–7(6)–1, 5–7(6)–1–3, and 7(6)–1–3–5. No matter what the order, the chord tones are always adjacent to one and other and fall within one octave. Jazz players often make substitutions to the root and 5th to add color to the closed position voicing. The chord quality determines the 3rd and 7th (6th). In Chapter 3B we will delve deeper into 4-note closed position chords.

Before dealing with 4-note voicings, compact 3-note voicings are examined in Chapter 3A. For the most part these structures are created by adding one note above the guide tones. Even though these structures are technically not in closed position, since not all of the chord tones are next to each other, all voices are contained within an octave. You can think of these 3-note voicings as 4-note closed position chords with one chord tone missing.

For our purposes, these 3-note voicings will be used as RH voicings over a LH root, so that you can clearly hear the tonality. At the end of Chapter 3A, we'll examine using them as stand-alone LH voicings for use with a bass player and/or when playing the melody in your RH.

In Chapter 3C, connecting sixth chords with diminished seventh chords will be discussed, as we highlight the importance of playing what Barry Harris terms, "little chords." In Chapter 3D, the sixth-diminished scale is briefly examined, with some basic applications. Finally, in Chapter 3E, more comping strategies are outlined presented as comping games.

Compact 3-note Voicings

By adding one note on top of our RH guide tone voicing from Chapter 2A, we can create a relatively full-sounding chord voicing. A 3-note structure that spans less than an octave and contains guide tones is called a compact 3-note voicing. They can be played as a RH voicing over a root, or as a LH voicing, especially useful when performing with a bass player and/or when playing the melody in the RH.

A basic seventh chord is made up of root, 3rd, 5th, and 7th. The non-chord tones (2nd, 4th, and 6th) create tension when played against the basic chord tones. When the 2nd, for example, is played "above" the chord tones, the effect is added color or tension to the chord sound. The 2nd is heard as an upper extension, and when played in the presence of the 7th is notated as a 9th. In the same way the 4th is notated as an 11th; and the 6th is a 13th. Therefore, the 9th, 11th, and 13th are known as **tensions** of the chord. If they are sharpened or flattened they become altered tensions. In Chapter 5 we will delve more deeply into the subject of chord tones, tensions, and chord scale theory. For now, we will present some of the mostly commonly used chords and the usual associated tension.

When creating our 3-note voicings we can add either a tension, root, or 5th above the guide tones. For two voicings, the b5 or b9 is actually added between the guide tones. Adding a tension will give the richest sound. Below are several charts showing some of the most common compact 3-note voicings for seven important qualities of chords: tonic major (maj7 or maj6/9), minor seventh (m7), dominant seventh with natural tensions (7 (13)), dominant seventh with altered tensions (7alt) or 7(b9), tonic minor (m6/9), half-diminished seventh (m7b5), and diminished seventh (o7).

To learn them, it's best to practice the voicings in context of major ii–V–I, minor ii–V–I, and a blues so you can see how they are usually played in a progression.

To play a major ii–V–I we will need a:
1. tonic major voicing for the I chord (which can be maj7 or maj6/9)
2. minor seventh voicing for the ii7 chord
3. dominant seventh voicing with natural tensions for the V7 chord (although, a dominant seventh with altered tensions will also work).

For tonic major learn these two positions. The first is maj6/9 or maj9. It has a 3rd in the lowest position with the 9 in the melody. The second is maj7 or maj13. It has a 7th in the lowest position and the 5 or 13 in the melody.

Tonic major	
9	5(13)
6(7)	3
3	7

For minor sevenths, place the 9 above the b7 or the 5 above the b3. If the minor seventh is a iii chord, the natural 9th can sound out of place in the key, and a clash sometimes occurs between the 9th and the melody. As a solution, simply play the root instead of the 9.

m7	
9(R)	5
b7	b3
b3	b7

Dominant sevenths give us the most flexibility when adding a third voice to our RH voicing. Above the guide tones you can add either natural tensions (13 or 9) or altered tensions (b13 or b9/#9). Dominant sevenths with natural tensions are usually used when resolving to major or when playing a blues.

7(13) Natural Tensions	
9	13
b7	3
3	b7

Dominant sevenths with altered tensions are darker, and are especially effective when resolving to tonic minor, or when moving to a minor chord in general. They have a stronger magnetic pull to the next chord. Altered dominant chords can also be used to resolve to major.

7(alt) Altered Tensions	
b9(#9)	b13
b7	3
3	b7

Practice major ii–V–I using compact 3-note voicings. You can either use a dominant seventh chord with natural tensions or with altered tensions. Listen to the difference.

Chapter 3 ◆ A

FIG. 1

Workout 22: Compact 3-note Voicings on the changes to "Broadway" as played by Ahmad Jamal. Practice "Broadway" with compact 3-note voicings in the RH over a root in your LH. The first eight bars are done for you. For now, play simple rhythms mostly on 1 and 3. As you get more comfortable experiment with incorporating the "and" of 4 and the "and" of 2 as you play along with the recording.

FIG. 2

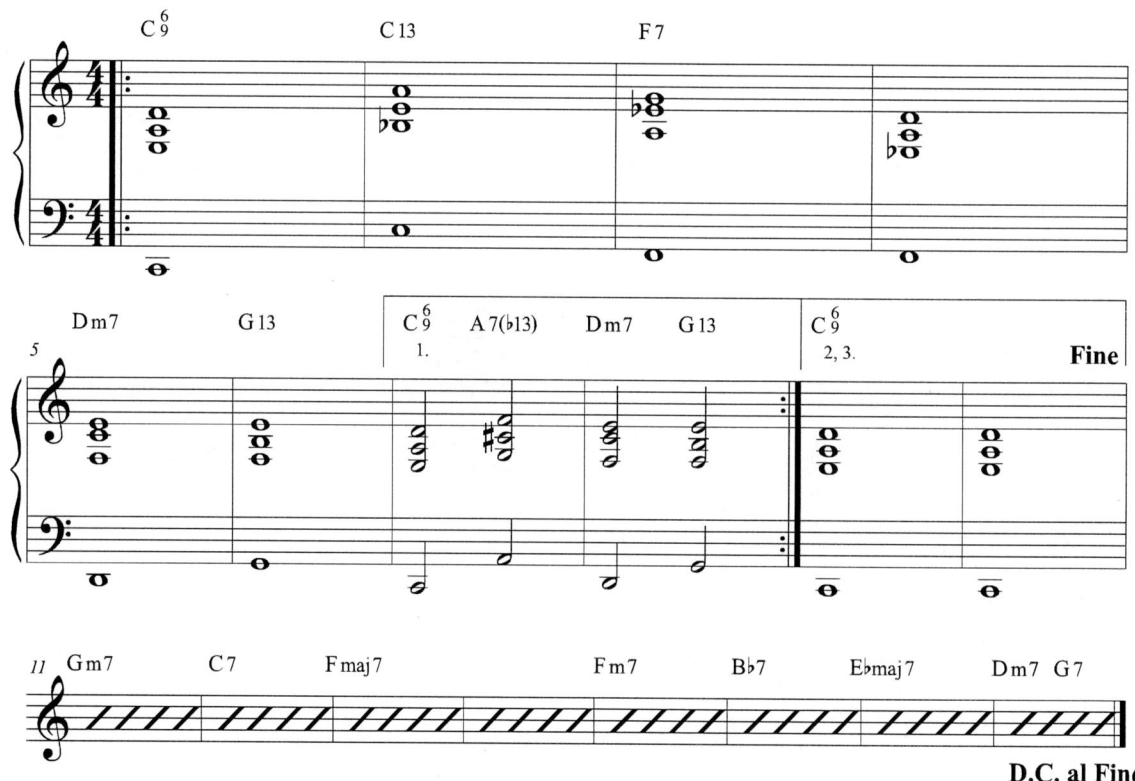

D.C. al Fine

To play a minor ii–V–i we will need a:
1. tonic minor voicing for the i chord (m6/9)
2. half diminished seventh voicing for the ii7b5 chord
3. dominant seventh voicing with altered tensions for the V7 chord

For tonic minor learn these two positions of m6/9. The first voicing has the flat 3rd in the lowest position with the 9 in the melody made up of fourths. The second has the 6th in the lowest position with the 5 in the melody.

Tonic minor	
9	5
6	b3
b3	6

For m7b5, avoid having the 9th in the melody. In Chapter 5 you will learn about the scales often used with this chord. For now, since the soloist may play b9 or natural 9 depending on the scale, it's better to leave it out entirely. Play the b5 either in between or on top of the guide tones.

m7b5	
b7	b5
b5	b3
b3	b7

Below is one last voicing for dominant seventh b9 built from the b7 that pairs nicely with the m7b5 voicing built from the b3. This voicing also contains the tension (in this case the b9) between the two guide tones. For minor ii–V feel free to mix and match any 3-note voicing for m7b5 with 7(alt) or 7(b9).

7(b9)
3
b9
b7

Practice the following minor ii–V–i progression in several keys.

FIG. 3

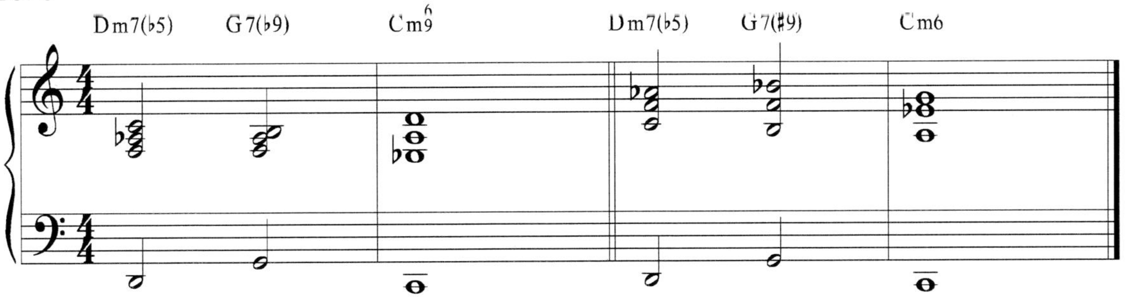

Chapter 3 • A

Workout 23: Compact 3-note Voicings on the changes to "Alone Together" as played by Sonny Stitt. Practice major and minor ii–V–Is in the context of this beautiful standard from Sonny Stitt's album, *New York Jazz*. The first 14-bar A section is done for you. Listen carefully to the great Jimmy Jones on piano, Ray Brown on bass, and "Papa" Jo Jones on drums. Usually at a jam session, this piece is called in D minor. It's always helpful to be flexible with keys, especially when playing with singers. Refer to **DL TRK 11-12** for a demo and play-along. For the 1st chorus, 3-note RH voicings are used.

FIG. 4

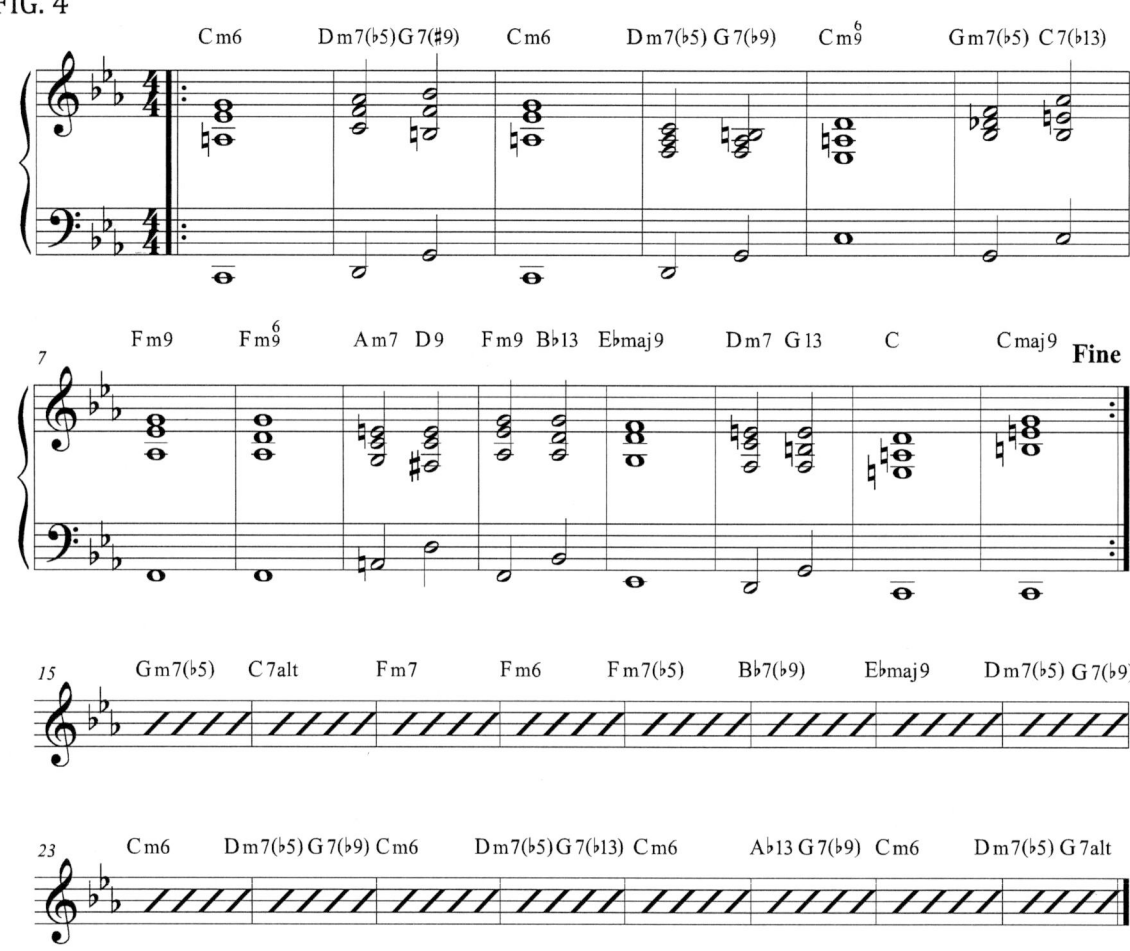

Finally practice these 3-note voicings for diminished seventh. Because it's lacking a b5, the first position is incomplete. Also, it's best at this point to avoid the 9. Begin by only playing the root or b5 over guide tones. After getting comfortable, you can experiment with substituting b13 for b5. Though incomplete at times, these simple diminished seventh voicings are useful, especially when playing the blues.

o7	
R	b5(b13)
6	b3
b3	6

Here is a basic jam session style blues with 3-note closed position chords notated in the key of F. Since we left the bluesy triad workout in Chapter 1, the blues has evolved a fair amount. For one thing, the V–IV turnaround in bars 9 and 10 has been replaced with a ii–V turnaround more common in straight ahead jazz. Also, the ii–V7alt/IV in bar 4 and ii–V7alt in bar 12 adds magnetic pull into bar 5 and bar 1 respectively. In addition, a V7alt/ii has been added to bar 8 to lead more smoothly into bar 9. Finally, notice the addition of the #ivo7 chords in m. 2 and m. 6 to give a touch of authenticity and downhome flavor reminiscent of Grant Green's "Sunday Mornin'" from Chapter 1.

Workout 24: Compact 3-note Voicings on the changes to Sonny Clark's "Blue's Blue." Employ some of the comping techniques from Chapter 2B. Groove along with the Sonny Clark Quintet from My Conception on this blues paying close attention to Art Blakey's cymbal beat and the placement of quarter notes by Paul Chambers. Note that this version "Blue's Blue" is in F instead of G. Use the chord sheet as a guide, but keep in mind that every chorus might be a bit different harmonically. Remember the blues isn't necessarily a set of specific changes that is unchangeable, but rather a set of changes that evolve as the solo develops. Try to hear the big picture. Start after the melody. Refer to **DL TRK 13-14** for a demo and play-along. For the 1st chorus of the demo 3-note voicings are played in the RH over the root in the LH. After playing along with Sonny Clark, use this voicing style to comp along with your favorite blues recording.

FIG. 5

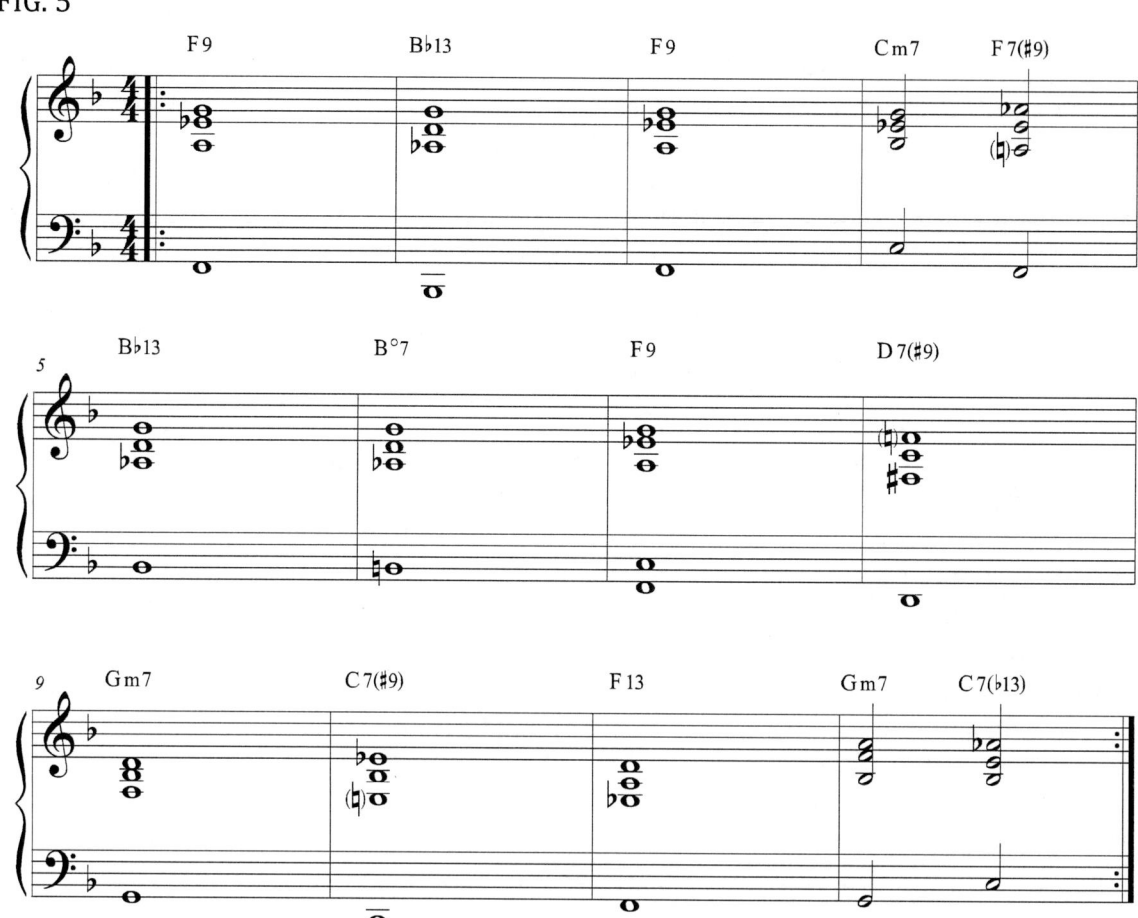

COMPACT 3-NOTE VOICINGS FOR THE LH

By playing 3-note compact voicings in your LH, you can free up your RH, enabling you to play melodies or solo. These 3-note structures are less heavy than 4-note closed position chords (to be studied in the next chapter) and work better when accompanying a single line in the RH.

Workout 25: LH Compact 3-note voicings on the changes of "Broadway" as played by Ahmad Jamal. Revisit Ahmad Jamal's version of "Broadway." This time play the 3-note voicings in the LH while playing the melody or embellishing the melody in your RH along with the recording. Note in m. 6 the G13 is changed to G7(b13) to accommodate the new embellished melody.

FIG. 6

Playing with a bass player often means not playing the bass note in the LH. Up to this point, all of the workouts have contained bass notes in the LH. In order to hear the entire chord sound, one has to play the root of the chord. Therefore, it is vital for young players not to advance to "rootless" chord voicings too quickly. On the other hand, playing the root with a heavy hand in the bass range can make it tough for bass players to enjoy playing together with you.

Throughout history, great pianists from Art Tatum, Bud Powell, Barry Harris, and even Bill Evans and Mulgrew Miller have played bass notes in their LH even though a bass player is present. The trick is, they might not be playing them constantly, they may play it as an accent off the beat, or (most importantly) the touch they have is so beautiful, notes in the bass range enhance the bass player's notes rather than clash with them.

There was a shift from the practice of stride pianists who played a constant "oom pah bass" figure with variations to the bebop pianist who played starker shell voicings played off the beat, modeled after the drummers' concept of "dropping bombs" to the post-bop pianist who played mostly rootless structures in the mid- range of the piano. All of these styles can be incorporated in your own LH style. I believe in variety, and that there's a time and place for many different LH voicing styles. Don't be limited to just one.

Compact 3-note voicings in the LH can also be used for comping behind a soloist with a bassist. Simply by adding root–5th–root or 5th–root–5th in your RH you can create effective, big band-style (think 3 trumpets and 3 trombones) comping voicings. Make sure that the tensions and 5ths in the RH match the tensions and 5ths in the LH. For altered dominants, sharp the 5 in the RH to match the altered tensions in the LH.

Here is "Broadway" again, using big band-style voicings. Observe the 1–5–1/5–1–5 right hand shape and how it's modified to 1–#5–1 for G7b13 and A7b13.

FIG. 7

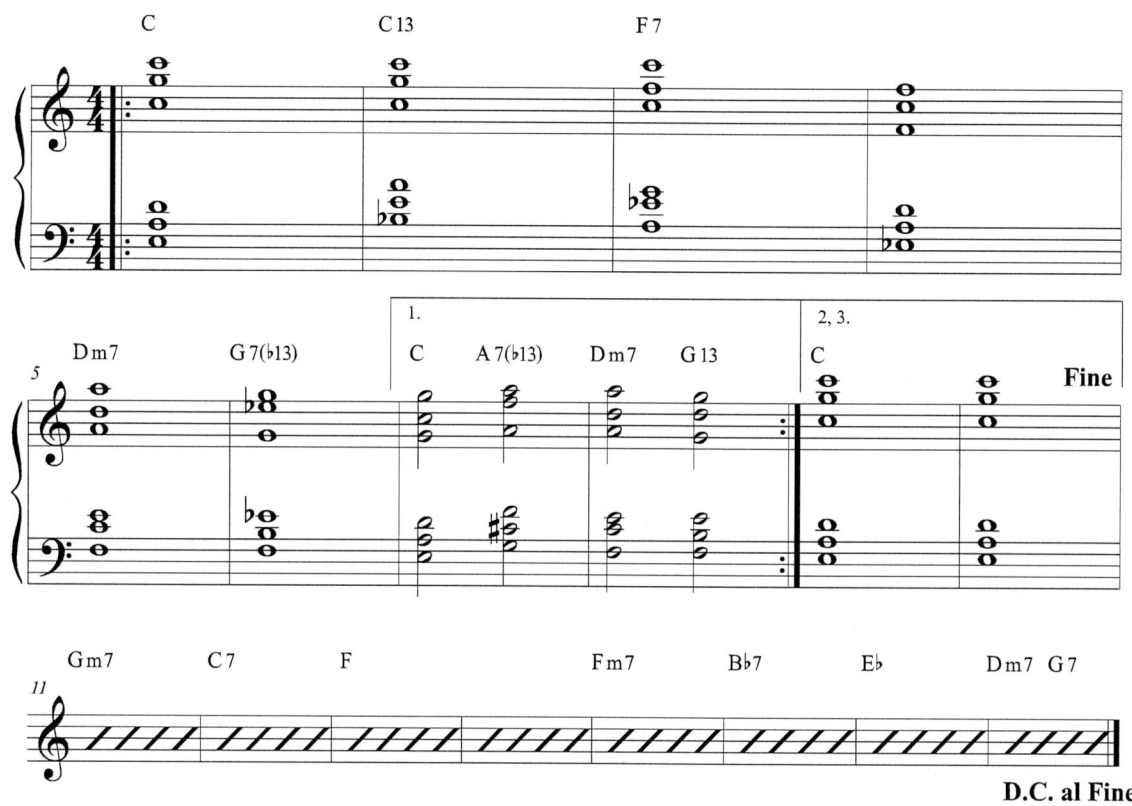

To minimize skipping around in the RH, you can use the same right-hand shape for each chord of ii–V–I. Simply play 1–5–1 or 5–1–5 of the V chord for ii, V, and I. Practice these major and minor ii–V–I progressions in all 12 keys.

FIG. 8

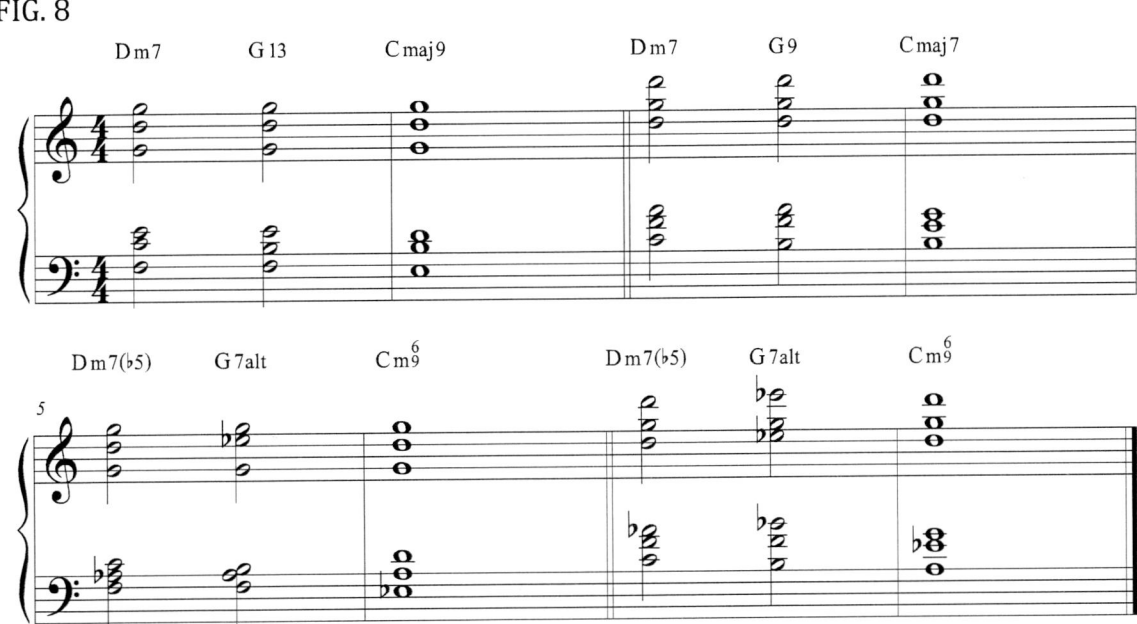

Besides being economical, this voicing strategy solves the problem created when playing 1–5–1 in the RH over the 3-note structure for maj7(9). Since there is no root in the new RH shape, the major 7 in the LH does not create an undesirable minor ninth interval.

Workout 26: Big band-Style Voicings on the changes to "Alone Together" as played by Sonny Stitt. Revisit "Alone Together," this time playing the 3-note voicings in the LH and adding the 3-note RH octave structures. Figure out the structures for the bridge and the last A. Play along with the recording. Refer to **DL TRK 11-12** for a demo and play-along. For the 2nd chorus, big band-style voicings are used.

FIG. 9

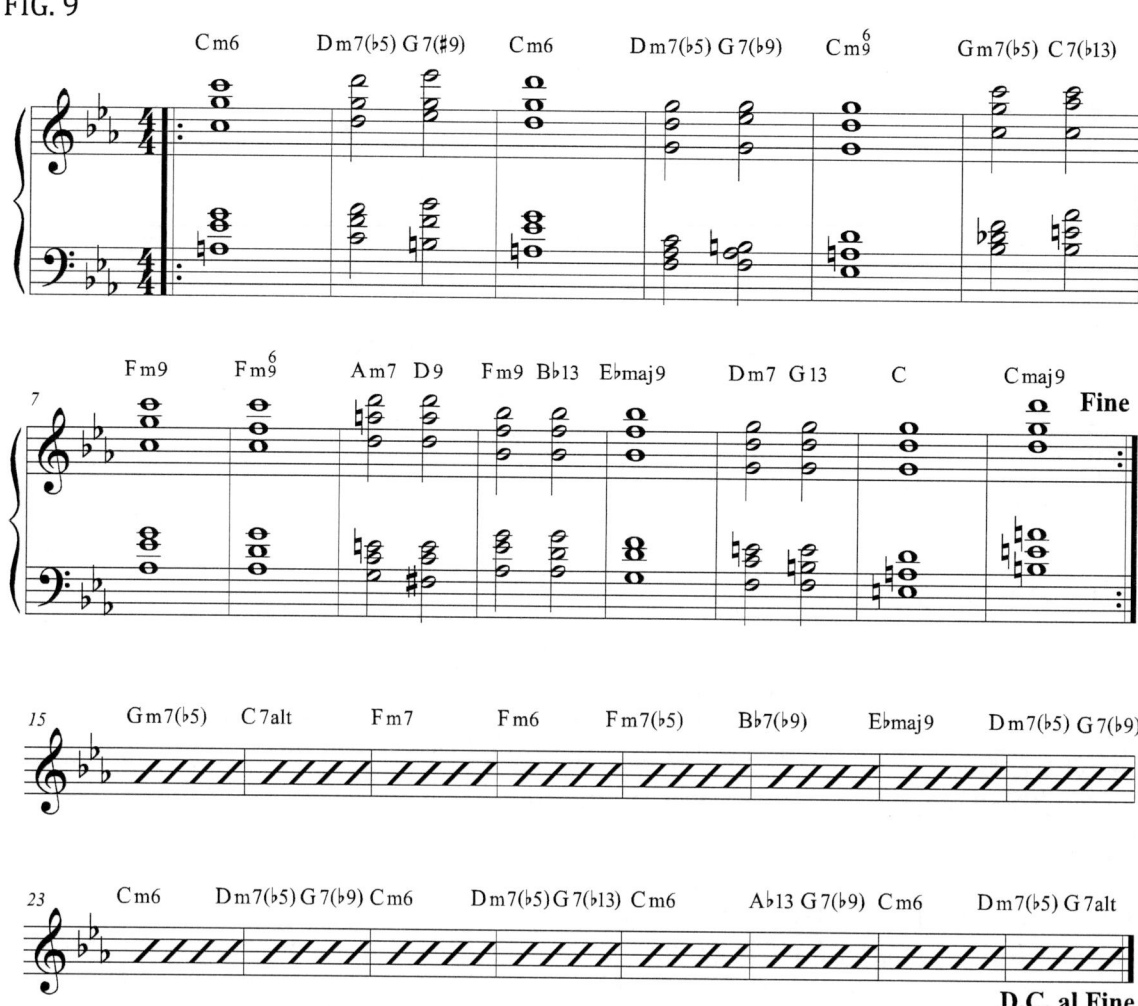

For the blues we can experiment with some simple substitutions for the RH octave structures. For dominant chords you can keep them as is (1-5-1) or replace the root with 9 and/or replace the 5 with 13. If it's an altered dominant, replace the root with #9 or b9 and replace the 5 with b13. For minor chords you can keep them as is, or replace the root with 9, but don't replace the 5 with 13. For diminished chords simply flat the 5th.

Workout 27: Big band-style Voicings on the changes to Sonny Clark's "Blue's Blue."
Revisit "Blue's Blue," this time playing the 3-note voicings in the LH and adding the 3-note RH octave structures. Practice several times through using different variations of root/9/b9/#9 and 5/b5/13/b13. Again, make sure the tensions and 5ths in the RH coincide with the tensions and 5ths in the LH. Observe the additional diminished seventh passing chord in the second measure. Refer to **DL TRK 13-14** for a demo and play-along. For the 2nd chorus of the demo, big band-style voicings are employed. Use this voicing style to comp through a blues in Bb.

FIG. 10

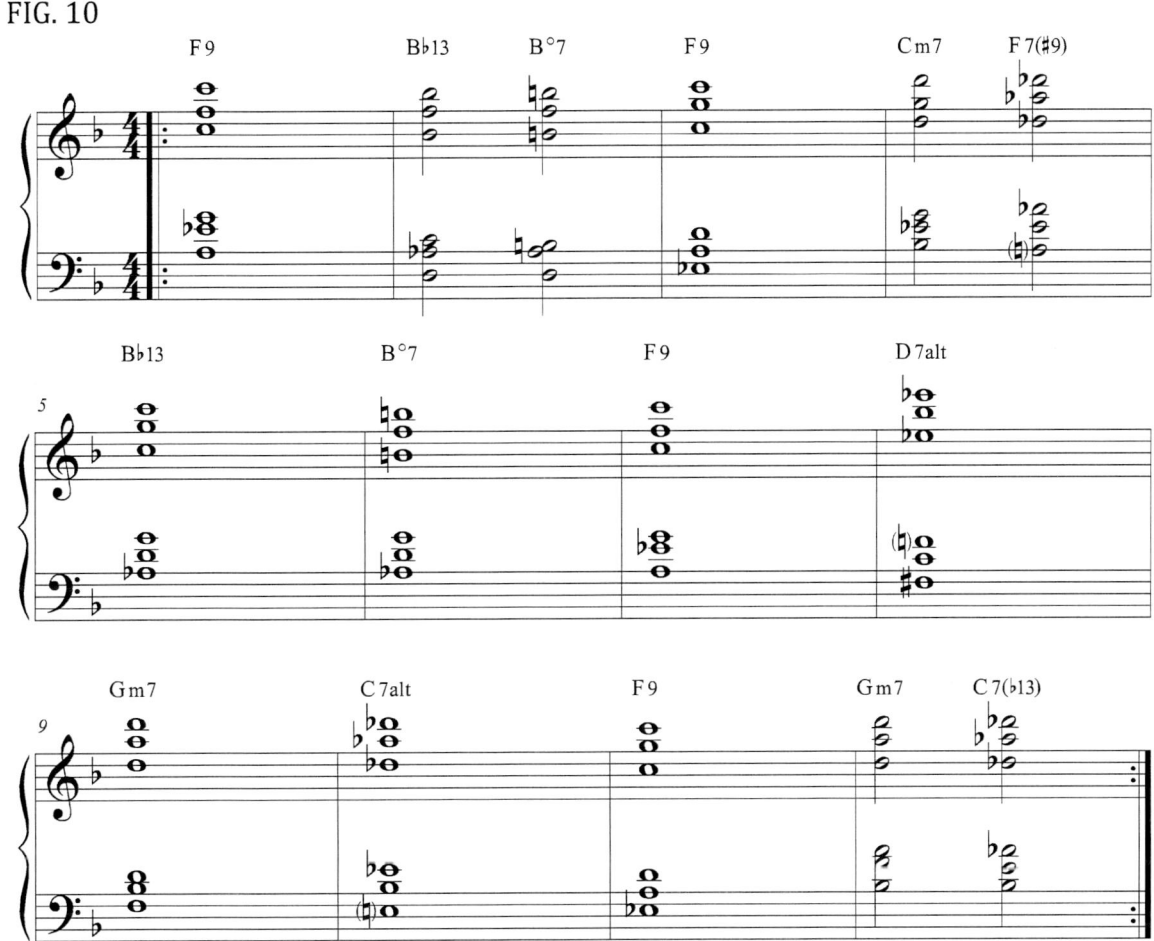

4-note Closed Position Voicings

Four chord tones or tensions stacked close together within one octave is called a 4-note closed position voicing. It is the voicing used often in big bands when writing for the different sections: 4 trumpets, 4 trombones, and 5 saxophones (the fifth voice is often the melody note doubled an octave below). Then arrangers sometimes manipulate these 4-note voicings to make them larger by moving notes down an octave (more on that later). But, when you are starting out at the piano, or reading chord symbols, or arranging for a band, the 4-note closed position voicing is all-important.

Specifically, we will be investigating the "A position" and "B position" voicing. Simply put, an A position voicing has the 3rd as its lowest note; a B position voicing has the 7th as its lowest note. These special kinds of 4-note closed position chords contain all of the information for a complete chord sound. They each contain a root, 3rd, 5th, 7th or acceptable substitution arranged in this basic configuration:

A position (from bottom to top): **3-5-7-1**

B position (from bottom to top): **7-1-3-5**

In their default position, these voicings are a bit dull. The fun comes when substituting acceptable tensions for the roots and 5ths. The 9 is often substituted for the root, and the 13 is often substituted for the fifth, especially when building dominant chords.

Here is a list of common templates when building A and B voicings for dominant chords. Comparing the templates to the definitions of A and B position above, notice how the 9 substitutes for the root, and how the 13 replaces the 5th. Also observe how the 3 and 7 are adjusted to match the chord quality–a dominant chord has a major 3rd and a flatted 7th.

	A position	B position
13 (7 w/natural tensions)	3-13-b7-9	b7-9-3-13
7alt (7 w/altered tensions)	3-#5-b7-#9	b7-#9-3-#5

Two dom7 voicings are provided: 13 and 7alt. The "13" chord symbol implies a dom7 with the 9 and 13 added. It contains natural tensions meaning the 13's and 9's are natural. The "7alt" chord symbol implies a dom7 with 5's and 9's either sharpened or flatted. It includes these altered tensions: #5 (or b13), b5 (or #11), #9, or b9. For our purposes we'll be concentrating on 7#5#9, which is one possible configuration of 7alt.

To begin, practice dominant chords with natural tensions through the cycle of 4ths. Alternate between A and B positions so that the upper guide tone is between G3 and G4 (give or take a half step). Play C13 (B pos)–F13 (A pos)–Bb13 (B pos) etc. Think four trombones as you keep the voicings near middle C.

FIG. 1

Next, extend the progression by inserting dominant seventh chords with altered tensions before advancing to the next key. Again, find the closest position of the next chord. Starting in the key of C play: C13–C7alt–F13–F7alt–Bb13–Bb7alt etc.

FIG. 2

Now instead of playing the altered dominant after each 13th chord, play the 13th chord a tritone away before advancing to the next key. In other words: C13–Gb13–F13–B13–Bb13–E13 etc.

FIG 3

Notice how the RH shape for C7alt is identical to the RH shape for Gb13. C7alt is sometimes explained as Gb13/C. Also, try the above exercises starting in B position.

Next, let's take a look at the templates for m7 and maj7. Observe that the basic configuration is the same as listed on p. 78. Again, the 9 replaces the root, but this time the 5 remains intact for all of the voicings with the exception of major (A position), in which 13 can be used instead of 5 depending on voice leading concerns. Because the 9's are present, m7 becomes m9 and maj7 becomes maj9. Also, notice that the guide tones are adjusted to fit the chord: b3–b7 for m7 and 3–7 for maj7.

	A position	B position
m9	b3–5–b7–9	b7–9–b3–5
maj9 (maj13)	3-5(13)–7–9	7–9–3–5

Now that we have minor, dominant, and major voicings we can construct ii–V–I progressions. Practice these two versions of ii–V–I in A and B position in all 12 keys. The first contains a dominant chord with natural tensions; the second contains a dominant chord with altered tensions.

FIG. 4

Try reading through several lead sheets of simple songs made up primarily of major, m7(9), dominant (with natural or altered tensions) using A and B position voicings. Suggestions include: "Afternoon in Paris", "Pent Up House", "Moonlight in Vermont", "The Way You Look Tonight", "The End of a Love Affair", "Tune Up", and about a hundred more. Start searching through fake books, etc. By placing these A and B position voicings over a bass line you can read through and get acquainted with hundreds of beautiful standards.

Workout 28: 4-note Close A and B Position Voicings on the changes to "Stompin' at the Savoy" as played by Clifford Brown. Here is an accompaniment for the first 8 bars of Clifford Brown's solo on "Stompin' at the Savoy" from *Brown and Roach Incorporated* using A and B position voicings discussed so far. Comp behind Clifford Brown's solo.

It's interesting to note the Gb13 in m. 2, which is different than the usual Dbmaj7. This adds some bluesy harmonic motion during the trumpet solo. The chord changes are approximate and serve as a starting point. This quintet with Harold Land (tenor), Richie Powell (piano), George Morrow (bass), and Max Roach (drums) was one of the most influential in history. Make sure to listen to more essential recordings by this incomparable ensemble.

FIG. 5

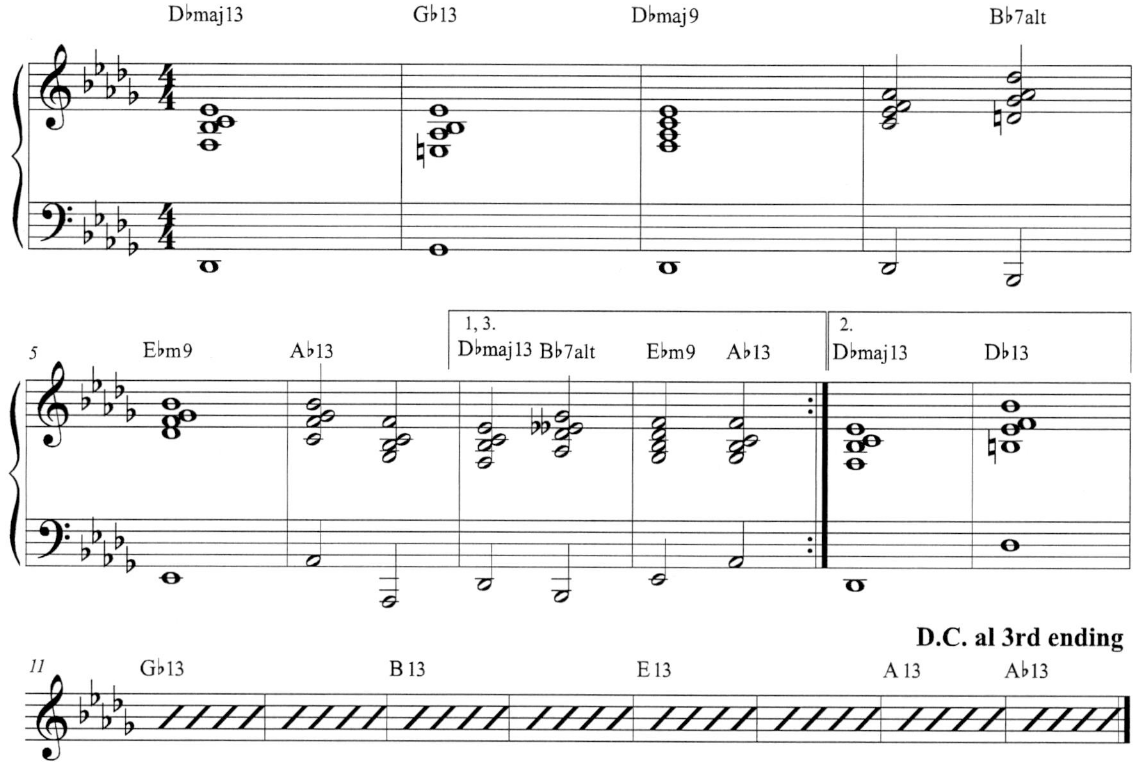

Returning to the initial description of A and B voicings, you can think of the numbers listed beside A position and B position as representing 4 chord tone categories: the root category, the 3rd category, the 5th category, and the 7th category. Each category contains possible chord tones and tensions to include in your voicing. To build a voicing, simply choose one note from each category and organize them in the prescribed order. [1]

Below is a chart showing the 4 chord tone categories with possible tension or chord tone substitutions for building voicings in A or B position.

7th	6, b7, 7
5th	11, b5(#11), 5, #5(b13), 13
3rd	3, b3, 4
Root	R, 9, b9, #9, 7*

When building diminished seventh chords, you can use 7 as a tension, since b3–6 are the guide tones. Besides this exception, the root category should only include R, 9, b9, and #9. For 7sus chords, (7 with a suspended 4th) choose 4 when choosing a note from the 3rd category. Sus chords are very similar to dominant, but with a suspended 4th. They can work instead of ii7 since they are identical shapes, only with V in the bass. That's why Dm7/G = G9sus and Dm9/G = G13sus.

---
[1] Gary Lindsay, Jazz Arranging Techniques (Miami, FL: Staff Art Publishing, 2005), 83-85.

The choice that you make for each category has to do with the chord type, the tensions desired or listed in the chord symbol, and the current musical context. Revisit ii–V–I progressions. This time experiment with some of the other possibilities of tensions listed in the above table. For example: Dm11–G7(#11b9)–Cmaj13.

FIG. 6

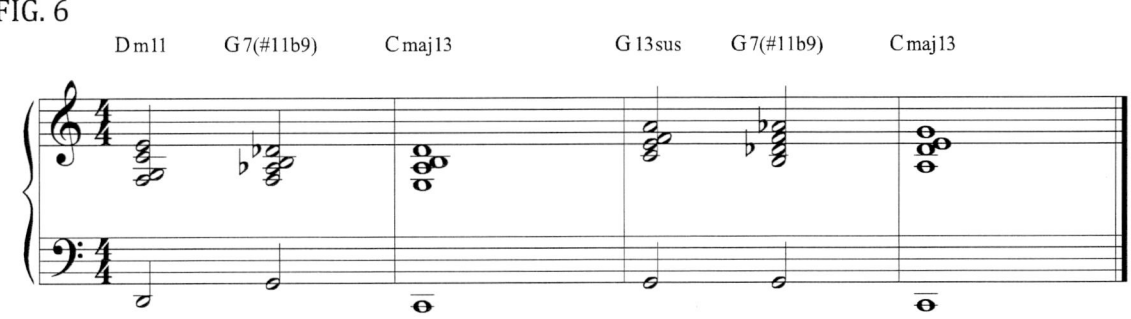

Workout 29: 4-note Close A and B Position Voicings on the changes to "Sweet Pumpkin" as played by Blue Mitchell. Play along with Wynton Kelly and company as you comp behind Blue Mitchell from *Blue's Moods*. Chord symbols are provided with clues regarding chord tone substitutions and tensions. For the diatonic walk down in the 2nd/3rd ending use guide tone voicings with doubled notes. Refer to **DL TRK 15-16** for a demo and play-along. Use A and B position voicings to play along with another standard of your choice.

FIG. 7

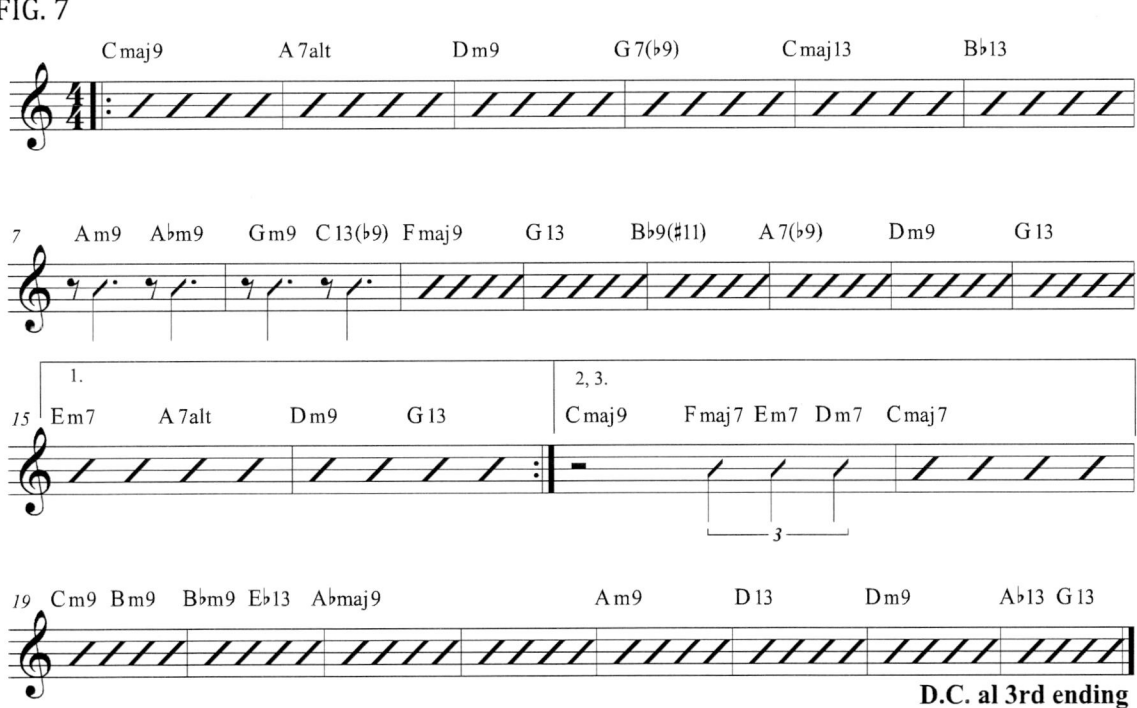

Chapter 3 • B

As an alternative for creating half-diminished chords, you can use a 4-note close voicing for dominant 13 chord a major third lower and play it over a 3rd in the bass. For example, for Dm7(b5) play Bb13 in A or B position over a D in the bass.

Workout 30: 4-note Close A and B Position Voicings on the changes to "Woody'n You" as played by Miles Davis. Comp behind Miles Davis on this jazz classic from *Relaxin' with the Miles Davis Quintet*. This time for all of the half-diminished chords play the 13 chord a major third below with a 3rd in the bass. Observe the comping rhythm below for the melody chorus. Feel free to add some comping rhythms from Chapter 2. Slow down the play back if using Youtube.

FIG. 8

Playing Mini Cadences using "Little Chords"

Alternating between dominant and tonic gives the feeling of tension and release. Maintaining this back and forth is the secret of creating motion on top of static harmony. Jazz pianists are constantly creating interesting mini cadences without disturbing the basic harmonic structure. A mini cadence is a turnaround or other circular harmonic progression that adds harmonic motion on the surface without affecting the underlying harmonic structure that can be played anywhere in the song.

Instead of getting bogged down with building complex 4-note structures using tensions and chord tone substitutions, we can create the same modern sounds using simple sixth and seventh closed position chords in the RH. These are mobile structures that are easy to invert. No longer do you have to be stuck with only "A" and "B" position chords. For these simple, "little chords" you are free to use any inversion. The idea of using "little chords" instead of complex structures is one encouraged by the great Barry Harris. He believes in always moving chords around melodically. If the chord is small and manageable, moving around becomes more intuitive.

The trick comes with placing these simple structures over alternate bass notes. Here is an outline of some of the most common "little chords" over alternate bass notes and their more complex jazz chord counterparts written in roman numeral notation and then in Bb major.

"Little Chords" over Alt Bass Notes for Making Mini Cadences

V6/I = Imaj9	F6/Bb = Bbmaj9
IV6/V = V7sus	Eb6/F = F7sus
IV6/ii = iim7	Eb6/C = Cm7
viio7/V = V7b9	Ao7/F = F7(b9)
iim6/V = V9	Cm6/F = F9

Below V7sus is created by placing IV6 (a "little chord") over V in the bass. To get started making mini cadences, practice alternating between I6/I and IV6/V. In the key of Bb major it's as if you are moving between Bb6 and F7sus. Practice in all inversions.

FIG. 1

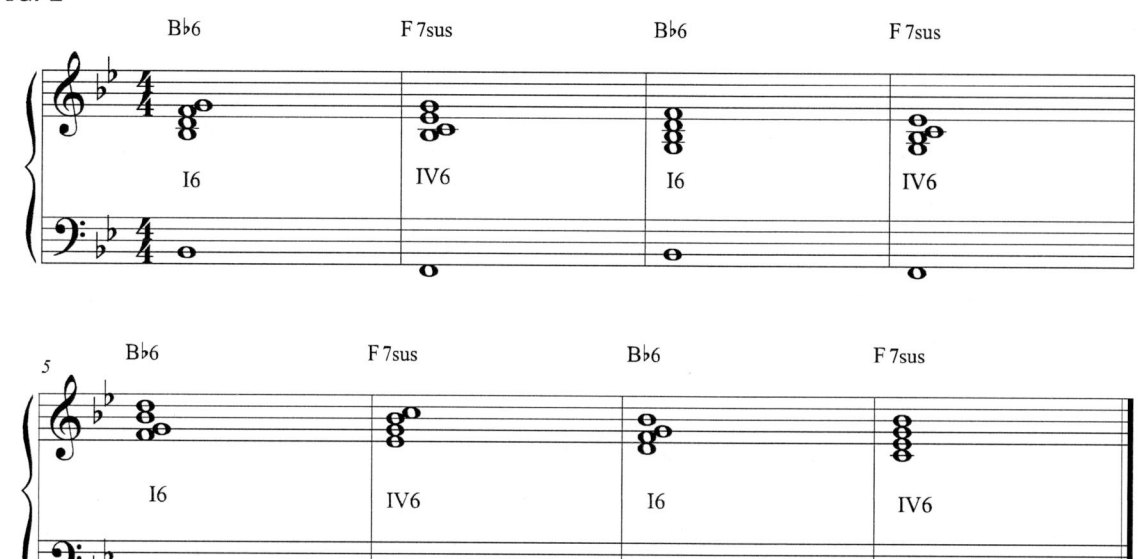

Next add spice to the tonic major chord by playing V6/I moving to IV6/V. Notice how more voices move between each chord. If you are in Bb major, it's as if you are playing Bbmaj9 to F7sus. Practice in all inversions.

FIG. 2

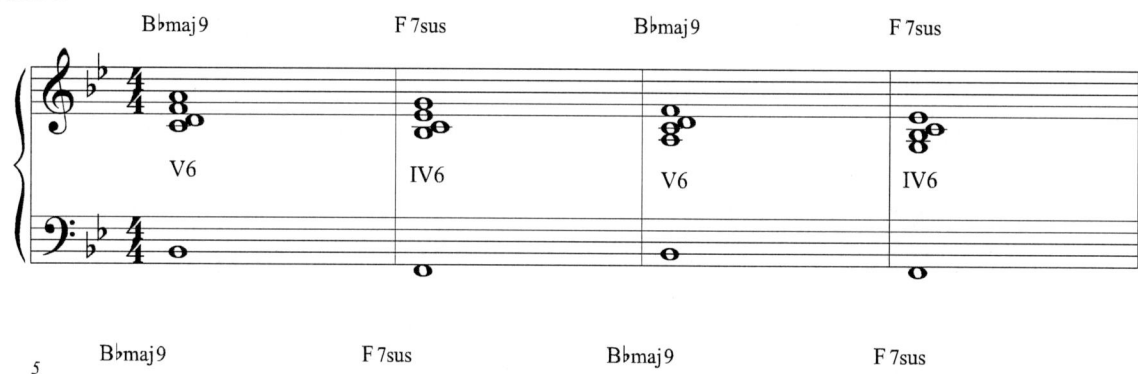

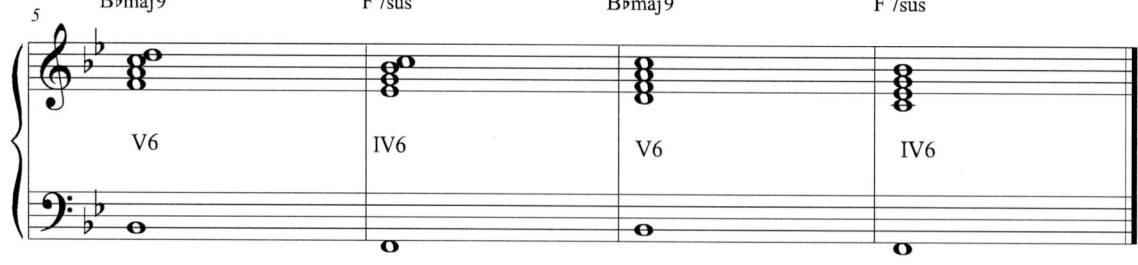

To expedite the trip back to the tonic chord (I6 or V6/I), add a passing diminished chord located a half step below tonic (viio7). In Bb major the viio7 implies F7(b9), the dominant of Bb major. The RH shapes, IV6–viio7–V6 imply ii–V–I. Again, practice in all inversions.

FIG. 3

Next, add a passing diminished chord in between tonic and iim7. Use #io7, a half step below the RH shape (IV6). In Bb major the #io7 implies G7(b9) which is the dominant of iim7. The RH shapes, V6–#io7–IV6–viio7 imply the common chord progression or turnaround: Bbmaj9–G7b9–Cm7–F7b9. Since the RH is made up entirely of "little" chords, they are easy to move around and invert. In this way you can generate many subtle variations of the I–VI–ii–V chord movement.

FIG. 4

The io7 is another very versatile passing diminished moving to and away from tonic. When reading chord symbols, the movement away from tonic to ii7 is often expressed as biiio7; the movement toward tonic is often expressed as #ivo7. Both biiio7 and #ivo7 are inversions of io7.

Practice the following Count Basic introduction employing the io7 moving to and from tonic. Transpose to several keys.

FIG. 5

Below is a chart showing this back and forth movement to and from home. The circle on the left signifies tonic major or home base. It can be expressed by either playing I6 or V6 in the RH. The circle on the right shows the subdominant (a location that is away from home), expressed by playing IV6 in the RH. The passing diminished chords help push you to both locations. Following the chart around clockwise, you can generate I–VI–ii–V–like chord movements. Experiment creating mini cadences. The roman numerals below refer to the RH "little chord."

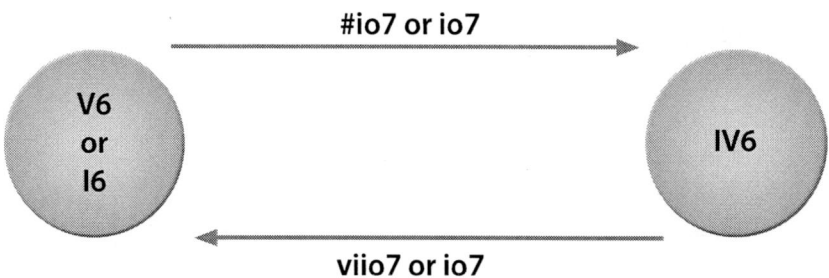

The A section of rhythm changes is a chord progression that can be derived from the chart. Below, one possible version of rhythm changes is illustrated. Experiment with finding your own way to navigate through rhythm changes by using the chart above. Transpose to several keys. Also try the RH progression over a V pedal.

FIG. 6

Workout 31: Comping with "Little Chords" on the changes to Lester Young's "Lester Leaps In." Below another possible solution is given for rhythm changes.
The A section to rhythm changes is all about making mini cadences around tonic, then venturing to IV in m. 6, only to come right back to tonic in m. 7. The rest of it is just about how to get to those destinations. Observe the alternate bass lines compared to FIG. 6, even though the RH pattern of "little chords" remains basically the same.

The B section modulates to III7 and from there circles back through the cycle of fourths every two measures back to I6. For each dominant chord in the bridge, play the m6 a fifth higher than the root. Am6 for D9 etc. By changing the m6 to o7 you create a 7(b9) that takes you to the next dominant chord. In this way the bridge becomes:

vm6/III–vo7/III–vm6/VI–vo7/VI–vm6/II–vo7/II–vm6/V–vo7/V. In the key of Bb: Am6/D–Ao7/D–Dm6/G–Do7/G–Gm6/C–Go7/C–Cm6/F–Co7/F.

For now, use comping strategies from Chapter 2. Keep it simple and light as you comp along with Lester Young from his 1946 Norman Granz recording: *New Lester Leaps In*. Joe Albany is on piano. Refer to **DL TRK 17-18** for a demo and play-along. For the 1st chorus of the demo, the following progression is used.

Chapter 3 • C

FIG. 7

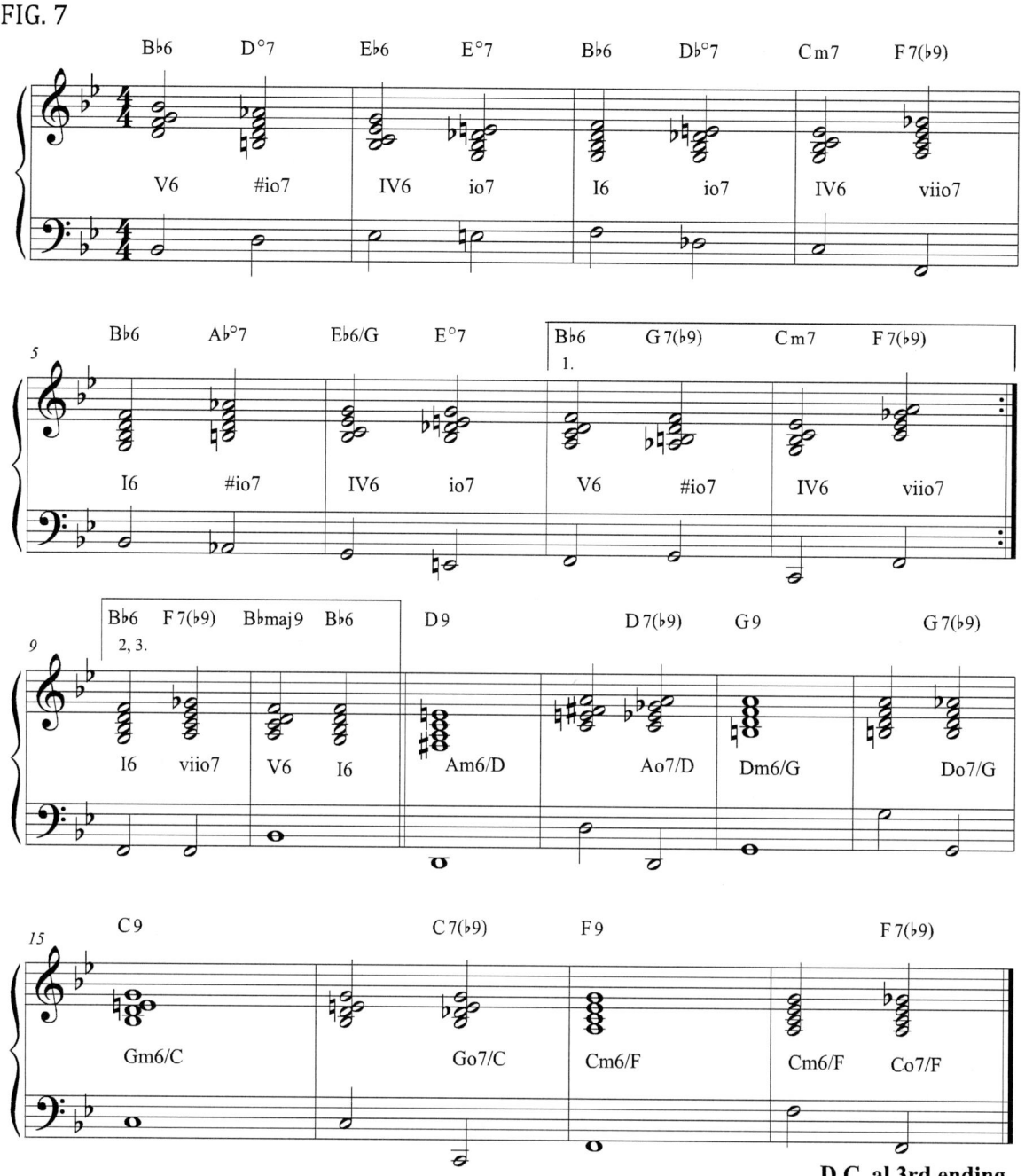

D.C. al 3rd ending

By introducing a few more "little chords" for expressing altered dominant and half diminished chords we can create more interesting motion in major and minor. Different inversions of 7(#5) and 7(b5) work well for alternate dominant voicings. To play 7(b13b9), play the m6 a half step above the root. For iim7b5, play ivm6 over ii in the bass.

"Little Chords" over Alt Bass Notes for Altered Dominant and m7b5

bvim6/V = V7(b13b9)	Gbm6/F = F7(b13b9)
ivm6/ii = iim7b5	Fm6/D = Dm7b5

The chart below illustrates how to create more varied mini cadences in major and minor. By moving clockwise, you can generate a variety of minor cadences (for ex. i–VI7alt–ii7b5–V7alt.) These altered dominants can also be used to move to iim7 and I major when creating major mini cadences. In addition, V6 can be used for iiim7 if played over III in the bass. The roman numerals below refer to the RH "little chord."

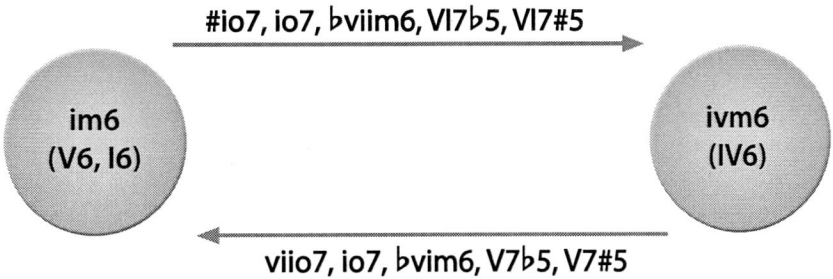

Workout 32: Using "Little Chords" for Altered Dominants on the changes to "Lester Leaps In" as played by Sonny Stitt. Experiment using little chords to express altered dominants to move to ii (bviim6, VI7b5, VI7#5) and to move to tonic (bvim6, V7b5, V7#5) when creating mini cadences in a major key. Also, use V6 with III in the bass to play iiim7. In the key of Bb, use G7alt (Abm6/G), G7b5, and G7#5 to move to Cm7; and Gbm6, F7b5, and F7#5 to move back to Bb major. Use F6/D to play Dm7. In addition, use little chords to express altered dominants in the bridge to add more motion. The first A is illustrated below. Play along with Lester Young. Refer to **DL TRK 17-18** for a demo and play-along. For the 2nd chorus of the demo, FIG. 8 and other variations are used.

FIG. 8

Workout 33: Comping with "Little Chords" on the changes to "Hot House" as played by the Quintet. Comp along with the bebop masters, Charlie Parker, Dizzy Gillespie, Bud Powell, Charles Mingus, and Max Roach from *Jazz at Massey Hall* with "little chords" incorporating altered dominants. The text below each chord refers to the RH shape. The first A is illustrated below. Use little chords to comp along with your favorite bebop recording.

FIG. 9

The Sixth-Diminished Concept: Playing Scales of Chords

Barry Harris believes fervently in having motion whenever you play at the piano. This is especially important when comping. He discourages pianists from incessantly playing pre-set complex shapes that don't move anywhere. Comping to him is much more about beauty, harmonic movement, subtlety, and telling a story. This concept isn't quite like the Modern Jazz Quartet in which John Lewis plays a full counter line while comping, but more about simple two or three-note melodies under the soloist, lurking elegantly beneath the surface, but always present urging the singer/soloist on in an encouraging way. The entire concept of this harmonic system is much too vast for this present section, but the following few examples offer an intro to the concept of the ***sixth-diminished scale.***

The basic idea, is that for every chord you play, you should have a complete scale of chords in mind. In other words, every chord goes somewhere, and was coming from somewhere. Thinking along these lines, any chord is merely an incomplete snapshot of a much bigger harmonic sequence. Therefore, chords are fleeting, and always changing.

To access the sixth-diminished scale, pick a "little chord" (usually a major or minor sixth chord) and pair it with a diminished seventh chord a half step below. By alternating back and forth between sixth chord and diminished chord you paint a more complete harmonic picture and generate a scale of chords.

For example, to express C major, I may pick C6 and pair it with Bo7 (a half-step below). By alternating between inversions of C6 and Bo7 I create a scale of chords called the C sixth-diminished scale since I'm alternating between a sixth chord and a diminished seventh chord.

Fascinating things happen when you begin to mix and match tones from the sixth chord and the diminished chord. But for our purposes, we will limit ourselves to a few common examples of sixth chord and diminished seventh pairs and how you can create sixth diminished scales to express harmony using scales of chords.

Here's a short list to get started. For each pair, practice them in succession in every inversion to create a scale of chords. The chords in the right column are produced by playing the sixth-diminished pair (left column) over a bass note.

C6–Bo7	over C	(I6–viio7)	C maj (I maj)
Dm6–C#o7	over G	(iim6–#io7)	G9 (V7)
F6–Eo7	over D or G	(IV6–#io7)	Dm7 or G7sus (ii7 or V7sus)

FIG. 1

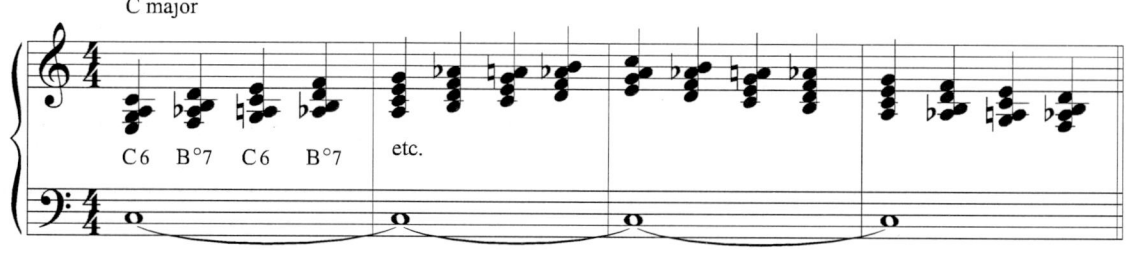

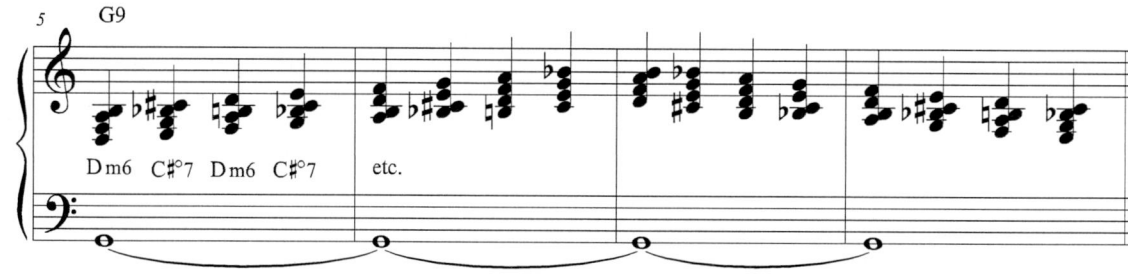

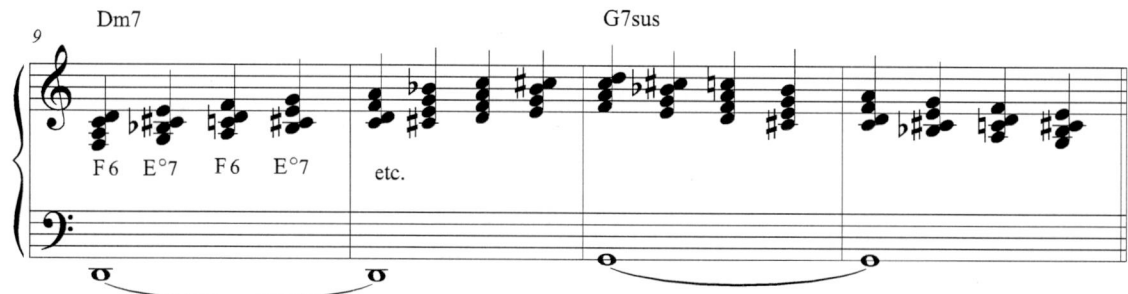

Not only do the sixth-dim pairs generate scales of chords, but bebop scales for single note soloing. C6–Bo7 generates the C6-dim scale, C major with the addition of b6. Dm6–C#o7 creates the Dm6-dim (D melodic minor ascending with the b6 added), and F6–Eo7 creates the F6-diminished scale (F major with b6 added). These scales, also called C major bebop, D minor bebop, and F major bebop respectively, will be discussed further in Chapter 6.

Create mini cadences by applying sixth diminished scales to add motion to I–V–I–V and ii–V–I. Most of the time the sixth chord is the target. The diminished chord is used to get to the next inversion of the target. It is possible, however, to start from the diminished chord and pass using the sixth chord.

For Cmaj use C6–Bo7; for G7(b9) use the inverse, Bo7–C6. For Dm7 or G7sus use F6–Eo7; for G9, Dm6–C#o7; and for Cmaj, C6–Bo7 or G6–Bo7. Try these variations in C major. Transpose to other keys.

FIG. 2

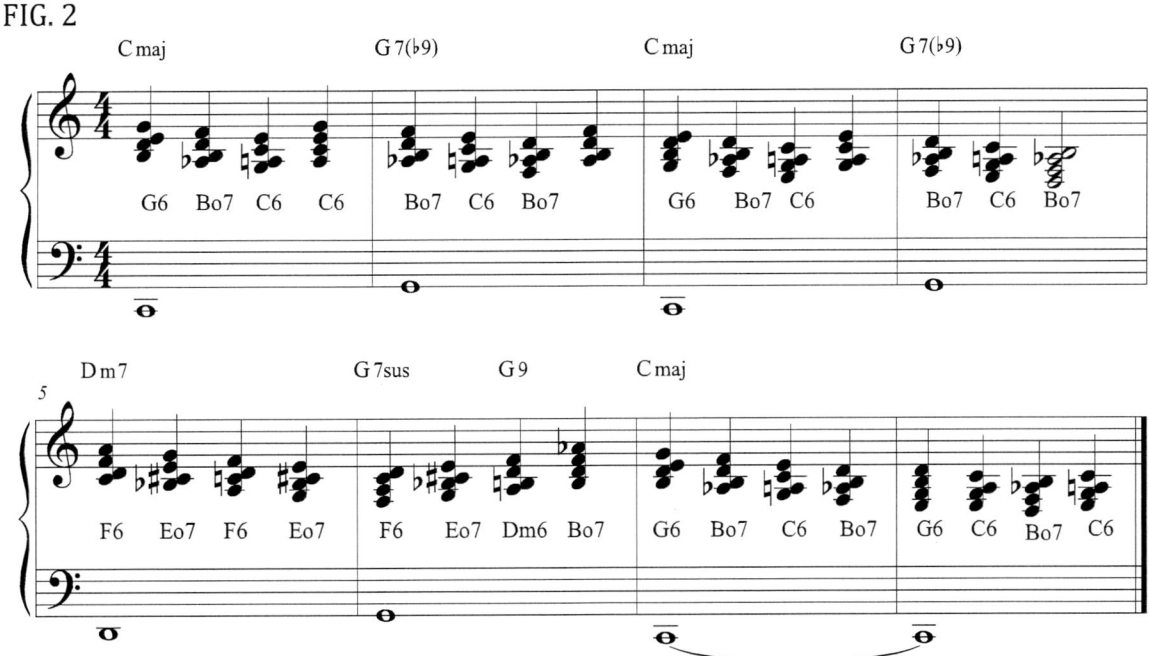

Here is a list of sixth-diminished pairs to add motion to minor chords. Practice them in the same way as in FIG. 1. Following that are some examples of mini cadences in minor.

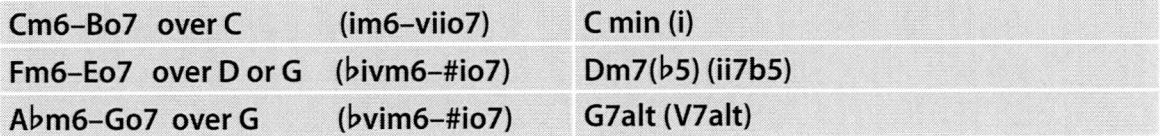

Cm6–Bo7 over C	(im6–viio7)	C min (i)
Fm6–Eo7 over D or G	(♭ivm6–#io7)	Dm7(♭5) (ii7♭5)
A♭m6–Go7 over G	(♭vim6–#io7)	G7alt (V7alt)

FIG. 3

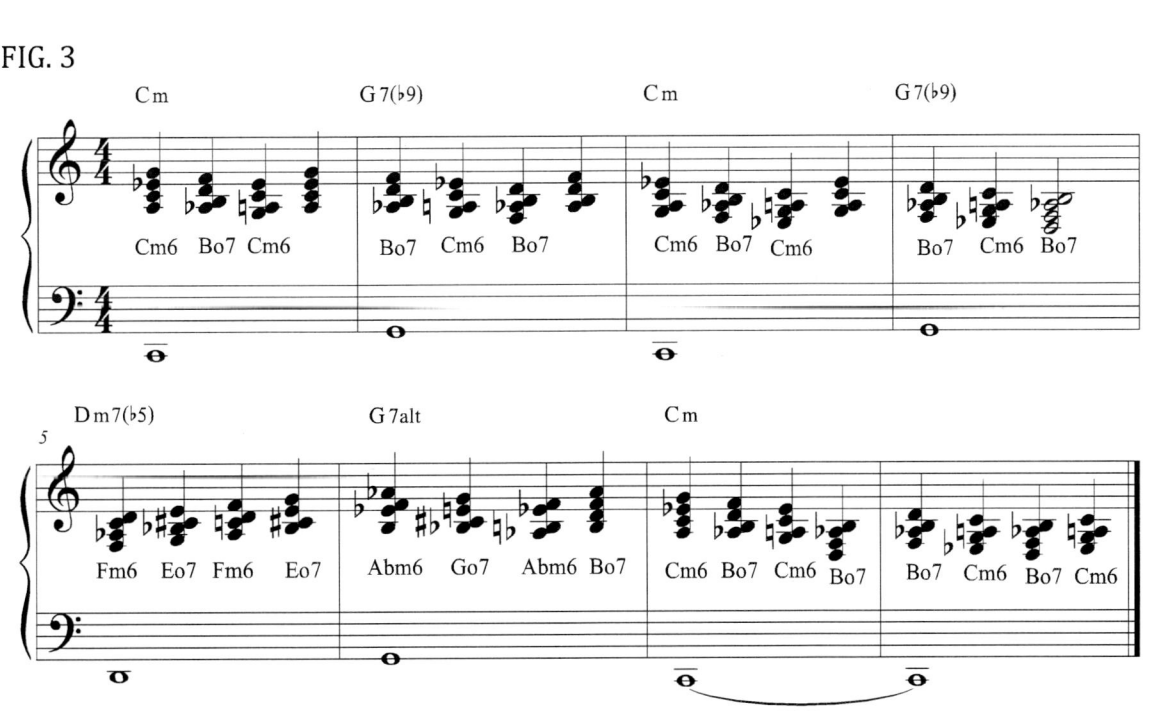

Chapter 3 ◆ D

Workout 34: Comping using "Little Chords" and the Sixth-Diminished Scale on the changes to "These Foolish Things" as sung by Frank Sinatra. The first eight bars are done for you. Suggested RH sixth-diminished pairs are provided along with an assortment of other "little chord" and A/B "pos" movements. Basic changes are given above. Glide along as you accompany Frank Sinatra on this beautiful ballad from his 1947 debut album, *The Voice of Frank Sinatra*. With this technique of adding motion to a ballad it's easy to get carried away. Don't play too much. When there's a pause in the melody or the soloist takes a breath, that's when you can fill.

FIG. 4

The Concept of Borrowing: In m. 5 the top G on beat 1 is "borrowed" from the Go7 and played on top of the three other notes from Ab6. This process of mixing and matching chord tones from both the sixth chord and the diminished chord is called **borrowing**. It's really the secret to unlocking the true potential of the sixth diminished concept, but is a bit outside of the scope of this book. For more information about borrowing, check out An Approach to Comping: The Essentials (2nd edition).

Comping Games

The following exercises are geared for improving your sense of time and overall comping language. The art of comping has a lot to do with learning the language of comping. This artform has been passed down for generations. Interestingly, even though the solo styles and voicings are quite different between many of the jazz piano greats, you'll find that the rhythmic language between Wynton Kelly, Bud Powell, Barry Harris, Sonny Clark, Horace Silver, Red Garland, and Bobby Timmons shares a lot of commonalities.

Many of the older musicians had names for comping rhythms. Rhythms come alive if you assign words to them. Check out these 5 one-measure rhythmic building blocks. They are written in normal notation, but all of the upbeats should be played closer to the third triplet of the beat to create a laid-back feel.

FIG. 1–5

"Charleston," "Who Parked the Car," and "Step Down," are real names I've heard over the years for these rhythms by the jazz masters. "Bud Powell" and "Red" are my own inventions. The two rhythms are meant to honor the great jazz pianists, Bud Powell and Red Garland, and represent rhythms that the pianists favored. You can come up with your own names, but assigning lyrics to rhythms serves both as a memory aid and a way to breathe life into something that would otherwise be notated in dry Western rhythmic notation (which is only approximate at best).

Note that for "Who Parked the Car" the rhythmic representation of the word, "the" is in parenthesis, indicating that it can be omitted. When you are just getting started having two eighth notes in a row when comping is too busy and should be avoided. If you listen to Sonny Clark, who uses this comping rhythm a lot, sometimes he inserts a single note on the "and" of two, as if he's saying "the" softly, but emphasizing "Car."

By connecting the one-measure rhythms like blocks, you can string together rhythmic phrases to create longer ideas.

Workout 35: Creating Comping Rhythms on the changes to "Cool Struttin." Construct a 4-measure combination and apply it to several choruses of the Sonny Clark classic F blues using voicings from earlier in the chapter. Feel free to repeat one-measure patterns, or leave one measure rest. The choices are: "Charleston", "Bud Powell," "Who Parked the Car," "Red," and "Step Down." Anticipate the harmony of the next measure if the chord falls on "and" of 4. Start after the melody. Try the following rhythms:

1. Charleston–Bud Powell–Charleston–Rest
2. Red–Red–Step Down–Red
3. Who Parked the Car–Red–Who Parked the Car–Step Down

Create your own. #3 is illustrated below. Add roots in the LH. For best results, play the pattern along with Jackie McLean's solo. Refer to **DL TRK 13-14** for a demo and play-along. Chorus 3 of the demo employs the comping rhythm below.

FIG. 6

INTERACTION

As you develop your comping language, you will become more able to listen to the musicians around you. Your first goal is to make it feel good, and lay down the groove, with relaxed swinging comping rhythms. After that, you can begin to interact with what is happening around you.

Have fun interacting with Charlie Parker melodies. You can either play with the accents of the melody, or play in the spaces. For now, practice scatting the hits of the melody away from the piano. After a while, apply simple guide tone or 4-note closed position voicings to the hits of the melody.

Workout 36: Comping the Accents on the changes to Charlie Parker's "Confirmation." Comp to match the accents of the melody as you play along with the recording. The first eight bars are illustrated below.

FIG. 7

Workout 37: Comping the Spaces on the changes to Charlie Parker's "Confirmation." Comp in the spaces between the accents of the melody as you comp along with the recording. The first eight bars are illustrated below using only upbeats.

FIG. 8

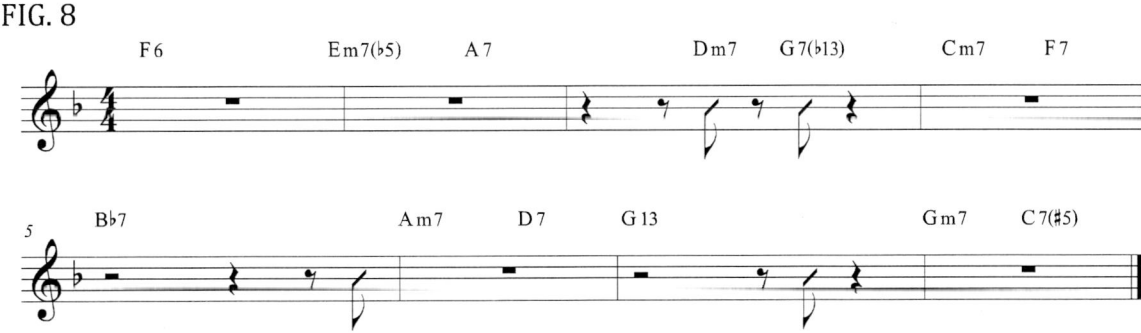

Practice comping the accents/spaces of your favorite Charlie Parker composition with the original recording.

Duet 3: Interacting with a Soloist on the Blues, Part 1. Comp for a friend on the blues. React to your friend by playing an upbeat or downbeat, 1, 1.5, or 2 beats after the end of each phrase. Have your friend wait to start his/her next phrase after hearing your rhythmic hit. After getting comfortable, switch rolls. You solo and have your friend play an upbeat or downbeat (even if it's on a single-note instrument or voice) after you finish your phrase. Start your new phrase after hearing the hit from your friend. You can do this exercise alone by having your left hand answer your right hand.

FIG. 9

At this time, we return to one of the 5 rhythms from the beginning of the section. Practice the Charleston starting on every beat or upbeat until you can play the rhythm anywhere in the measure.

FIG. 10

Apply each one-measure "Charleston" rhythm to an entire chorus of "Cool Struttin'" during one of the solos.

Duet 4: Interacting with a Soloist on the Blues, Part 2. Now that you feel comfortable displacing "Charleston" repeat the interaction exercise from Duet 3. This time answer using the "Charleston" rhythm starting on any upbeat or downbeat 1, 1.5, or 2 beats after the end of your friend's phrase.

Chapter 4
Open Position Chords

Open position means that the chord tones have been spread out, and are not all adjacent to each other. Instead of being bunched up together, the chord tones now span more than an octave. Moving certain chord tones contained in a closed position chord up or down an octave creates an open voicing. In most cases, open position chords are played with two hands, in contrast to closed position chords that are often played with one hand.

FIG 1

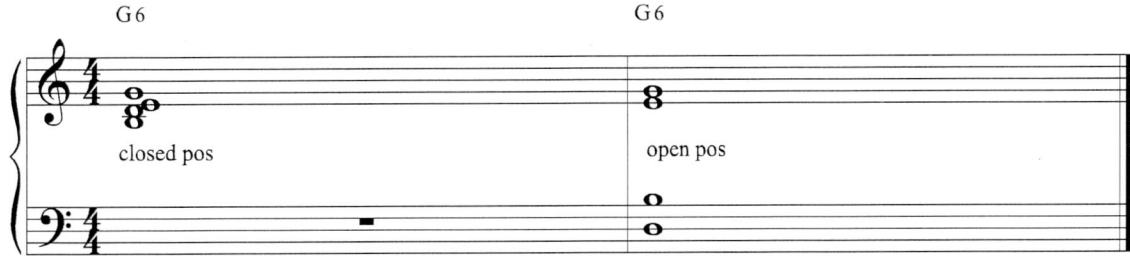

By opening up your voicings, you can begin to take advantage of the piano's beautiful sonority. Open position voicings often have the fullest and clearest sound, and often share these characteristics:

1. Contain guide tones around the middle of the piano split between the hands
2. Integrate wider intervals within the voicing, such as fourths, fifths, sixths, and/or sevenths.
3. Consist of notes evenly spread out throughout the voicing.
4. Span a distance greater than an octave between the outer two notes

In this section, we will examine voicings produced by playing melody and guide tone over a shell, chord tone/tension and guide tone over a shell, upper structure triads over a shell or guide tones; spread voicings, drop-2 voicings derived from "little chords," and 4th-like voicings. As always, these voicing styles will be used to comp along with real jazz recordings.

At the end of the chapter a comping transcription is presented containing actual rhythms as played by Red Garland on *Workin' with the Miles Davis Quintet*. The idea here is for you to assign closed or open position chords, and proceed to comp along in real time. The benefit in doing this cannot be underestimated. By intensely listening and playing along you can pick up so many subtleties that cannot be put into words or notated musically.

Simple Open Position

In this first section, elegant yet economical 4-note open position voicings are explored. Unlike the 4-note closed position chords from Chapter 3, not all of the chord tones are adjacent within the voicing. This creates a more transparent and open sound. Since two notes are usually played in each hand, this style voicing is referred to as "2 and 2."

MELODY + GUIDE TONE OVER SHELL

A basic way to realize a melody with open voicings is to play the melody in the right hand about 1.5 or 2.5 octaves above a root in the left hand. Then simply fill in two near-by guide tones (GTs) with your two thumbs. This should give you the melody note and guide tone in the RH over a 1–3 or 1–7 LH shell. If the melody is low (and happens to be a 3rd or 7th), then play the melody alone over a shell, creating a 3-note voicing. Only create voicings under the melody notes that line up with a change of harmony.

These two steps are shown below for the first four bars of "Polka Dots and Moonbeams." Learn the melody and changes of this tune in this manner. Besides referencing a lead sheet, listen to several recordings of this tune. Also, listen to vocal versions so that you are aware of the lyrics. Keep in mind that the chord changes can vary. The important thing is to keep it simple and clear, and play chords that support the melody.

FIG. 1

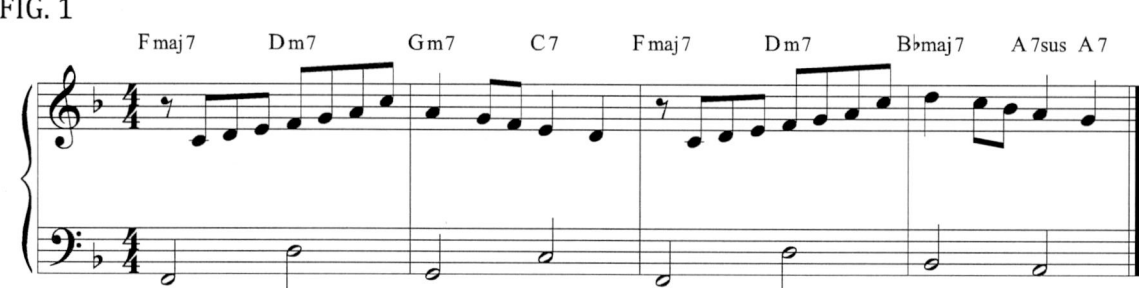

FIG. 2

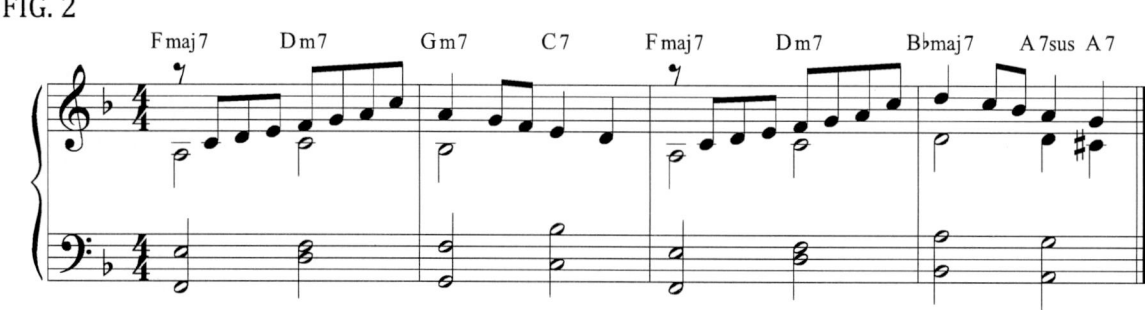

Play the melody of "Polkadots and Moonbeams" using simple open voicings on strong beats. Here are the second four bars with the melody omitted. Add the melody on top of these structures. For plain triads, play one nearby chord tone in each thumb making sure that the 3rd is played somewhere in the voicing.

FIG. 3

Try this technique with several different standards. It's all about having the voices relatively well-distributed without huge spaces between the two hands. Remember, sometimes it is necessary to transpose the root up an octave, or bring the melody down an octave.

Most of the time, you can simply put guide tones between the melody and bass note. There are a few additional options to consider, however. If the melody is a guide tone, you can replace the duplicate guide tone in the LH with the fifth. As an alternative to the LH 1-3 shell, 5-3 can be used; especially effective when 1-3 is too low. Be careful not to over use this voicing since it sometimes obscures the root of the chord. If putting the 5th in the bass, make sure to make it b5 for alt, m7b5, or dim7. For m7b5 you have a few options: play GT's and root under the melody if the melody is b5; play the b5 in the bass if the melody is not b5; replace the 3rd with b5, or leave the b5 out, and play m7.

Apply the following techniques to another standard.

1. Play the melody over a bass note with two guide tones in between.
2. If the melody is a 3rd or 7th, you may replace the duplicate LH guide tone with the fifth.
3. If the melody is low, and a 3rd or 7th, you can play it alone over a shell, creating a 3-note voicing.
4. For triads play chord tones with your thumbs, making sure the 3rd is somewhere in the voicing.
5. For m7b5 see options above.

Chord tone/Tension + Guide Tone over Shell

Simple open voicings can also be used to accompany a melody. This time instead of playing the melody in the top voice, choose any available tension or chord tone within reach.

Below is a chart illustrating the construction of common jazz chords (maj7, maj6, dom7, min7, min7b5, m6, and o7) using the 2 and 2 voicing. For all of the voicings below, the left thumb and right thumb are playing the two guide tones. The chart only lists 3 out of the 4 notes in the voicing. You choose the top voice, marked with an X.

major	RH	X	X	X
		3	7 (or 6)	7 (or 6)
	LH	7 (or 6)	3	3
		1	1	5
dominant	RH	X	X	X
		3	♭7	♭7
	LH	♭7	3	3
		1	1	5
min7 or min7(♭5)	RH	X	X	X
		♭3	♭7	♭7
	LH	♭7	♭3	♭3
		1	1	5 (or ♭5)
tonic minor or dim7	RH	X	X	X
		♭3	7 (or 6)	7 (or 6)
	LH	6	♭3	♭3
		1	1	5 (or ♭5)

X = available tension or chord tone

Below are some examples of common jazz chords voiced 2 and 2 in the key of C. Call out the chord symbol as you play through the voicings with the different tensions.

FIG. 4

Here are a few tips:

1. Choose the top voice based on the color preferred. Adding too much color can get in the way of the soloist or singer. Have a purpose when adding tension.

2. Keep the RH interval rather small. The interval between the soprano and tenor should be equal to or less than an octave.

3. The tenor should never be above middle C (C4) or below the C3. Playing the 5–3 shell in the LH (i.e. playing the 5th in the bass) creates a somewhat unorthodox voicing. If you are just starting out, stick with 1–7(6) or 1–3 shells. The 5–3 shell offers a rich alternative, however, allowing you to play a lower bass note while keeping the tenor voice in a good range.

For plain triads, play two chord tones in each hand while preserving the parameters listed above. Be sure to include the 3rd of the chord somewhere.

Here are the first 8 measures of "Polkadots and Moonbeams" voiced 2 and 2. These harmonic pads work well if singing the melody or accompanying a horn player. Note some of the different chord changes this time. Also, notice the plain triad in m. 5.

FIG. 5

As an alternative, it is possible to sometimes tuck a 9 or b9 in between the guide tones, often creating a M2 or m2 in the RH over a 1–7(6) shell. When using a m2 on the top of the voicing proceed with caution. This dissonant sound should not be over used, but saved for a delicate moment.

Create major, dominant, non-tonic and tonic minor chords using this tucking method:

maj9 6/9	RH	3	3
		9	9
	LH	7	6
		1	1
7(9), 7(♭9) 7sus, 7sus(♭9)	RH	3	4
		9 (or ♭9)	9 (or ♭9)
	LH	♭7	♭7
		1	1
m9	RH	♭3	
		9	
	LH	♭7	
		1	
m9(maj7) m6/9	RH	♭3	♭3
		9	9
	LH	7	6
		1	1

FIG. 6

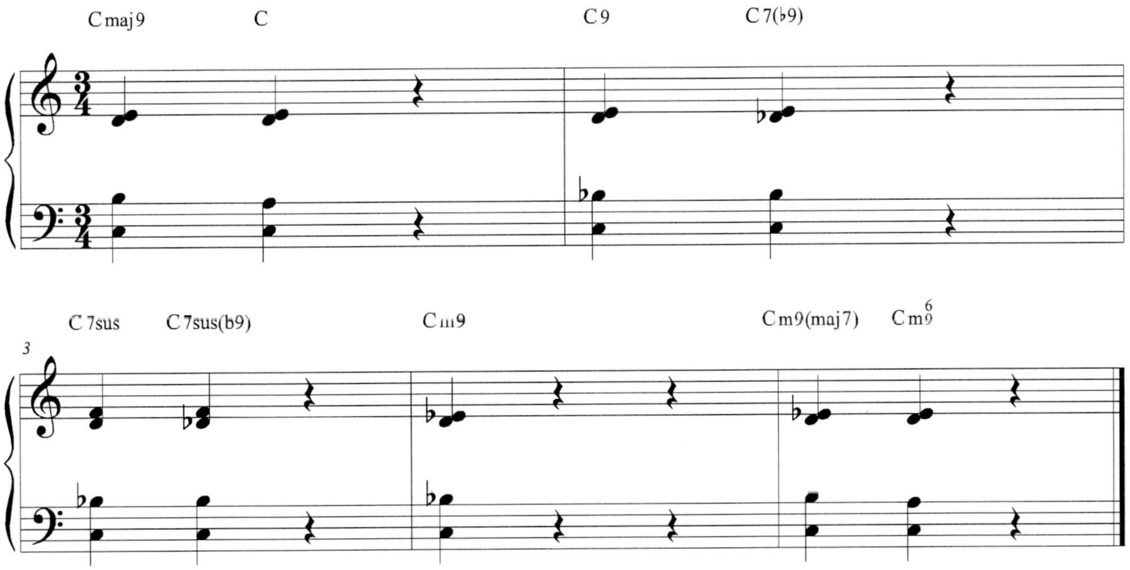

We now return to "Polkadots and Moonbeams". Here are the second 8 bars of the "A" section using the tucking method outlined above. Check out the slightly different harmonization.

FIG. 7

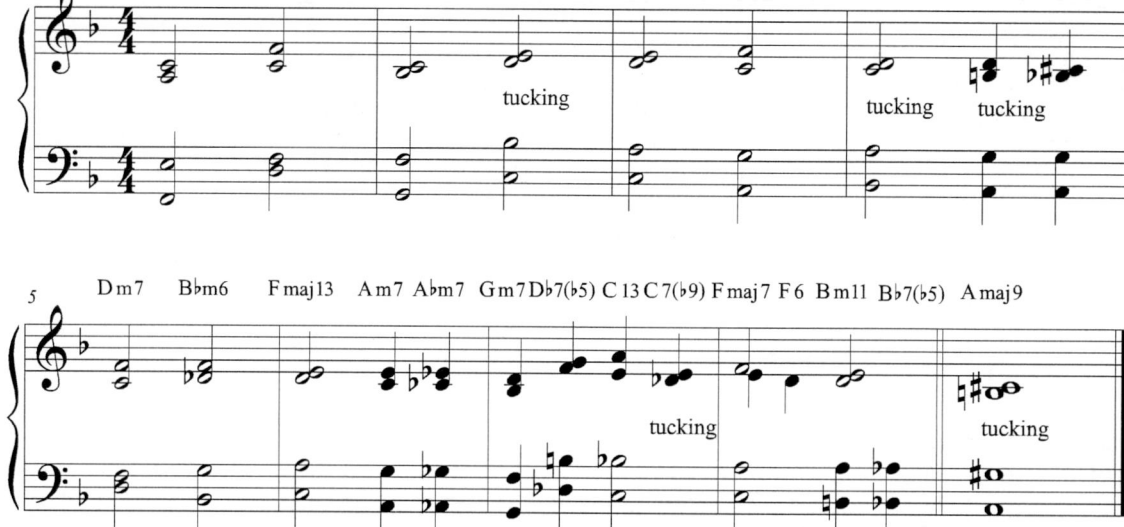

Workout 38: Playing Simple Open Position chords on the changes to "Polka Dots and Moonbeams" as played by Chet Baker. Choose any chord tone or tension as the top voice of your 2 and 2 voicings as you play along with Chet Baker's version of "Polka Dots and Moonbeams." Keep track of the guide tones as you create your voicings. Feel free to tuck 9s or b9s between the guide tones at times to add variety.

The changes below are loosely based on Chet Baker's version from *Chet Baker Quartet - Polka Dots and Moonbeams* (1958). Some of the changes have been simplified or are a bit different than the recording. Use your ears and see if you can identify the places where the bass and piano play slightly different changes. Often the rhythm section is not reading off a lead sheet on these recording sessions. The leader simply calls a tune and the piano and bass have to navigate through the form and come to some agreement regarding the changes. This valuable process is something that is often missing these days, as everyone simply reads chord changes from their phones. Learn to enjoy relying on your ears.

FIG. 8

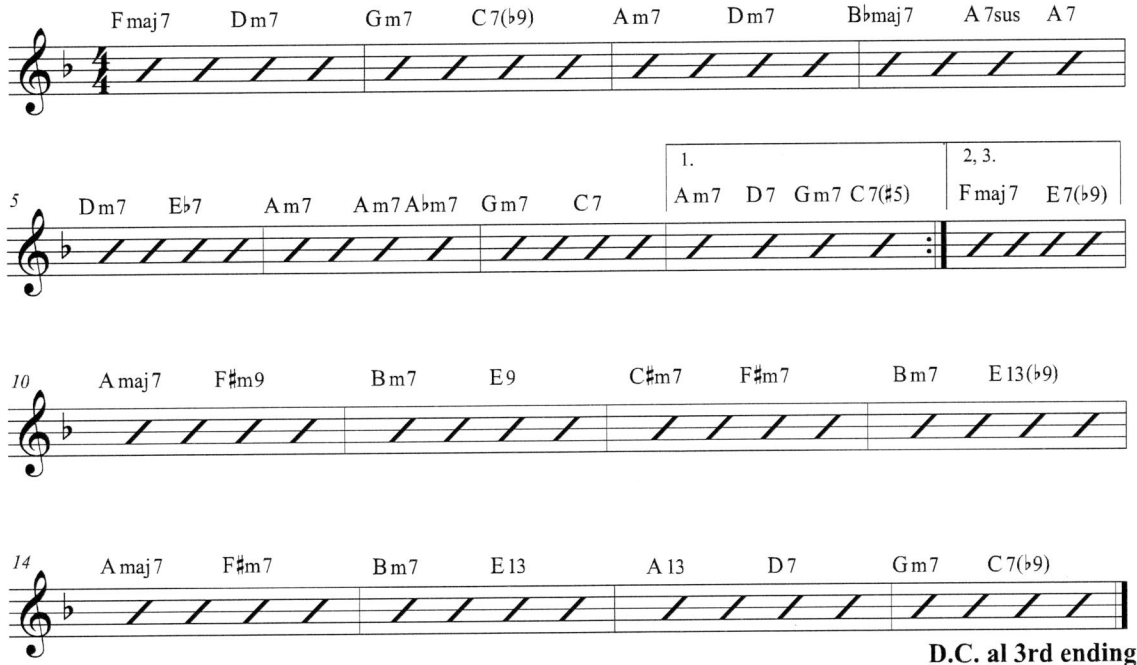

Refer to **DL TRK 20** for play-along track. Use simple open position voicings (voiced 2 and 2) to comp through an entire chorus.

Upper Structure Triad Voicings

Voicings consisting of triads built on top of other foundational structures such as roots, shells, and guide tones are called upper structure triad (UST) voicings.

Here are some common UST voicings for tonic major and tonic minor. Build the following triads from the scale step given and place over the root, shell, or guide tones of the chord symbol indicated. Make sure each voicing contains both guide tones. Feel free to double the melody of the upper structure triad in order to more evenly distribute the notes of the chord. Finally, be aware of octave doublings. It's ok to double the top voice down an octave; avoid doubling the bottom voice up an octave.

For 6/9 and m6/9 chords, the 7 is added as a tension note.

maj7: minor triad (mt) built off the 3rd and placed over a shell (S) or root (R)
maj6/9: major triad (Mt) built off the 5th and placed over guide tones (GTs) or (R & GTs)
m6: minor triad (mt) built off the root (R) and placed over (1–6 S) or (GTs)
m6/9: major triad (Mt) built off the 5th and placed over (GTs) or (R & GTs)

FIG. 1

Here are some of the several UST possibilities for dominant voicings. Place the following triads over the root, shell, or guide tones of the chord type indicated.

7(9): minor triad (mt) off 5
13: minor triad (mt) off 6
7sus: major triad (Mt) off ♭7 or minor triad (mt) off 5
7♭13): aug triad (At) off 3
7(#11,9): aug triad (At) off ♭7
7(♭13#9): major triad (Mt) off ♭6
13(#11): major triad (Mt) off 2
7(♭13♭9): minor triad (mt) off ♭2
7sus(♭9): minor triad (mt) off ♭7

Transpose these various dominant–tonic progressions.

FIG. 2

Here are some additional UST voicings for 7(♭9) and o7 employing diminished triads.

7, 7(♭9)	o7
dt off 3, 5, ♭7, or ♭9	dt off ♭3

FIG. 3

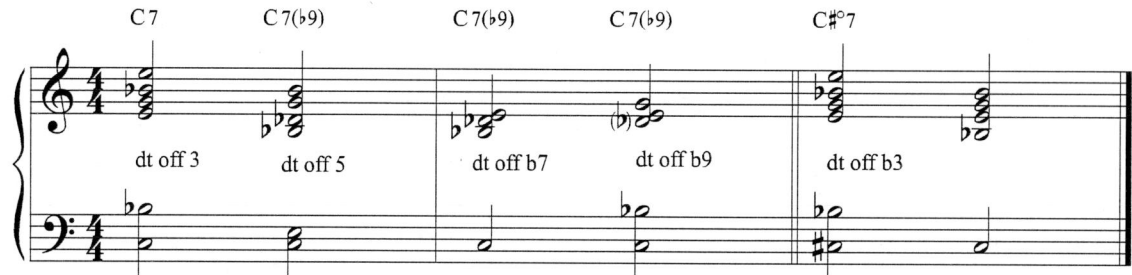

Try these voicings for minor seventh and half diminished chords.

m7	m9	m7♭5	m9♭5
Mt off ♭3, ♭5, or 6	mt off 5, Mt off ♭7	mt off ♭3	Mt off ♭7

Use the following six UST formulas to create easy comping patterns containing 3-note RH triads over LH roots. Apply to several standards; invert the RH triad as needed.

FIG. 4

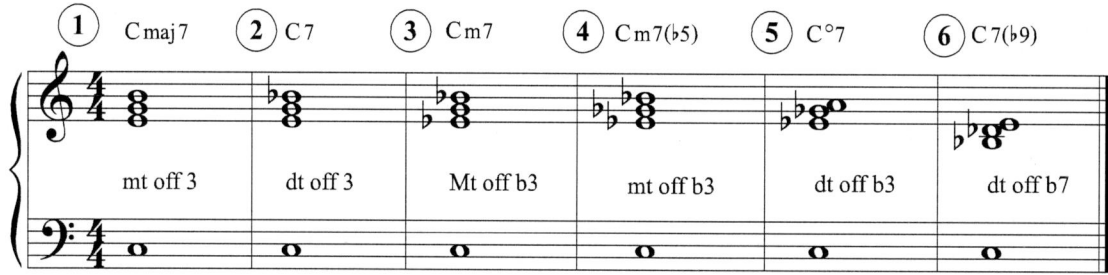

We can also create UST voicings for 7b9 and o7 by extracting major triads from the symmetric diminished scale and building off the tensions (see Ch. 5D for more about the diminished scale). The slash chords below imply diminished sevenths

7♭9 (half-whole)	o7 (whole-half)
Mt off ♭3, ♭5, or 6	Mt off 7, 2, 4, or ♭6

FIG. 5

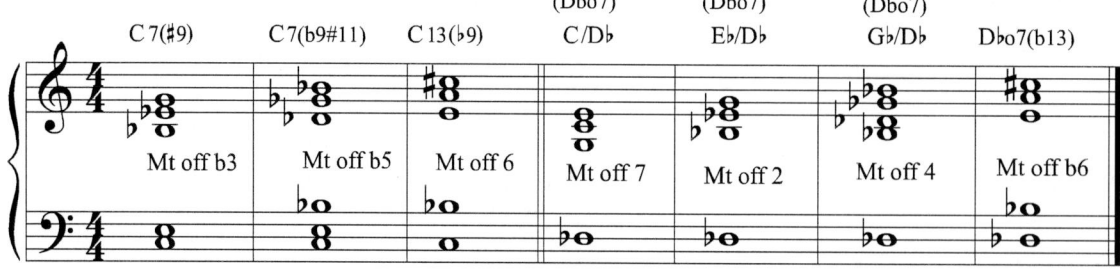

FIG. 6i

FIG. 6ii

The following chart summarizes the UST voicings discussed so far. The type of triad (t) is indicated to be built off a certain chromatic scale degree and placed over the listed foundational structure: root (R), shell (S), or guide tones (GTs) to generate a type of chord.

Min7, Min7b5	Dom7, 7sus	Tonic Major/Tonic Minor
m7: Mt off b3/(R or S)	7: dt off 3/(R)	maj7: mt off 3/(R or S)
m7: mt off R/(1–7 S)	7(13): mt off 6/(1–7 S or GTs)	maj6/9: Mt off 5/ (1–3 S, R & GTs, or GTs)
m7(9): mt off 5/(1–3 S)	7(9): mt off 5/(1–3 S)	m6: mt off R/(1–6 S or GTs)
m7(9): Mt off b7/(R & GTs)	7(b9): dt off 5, b7, b9/ (R or S)	m6/9: Mt off 5/ (1¬–3 S, R & GTs, or GTs)
m7b5: mt off b3/(R or S)	7(#9): Mt off b3/ (1–3 S or GTs)	
m9b5: Mt off b7/ (1–b5 S)	7(#11)(9): At off b7/ (1-3 S)	
	7(13#11): Mt off 2/(GTs or R & GTs)	
	13(b9): Mt off 6/ (1–7 S for GTs)	
	7(b13): At off 3/ (1–7 S or GTs)	
	7(b13#9): Mt off b6/ (GTs or R & GTs)	
	7(#11b9): Mt off b5/ (1–3 S, R & GTs or GTs)	
	7(b13b9): mt off b2/ (1–7 S or GTs)	
	7sus: Mt off b7/(R or S)	
	7sus: mt off 5/(1–4 S)	
	7sus(b9): mt off b7/(R)	

Select one voicing from each column to create your own ii–V–I-related progressions. Transpose to several keys. Here are two examples.

FIG. 7

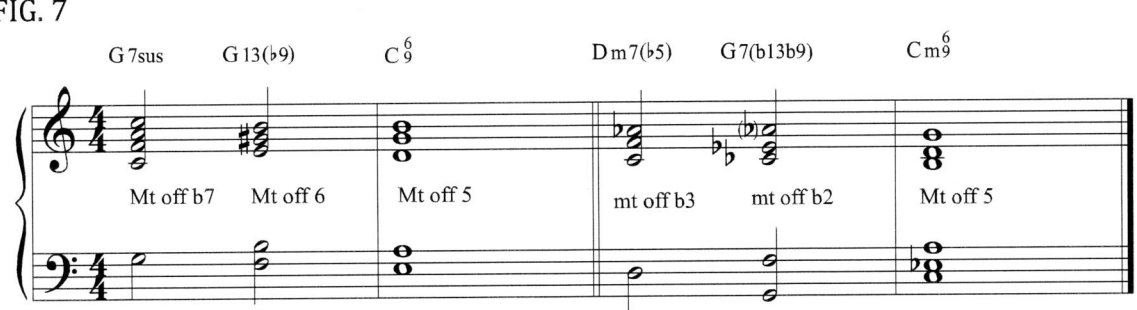

Chapter 4 • B

Workout 39: Playing Upper Structure Triad Voicings on the changes to "Polka Dots and Moonbeams" as played by Chet Baker. Build open voicings with upper structure triad voicings. This time don't worry about playing the melody. Instead, concentrate on laying down beautiful pads of UST voicings for the entire standard as you play along with the recording. Below is one possible solution. The 1st four bars are labeled. Label the rest of the USTs. Refer to **DL** **Trk 19-20** for a demo and play-along track. For the first eight bars of the chorus on the demo track, see FIG. 7 below.

FIG. 8

Spread Voicings

Spread voicings are 5-note open structures containing a root, in which the guide tones are split between the hands. They can be created in two ways:

1. First, by dropping the second voice of an A or B position chord down an octave, and playing it over a root. Below the ii–V–I's from Chapter 3B FIG. 4 are illustrated as spread voicings. Note that in m. 2 and 6, Fmaj13 is used instead of Fmaj9. The stack of 4ths in the RH makes for a more evenly spread voicing and creates a richer sound.

FIG. 1

2. Second, by building it from the bottom up. On top of a root add one note from each chord tone category (from Chapter 3B) in the following configurations from bottom to top: 3–7–R–5 and 7–3–5–R. The chord type will limit the choices.

5th	11, #11, 5, b13, 13	Root	R, 9, #9, b9, *7
Root	9, #9, b9 *7	5th	11, #11, 5, b13, 13
7th	6, b7, 7	3rd	3, b3, 4
3rd	3, b3, 4	7th	6, b7, 7
Root	R	Root	R

Experiment choosing various combinations of chord tones and subs to create 5-note spread voicings for different chord types. The root and guide tones for each chord are shown as whole notes and half notes and make up the bottom three notes of each voicing. The tensions and fifths are reserved for the soprano and alto voices, and are written as quarter notes.

Be careful to avoid: minor ninths (except for 7b9); doubling notes unless it's between the melody and the root; or using more than one note from each category for the upper four notes except for when one of the guide tones is a 6, in which case, 7 can be part of the root category and have the effect of being a tension note.

FIG. 2

For **tonic major** choose R (root), 3, 7(6) or R, 7(6), 3 for the LH shell and RH thumb. For the soprano and alto choose between 9, R, 7*, 5, 13, and/or #11. 7 can be used as one of the upper two voices for M6 or M6/9.

For **tonic minor** choose R, b3, 7(6) or R, 7(6), b3 for the LH shell and RH thumb. For the soprano and alto choose between 9, R, 7*, 5, 13, and/or 11. 7 can be used as one of the upper two voices for m6 or m6/9.

For **minor 7** choose R, b3, b7 or R, b7, b3 for the LH shell and RH thumb. For the soprano and alto choose between 9, R, 5, and/or 11.

For **dominant 7** choose R, 3, b7 or R, b7, 3 for the LH shell and RH thumb. For the soprano and alto choose between 9, R, b9, #9, 5, #11, b13 and/or 13.

For **minor 7b5** choose R, b3, b7 or R, b7, b3 for the LH shell and RH thumb. For the soprano and alto choose between 9, R, b5 and/or 11

For **diminished 7** choose R, b3, 6 or R, 6, b3 for the LH shell and RH thumb. For the soprano and alto choose between 9, R, 7, b5, 11, and/or b13. Tensions include notes a whole step above or half step below chord tones.

Hybrid Spread Voicings

It is relatively common to have a doubled 3rd or 7th in the soprano voice when voicing 5-note rooted chords. Technically, this isn't a complete spread voicing since the top four voices do not include R, 3, 5, and 7 or acceptable sub. This voicing can be thought of as a hybrid between a guide tone voicing with doubled notes and a spread voicing.

FIG. 3

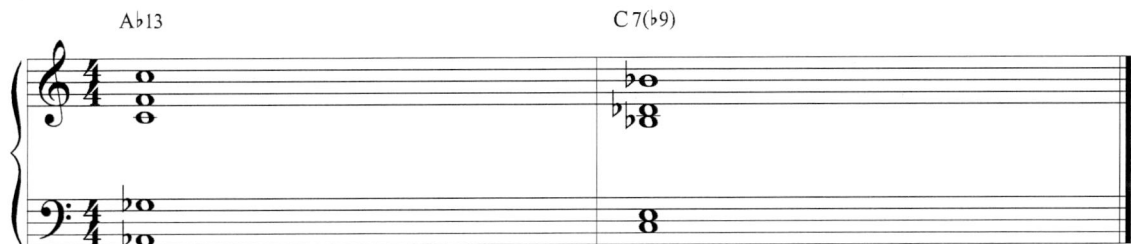

The spread voicings for half-diminished chords illustrated in FIG. 2 are a bit limited. UST voicings usually work much better and allow for full-sounding half-diminished voicings with the b5, but without a natural 9th. As an alternative, spread voicings for half-diminished chords can be created by placing b5–b7–11 in the RH over a LH 1–3 or 1–7 shell. Note that these voicings do not contain the b3; the 11 is used instead. Red Garland uses this sound during his intro to Woody'n You found on *Relaxin' with the Miles Davis Quintet*.

FIG. 4

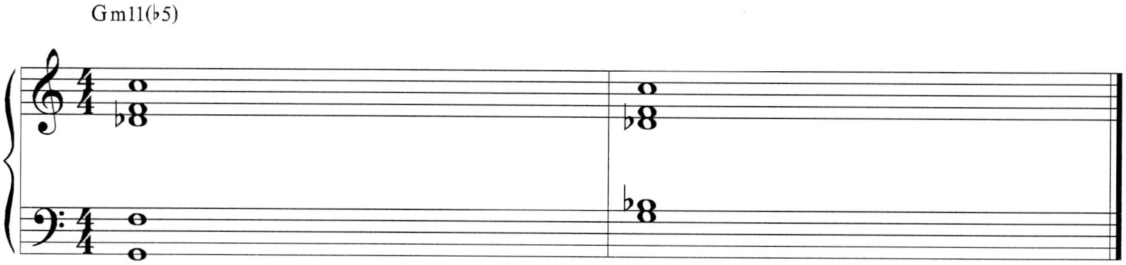

Play through the "A" section of *I Hear a Rhapsody* using mostly spread voicings. Add the melody in the top voice. The first two bars include the melody and the chords. For the rest of the "A" section, the chord voicing is illustrated without the melody. SPR=spread voicing; UST=upper structure voicing; D2=drop-2 (more on drop-2 voicings in the next section.)

FIG. 5

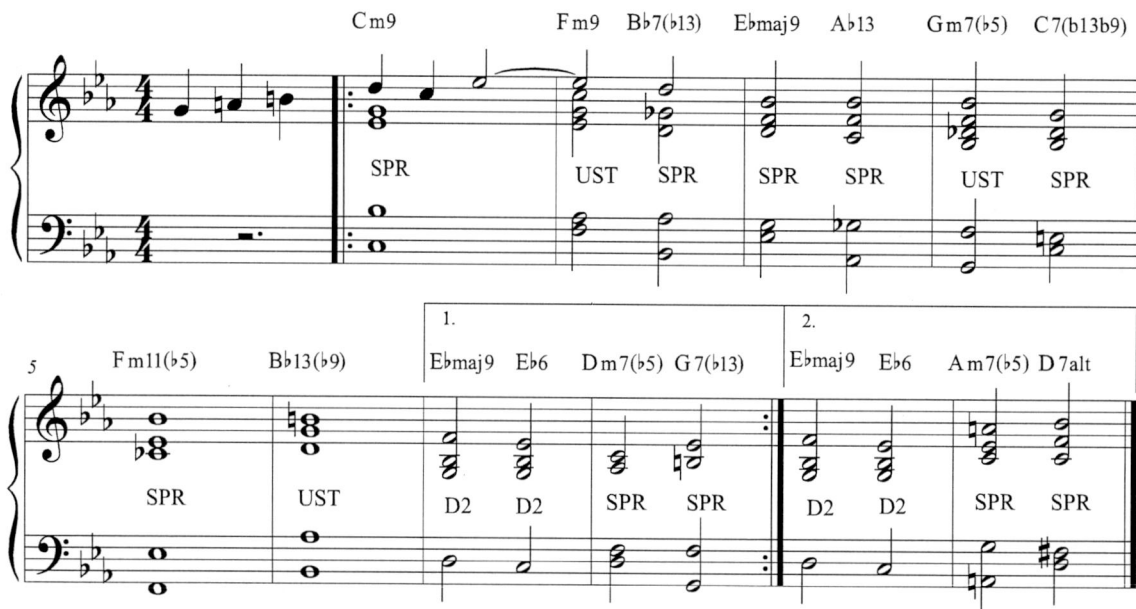

Continue playing through the second half of the tune. Since the melody is low, consider using simple open position chords for the first four bars of the bridge. Then for the last four bars spread voicings will work well.

Using spread (SPR), UST and simple open position (SOP) voicings, read through several standards incorporating the melody in your chord voicings.

Workout 40: Playing Spread Voicings on the changes to the Bridge of "Polka Dots and Moonbeams" as played by Chet Baker. Use spread voicings or UST voicings to play the straight melody along with Chet Baker for the B section of "Polkadots and Moonbeams". Here is the bridge using a combination of spread (SPR) and (UST) voicings. In general, SPR voicings are ideal when the melody is a tension or fifth; UST voicings work well when the melody is the 3rd or 7th.

Add the melody (with your 4th or 5th finger) to the voicings as you play along with the recording. The first two bars are done for you. At times 6-note spread voicings (SPR-6) are used in which the 5, 9 and 11 are all played together. Rolling the chords or playing the root in a separate pedal may be necessary to play some of the larger voicings.

Refer to **DL TRK 19-20** for a demo and play-along track. For the bridge on the demo track, spread voicings are used from FIG. 6 below.

FIG. 6

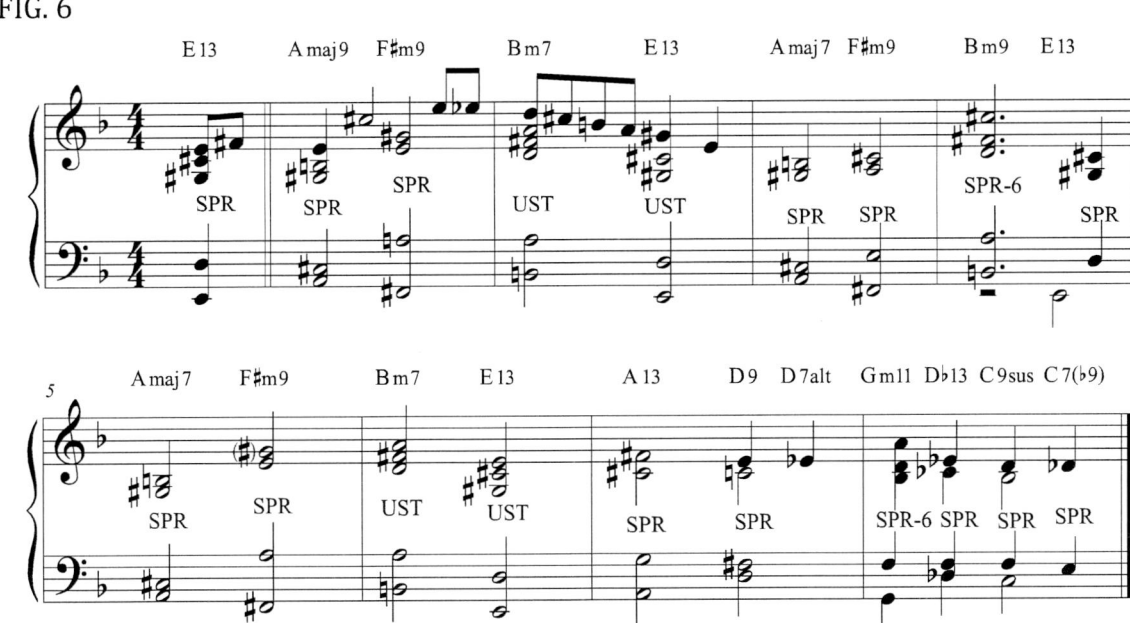

Use SPR, UST, and SOP voicings to play along with a recording of your favorite jazz standard.

Drop-2 Voicings

A drop voicing is an open position chord created when you move one or more of the 4 voices of a closed position chord down an octave. Thinking of the standard SATB configuration, moving the 2nd voice from the top (alto) down an octave creates a **drop-2 voicing**.

To get started, practice "little chords" (M6, m6, and o7) in drop-2 position like this:

FIG. 1

Transpose the above progression up in half steps. Also try this ii–V–I progression in drop-2 using a o7 chord for V7(b9) in all 12 keys. Notice how only two voices move at a time.

FIG. 2

Let's review how to convert common jazz chords to "little chords."

I (tonic major)	V6 or I6	M6 a fifth above, or parallel M6	Cmaj9 = G6/C
iim7	IV6	M6 a m3 above	C6 = C6
V7(9)	iim6	m6 a fifth above	Dm7 = F6/D
V7(b9)	viio7	o7 a M3 above	G9 = Dm6/G
V7alt	bvim6	m6 a m2 above	G7(b9) = Bo7/G
V7sus	IV6	M6 a m7 above	G7alt = Abm6/G
i (tonic minor)	im6	Parallel m6	G7sus = F6/G
iim7b5	ivm6	m6 a m3 above	Cm6 = Cm6

Now convert the chords in the bridge of "Polka dots and Moonbeams" to "little chords" in drop-2. Play through the example below while singing the melody. Experiment with other inversions.

FIG. 3

From Chapter 3D we learned that by adding a dim7 chord a half step below any sixth chord you can create a smooth scale of chords alternating between sixth and diminished. Try these ii–V–I drop-2 progressions in major and minor. Experiment going up or down the piano using the IV6-dim scale for ii–V and the I6-dim scale for I. For minor ii–V use the ivm6-dim scale and the im6-dim scale for i.

FIG. 4

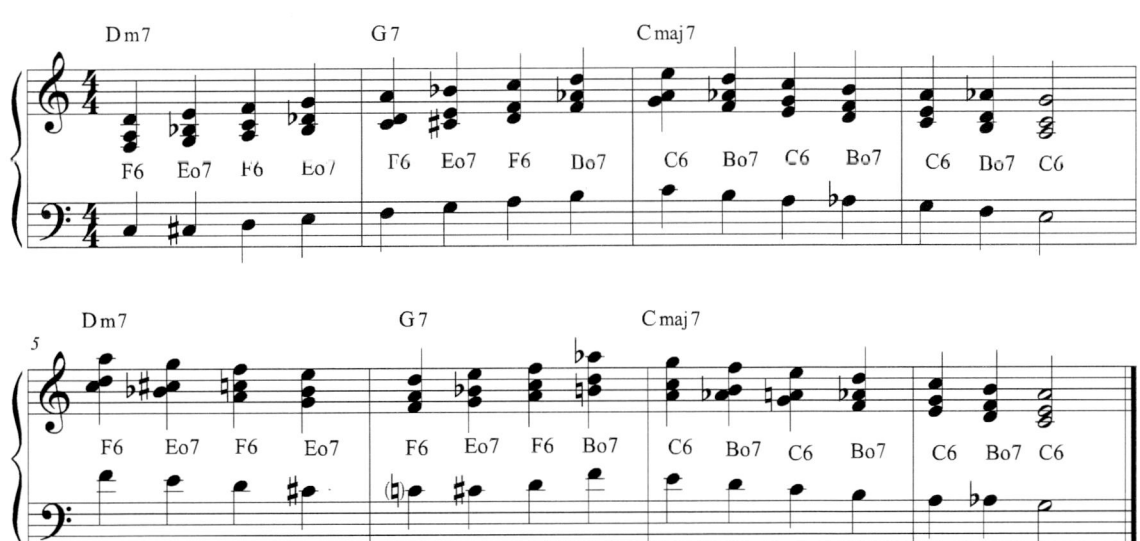

Revisit Chapter 3B, 3C, and 3D, and move the 2nd voice from the top in all "little chords" and A and B position voicings down an octave, thus creating drop-2 voicings. Here the accompaniment to Frank Sinatra's "These Foolish Things" is shown using drop-2 voicings. For much of it, the original closed position chord is transposed up an octave so that the resulting drop-2 will be in a good range and not too muddy.

FIG. 5

Use drop-2s and the sixth-diminished scale to play along with your favorite ballad recording.

Workout 41: Playing Drop-2 Voicings on the changes to "Polka Dots and Moonbeams" as played by Chet Baker. Use drop-2 voicings and UST voicings to comp along with Chet Baker on "Polka Dots and Moonbeams." Experiment with filling in with different inversions of drop-2 configurations of little chords or A and B position voicings. Also, try applying the sixth-diminished scale using drop-2 voicings.

When A and B closed position voicings are converted to drop-2, A pos switches to B pos and vice versa. This is because the top guide tone is in the alto voice and gets dropped an octave.

The first eight bars are shown below using these types of open voicings. The melody is referenced from time to time. In the second half of m. 1, the melody appears as the top voice of the drop-2 voicings. In m. 4 the melody is placed on top of the UST voicings on beats 1, 3, and 4. Continue through the rest of the tune. Refer to **DL TRK 19-20** for a demo and play-along track. For the second eight bars of the chorus on the demo track, drop-2 voicings are used from FIG. 6 below.

FIG. 6

4th-like Voicings

Building structures with fourths is an excellent way to create sonorous, modern and sleek structures that can be easily moved around and connected to other open chords.

One of the most iconic 4th-like voicings is called the "So What" voicing made up of One of the most iconic 4th-like structures is called the "So What" voicing made up of 4ths built up from the root with a major third on top. This voicing works well for most minor chords. Below, "So What" voicings are built off the 1st and 2nd degrees of D dorian followed by 4th-voicings built off the 3rd, 5th, and 6th scale degrees. This 5-chord movement is useful when comping on modal tunes or when there is a long stretch of a single minor chord.

FIG. 1

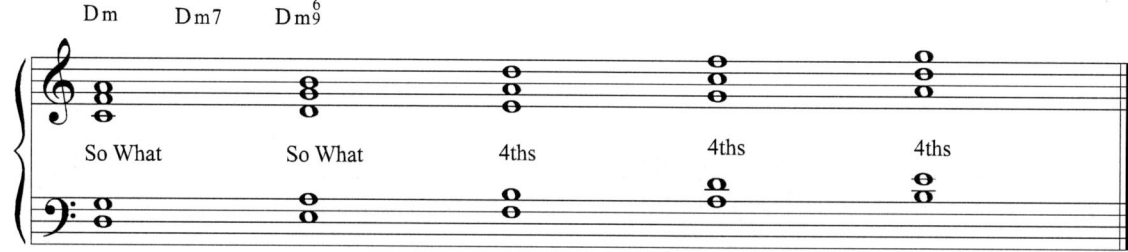

Here is a basic template for major ii–V–Is.

FIG. 2

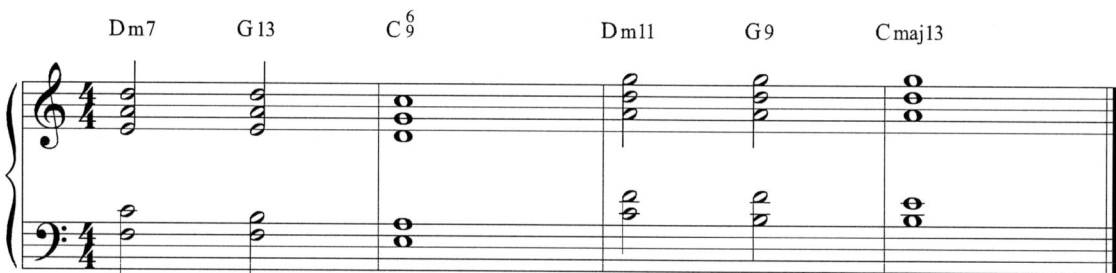

These voicings contain 4ths in the RH over GTs in the LH. For dominant and major chords, drop 4ths from the root or 5th and place over guide tones. For minor 7 chords, drop 4ths from the root or 11. Note that the voicings are primarily made up of 4ths but sometime contain 3rds or 5ths, hence the *4th-like* classification. Avoid 3rds on the bottom.

For m7b5 use the 4th-like voicing for the dominant chord a major third lower. For example, for Em7b5 play C7, etc. Try these variations for minor ii–V–i.

FIG. 3

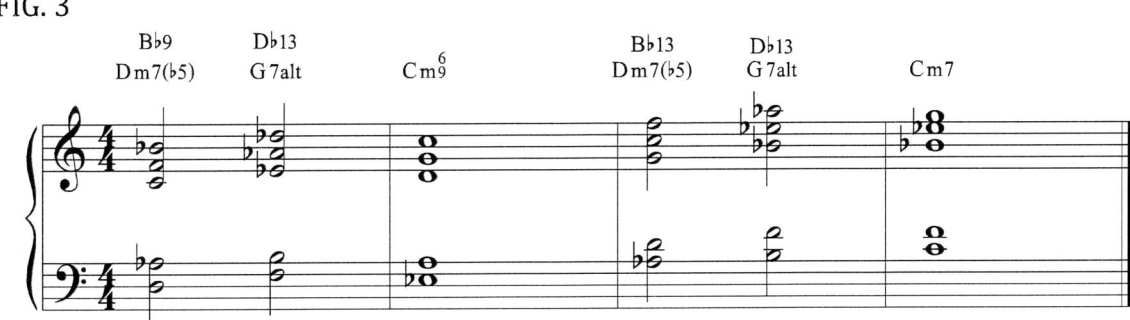

Workout 42: Playing 4th-like Voicings on the changes to "On Green Dolphin Street" as played by Miles Davis. Use 4th-like voicings to comp along with Bill Evans on the famous 1958 recording. For diminished chords use drop-2 voicings. The last 16 bars are done for you.

FIG. 4

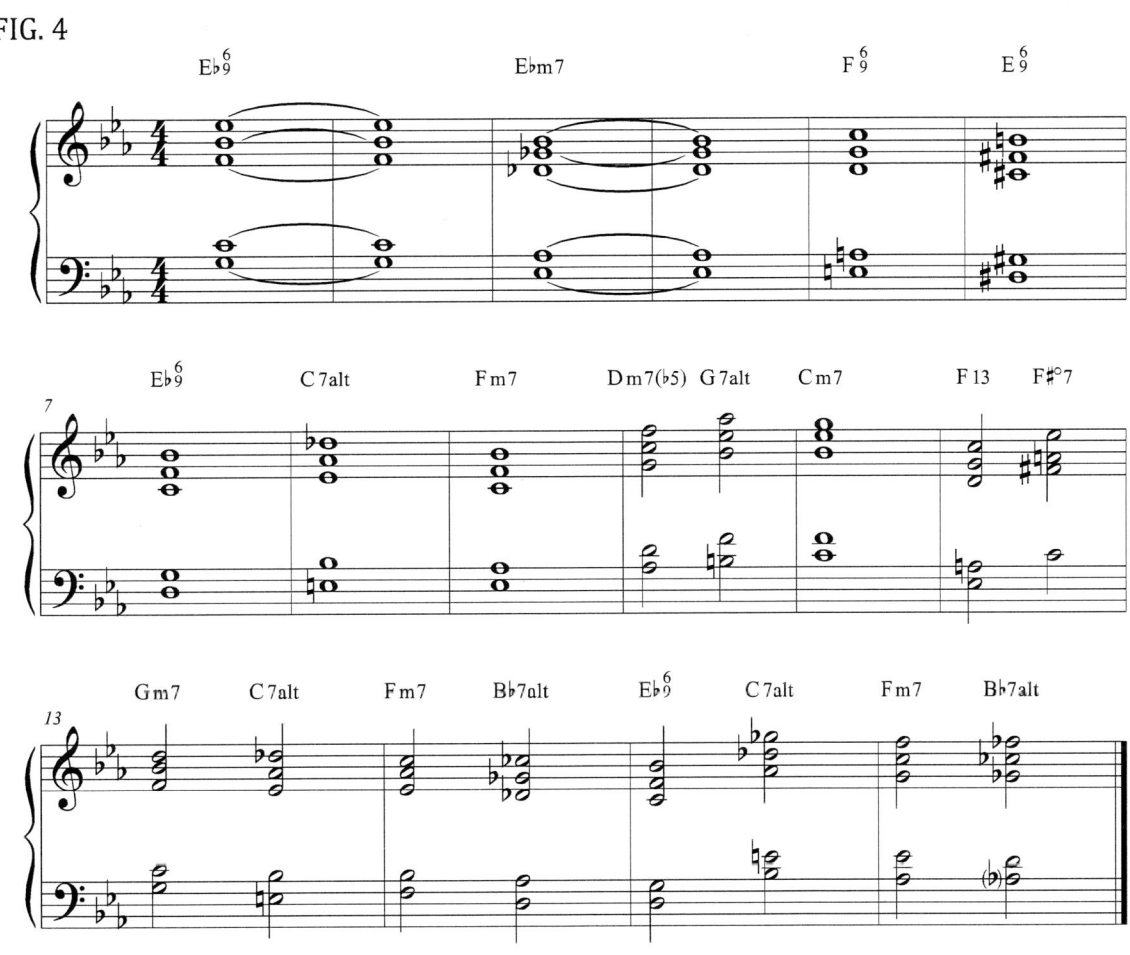

Duet 5: Accompanying a Soloist using Open Voicings. Player 1 plays a melody in octaves or as the top voice of open voicings. Player 2 accompanies using a variety of open voicings.

Comping Rhythm Transcription

By comping along to recordings using the precise rhythms as played by the jazz masters, you can more easily soak up the feeling, touch, and other subtleties. For many more comping rhythm transcriptions along with fully notated, complete 2-handed transcriptions see *Approach to Comping Vol. 1 and 2*, also available from Chuck Sher Music (www.shermusic.com).

Workout 43: Comping along with Red Garland during Miles Davis' Solo on the changes to "Trane's Blues" from the album, *Workin' with the Miles Davis Quintet*. Apply open or closed position chords to the rhythms. Follow the changes. Red Garland's comping progression is rich with mini cadences. For 6, m6, and o7, little chords work the best. At times, no chord is necessary. Instead, play a simple bluesy line, possibly in thirds. Listen to the original recording to get some ideas. Think of it as a conversation between Red Garland and Miles.

As you comp along with this recording, try to fuse your sound with Red Garland's even if your individual voicings are a bit different. Pay close attention to the touch and the relaxed placement of his upbeats.

Chapter 4 • F

FIG. 1

Chapter 5
Practicing Scales

As jazz players it isn't enough to learn scales by playing them up and down. It's much more than an exercise in muscle memory and technique. Rather, you need to understand every corner, every nook and cranny of the scale. It needs to be something that's second nature, something that you hear. Only then, can you truly unlock the potential of scales when it comes to improvisation.

In this section we'll explore five very important scales: major, tonic minor (the ascending form of melodic minor), harmonic minor, diminished, and whole tone. Each scale has its own sound, and a unique arrangement of whole steps and half steps.

Selected modes will be explored for each scale. In addition, chord scale theory, chord tones, and tensions will be introduced as a powerful tool in order to find options for scales when improvising on specific chords.

To get acquainted with each scale we have to deal with four levels of mastery. First, we need to learn it from different starting points using stepwise motion. Second, we have to be able to play ascending or descending diatonic intervals starting anywhere within the scale. Third we have to be able to play continuous broken thirds, arpeggiated triads and seventh chords with or without diatonic/chromatic approach tones. Finally, we have to be able to create block chords from the scale and move these chords freely up and down while staying within the scale. This way we can internalize each scale's topography, and begin to truly hear the scale so that we can access it more freely.

The Major Scale

The C major scale is made up of the following intervallic pattern of whole steps and half steps: W/W/H/W/W/W/H.

FIG. 1

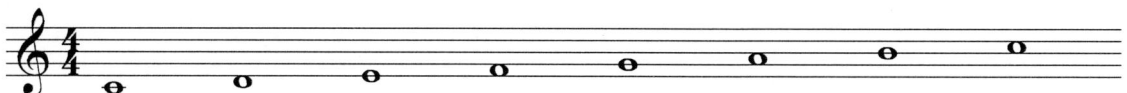

It's important to practice scales in a way that makes sense rhythmically and harmonically. Since swing is typically in 4/4, players often add or subtract notes from the 7-note scale to make it even, or play the notes in a specific order. For now, play the scale in ascending eighth notes. Start on C and play up to B and come back down without stopping. When you get back to C you should be on beat 3 of the second measure. Practicing in this way allows you to play each chord tone on a beat and the passing tones (or tensions) on upbeats. This makes for a strong, centered line that firmly emphasizes C major.

FIG. 2

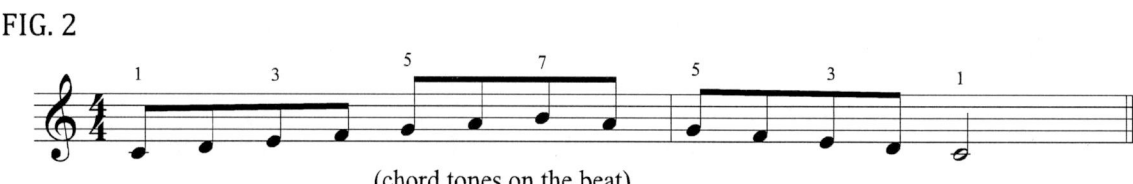

(chord tones on the beat)

When you start the scale on a note other than the root, you are playing one of its modes. If you start on D and play up the C major scale to the D an octave above, you've just played the second mode of C major. Each 7-note scale has 7 modes. In other words, you can start a scale from 7 different starting points to create 7 unique modes of a scale. Each mode of a major scale has a unique name, sound, and characteristics. Because the starting note is different, each one has a different center of gravity. Some sound minor, some major.

Here are the modes of the C major scale along with corresponding diatonic seventh chords:

FIG. 3

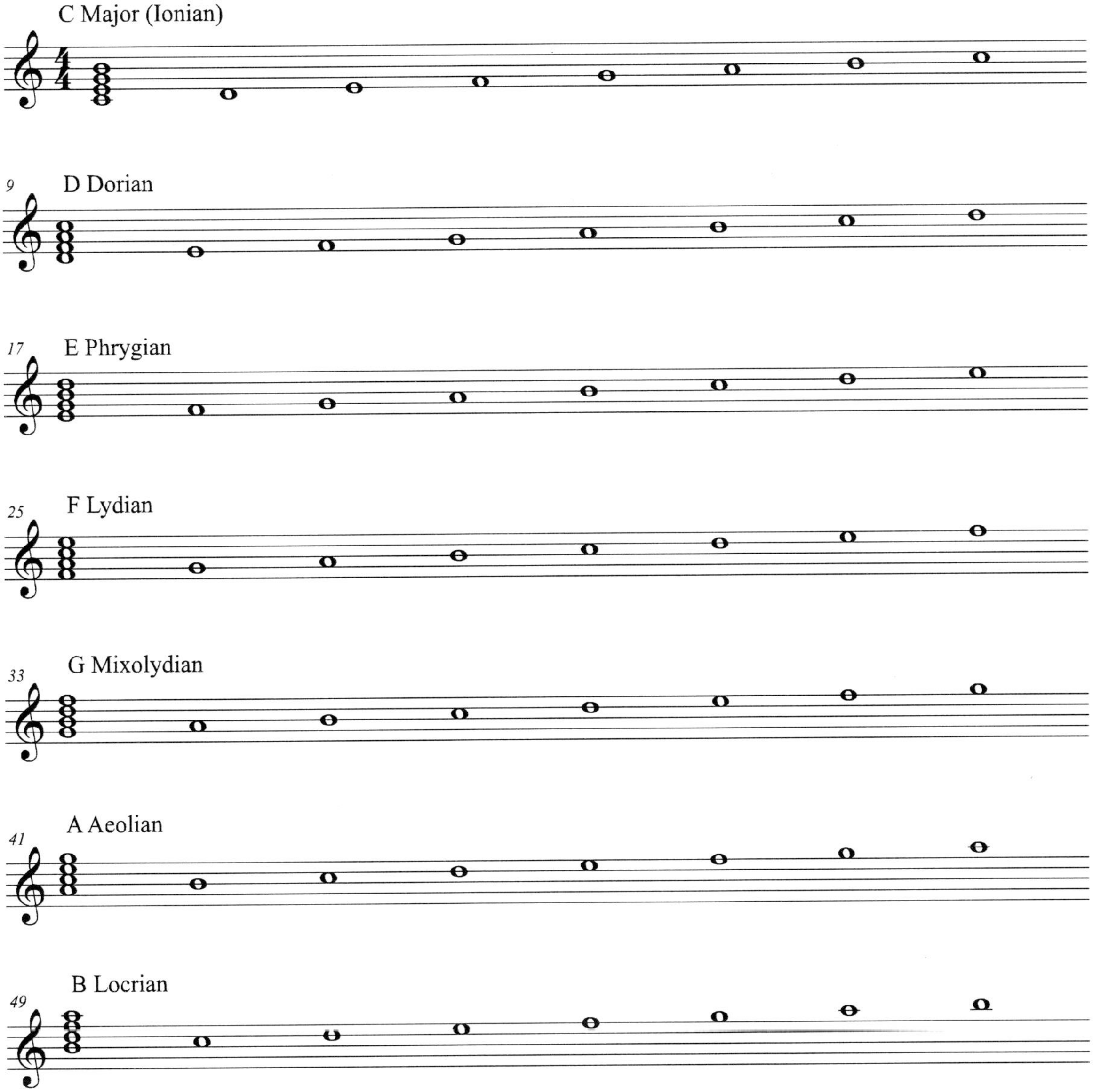

C Major (Ionian)

D Dorian

E Phrygian

F Lydian

G Mixolydian

A Aeolian

B Locrian

Jazz theorists assign scales to use for improvising on certain chords. A chord is contained within a scale. A scale or scales can be used to express a chord.

A quick review: the 1st, 3rd, 5th, and 7th degrees of a scale correspond to the root, 3rd, 5th, and 7th of the chord, and are known as **chord tones**. The other notes of the scale (2nd, 4th, and 6th) are called passing tones or **tensions**. When heard against the basic chord, these tones create dissonance or tension. Instead of being heard as merely passing tones, they are heard as upper extensions of the harmony. For this reason, they are often renamed (9th, 11th, 13th) to show that they float above the basic harmony of the seventh chord adding a distinctive color or characteristic.

We now have seven scales that correspond to the seven diatonic seventh chords. For example, the C major scale could be used when improvising on Cmaj7. C major scale is the "parent" scale. If you look closely at the scale, Cmaj7 is embedded in the scale. Dm7 is found in the D dorian scale, meaning D dorian can be used to express Dm7. Em7 is found in the E phrygian scale, meaning E phrygian can express Em7 and so on. If you find a scale that contains the chord that you wish to solo on, you can use the "parent" scale as source material for improvisation.

It quickly becomes apparent that chords often have more than one chord scale. For example, Dm7 is found in the D dorian scale derived from C major, but is also found in the D phrygian scale derived from Bb major and the D aeolian scale derived from F major. Dm7 is a diatonic seventh chord found in three different keys: it's the ii7 of C major; the iii7 of Bb major; and the vi7 of F major, and therefore can be expressed using three unique chord scales.

Cmaj7 is obviously found in the C major scale, but also is found in the G major scale, as the seventh chord built on the 4th scale degree. Cmaj7 can be expressed using two different chord scales derived from the major scale.

Here are the chord scale options for the chord types found in the seven modes of the major scale:

Maj7: major or lydian
m7: dorian, phrygian, or aeolian
7: mixolydian
m7b5: locrian

Different scales imply different tensions in the chord. In other words, the underlying seventh chord may be identical, but the tones in between the chord tones might be different. If a certain scale is desired for a chord sometimes it will be reflected in the chord symbol.

Cmaj7(#11) = C lydian
Cm7(b6) = C aeolian

Other times, the context or personal taste of the player is what decides the particular scale. An improviser could use C dorian, C phrygian, or C aeolian to express Cm7. Traditionally, if you are in the key of Bb, C dorian is often the choice; if you are in Ab, C phrygian fits better; and for a vi7 chord in Eb, C aeolian works well. Keep in mind, jazz players break this rule all the time, but it's nice to be aware of the difference in sound so that you can make a conscious decision instead of plugging in C dorian automatically whenever you see the Cm7 chord symbol.

Here are the parallel major modes starting from C described in terms of the C major scale. The chord symbols often associated with these scales are listed as well. Notice the chord tones (odd scale degrees) and tensions (even scale degrees) for each scale. Also, notice how the chord symbols are embedded in the corresponding scale.

FIG. 4

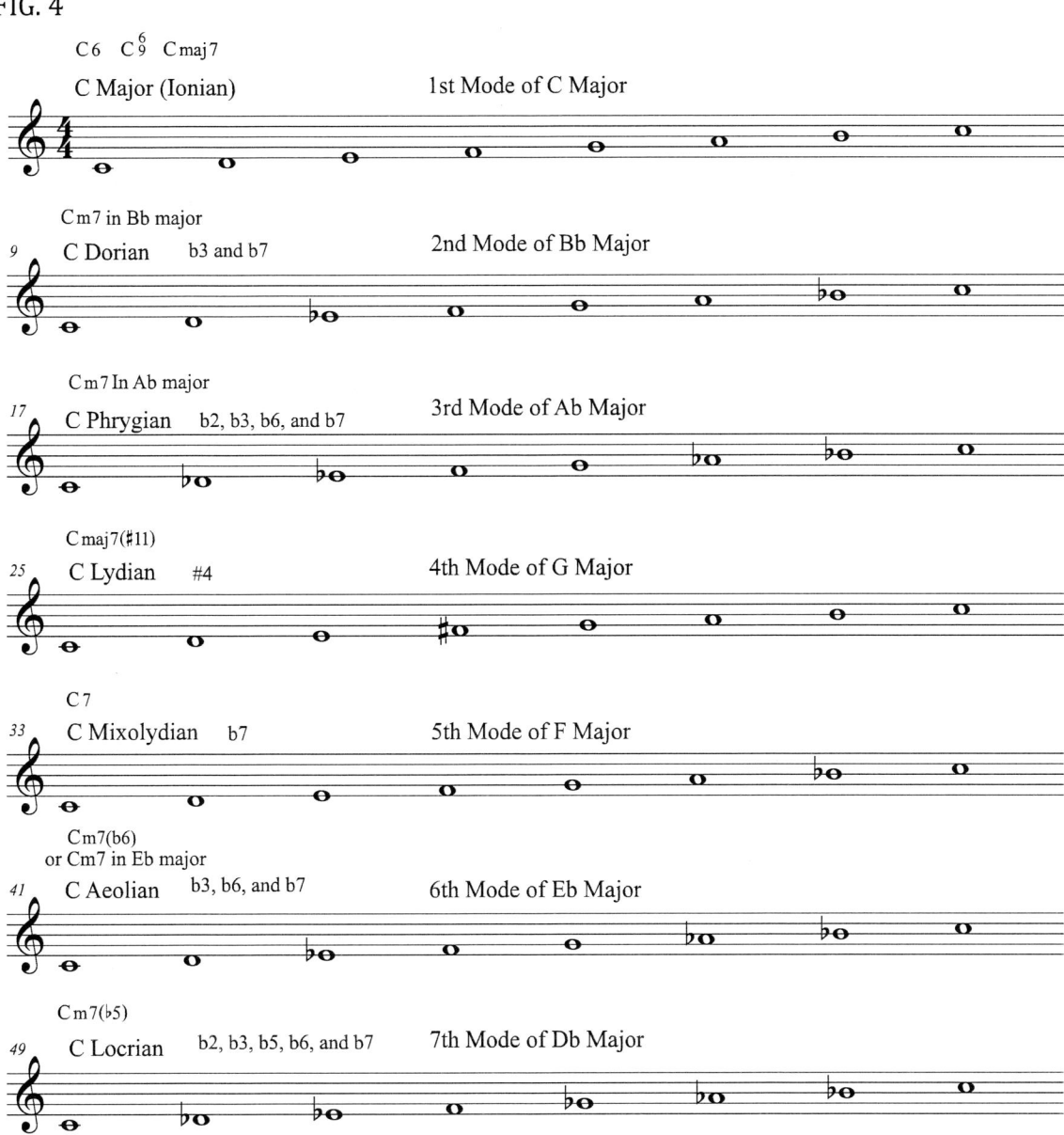

Often tensions are part of the scale but cannot be used in the chord voicing. When played together as part of a chord, tensions clash with the basic seventh chord underneath creating an undesirable minor ninth interval. This is true in the case of the 11th as part of C major to express Cmaj7; the b9 as part of C phrygian to express Cm7; the 11th as part of C mixolydian to express C7; and the b9 as part of C locrian to express Cm7b5.

These special tensions are called **unavailable tensions**. Keep in mind, these notes are often the most expressive and beautiful when used in the right way when improvising. I would caution against avoiding them all together.

Choosing the appropriate chord scale therefore has to do with context, choice of tension note(s), and personal taste. It's not quite as easy as plugging in a scale for a chord. But perhaps that's a good thing. An improviser must make choices in the moment.

Practice the 7 modes of the major scale in ascending eighth notes stopping on the 7th scale degree and then coming back down like you did for C major. First play all of the modes of C major, then, play all of the parallel modes starting from C. Transpose to all 12 keys. Listen for the different tonal characteristics of each mode. For example, major (ionian) is happy, mild; dorian is minor but not too dark; phrygian is exotic with a Japanese tinge; lydian is quirky and Bartok-like; mixolydian is bluesy; aeolian is ancient, distant, and minor; locrian is the darkest minor mode of the major scale. You'll have your own adjectives; just be aware of these subtle differences.

To gain fluency with a scale, in this case the major scale, it takes more than simply playing its modes up and down.

To really master a scale as an improviser you must be able to:

1. Create stepwise motion from anywhere in the scale
2. Freely play diatonic intervals from anywhere within the scale
3. Play continuous diatonic broken thirds, arpeggiated triads and seventh chords with or without approach tones
4. Move block chords through the scale

STEP 1: CREATING STEPWISE MOTION FROM ANYWHERE IN THE SCALE.

Practice 5-note fragments up and down the scale in 3-beat phrases with a simple LH shell pattern alternating between 1–5 and 2–5.

FIG. 5

STEP 2: FREELY PLAYING DIATONIC INTERVALS FROM ANYWHERE WITHIN THE SCALE.

The challenge here is to start anywhere in the scale and play a given diatonic interval either ascending or descending all while keeping time and preserving the gentle 3 against 4 cross rhythm. Besides the intervals illustrated below, try this with seconds, fourths, fifths, and sixths.

FIG. 6

STEP 3: PLAYING CONTINUOUS DIATONIC BROKEN THIRDS, ARPEGGIATED TRIADS AND SEVENTH CHORDS WITH OR WITHOUT APPROACH TONES.

Try the following sequence of diatonic broken thirds in several keys. For this exercise and the exercises that follow feel free to add a LH shell pattern like before.

FIG. 7

Next, add approach tones. This means adding a note a half step below each third. Playing notes outside of the scale in a pattern together with scale tones actually reinforces your knowledge of the notes that are *in* the scale.

FIG. 8

Play the following sequence of diatonic arpeggiated triads. Experiment with changing the direction of the arpeggio i.e. playing bottom to top vs. top to bottom.

FIG. 9

This time add a diatonic approach tones from above of each triad arpeggio. Play the pattern up and down the scale.

FIG. 10

Finally, play a sequence of diatonic seventh chords up and down the scale. Again, experiment with changing the direction of the arpeggio.

FIG. 11

Advanced students can add either one of the following syncopated LH shell patterns to the RH patterns above.

FIG. 12

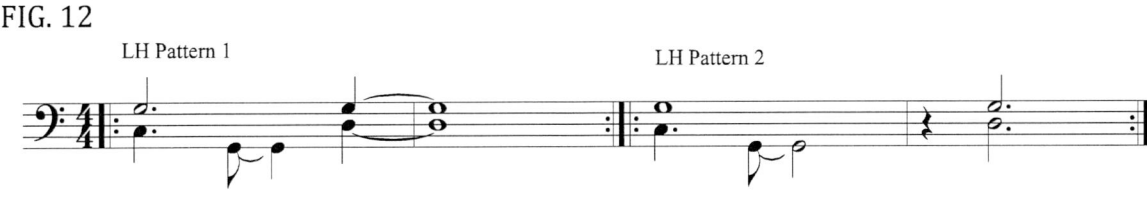

STEP 4: MOVING BLOCK CHORDS THROUGH THE SCALE

For our purposes, a **block chord** refers to a 5-note chord voicing in which a four-note root position seventh chord is played in the RII over a doubled melody note in the LH directly under the lowest note of the RH. There should be an octave between the top melody note of the RH and the note in the LH.

To begin generating block chords, play Cmaj7 in root position in the RH. With your LH, double the top voice an octave below, right underneath your right thumb. Next move the doubled 7th to a 6th and continue the pattern down the C major scale.

FIG. 13

Here is the pattern ascending.

FIG. 14

A simple ii–V–I can be played in block chord style by using seventh chords derived from the first and second modes of the major scale. For ii–V use seventh chords built on the tonic or 3rd of the dorian scale. For I use seventh chords built on the tonic or 3rd degree of the major scale. Apply the following block chord pattern for ii–V–I through the keys:

FIG. 15

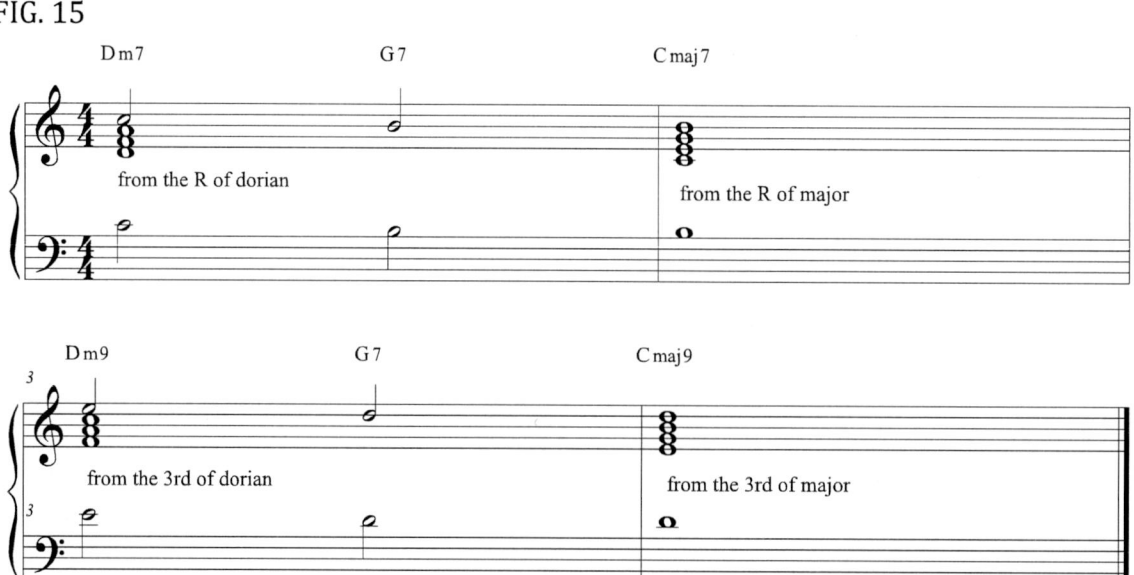

The point of this exercise is to show how to play chords through the scale or scales to "make the changes." For all of the block chord exercises that follow, there will be dissonances to resolve. Remember that this way of playing is all about moving, tension and release. Don't be alarmed by a momentary dissonance. There's a freedom when approaching harmony like this, and can help get out of the trap of having set voicings that are always the same.

Try this ii-V-I exercise using seventh chords built from the tonic, 3rd, and/or 5th of the major, dorian, and mixolydian scales. Continue the pattern down in whole steps. Experiment with starting the block chord patterns on different chord tones for each mode.

FIG. 16

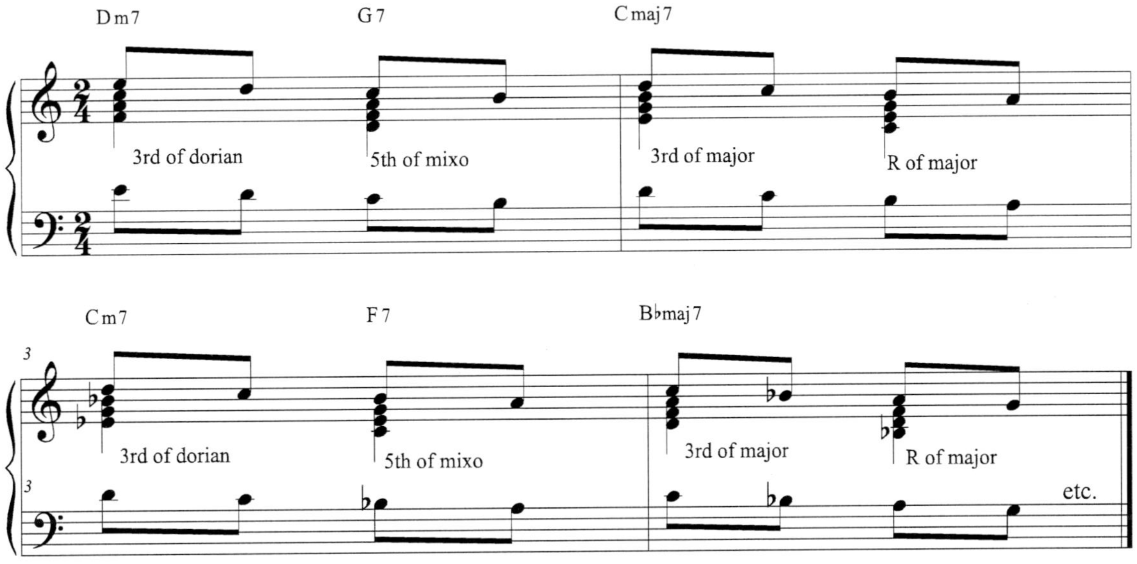

Workout 44: Playing Block Chords on the changes to "Afternoon in Paris" Apply this block chord pattern to the "A" section of this lovely standard as you play along with J.J. Johnson on trombone, Sonny Stitt on tenor sax, John Lewis on piano, Nelson Boyd on bass, and Max Roach on drums.

Use the chord symbols to help select the appropriate chord scale. The root of the given chord symbol corresponds to scale degree 1 of the appropriate mode. For example, Cmaj7 corresponds to the C major scale; Dm7 corresponds to the D dorian scale, etc.

For maj7 chords build seventh chords from the root or 3rd of the major scale. For iim7–V7, build seventh chords from the root or 3rd of the dorian scale. The chord pattern derived from the dorian scale will accommodate both the ii chord *and* the V chord in the case of one-measure ii–Vs.

FIG. 17

By arpeggiating the RH seventh chord embedded in the block chords above, you can create a compelling solo line. Feel free to mix and match ascending and descending seventh chords. Practice over a simple LH shell pattern. Play the "A" section along with the recording. Refer to **DL TRK 21-22** for a demo and play-along track. For now, only play the "A section." On the demo, block chords are used during the 1st "A section"; arpeggiated block chords are played during the 2nd "A."

FIG. 18

The Tonic Minor Scale

The tonic minor scale is created by lowering the 3rd scale degree of the major scale. Different than the dorian scale used for ii7, tonic minor feels like you arrived home and is used for minor compositions or key areas. It can also be thought of as the ascending form of the melodic minor scale with b3, natural 6, and natural 7. It's made up of the following intervallic pattern: W/H/W/W/W/W/H.

FIG. 1

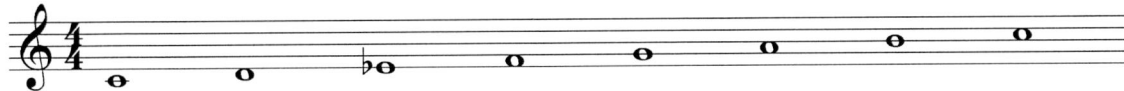

Practice the scale in rhythm like before: in eighth notes from the root up to the 7th scale degree and back down to the root.

For our purposes we'll concentrate only on four modes of the tonic minor scale that are often used for improvisation: the first, fourth, sixth and seventh, also known as melodic minor, lydian dominant, locrian natural 2, and altered respectively. Melodic minor refers to the ascending form of the third type of minor scale. The middle two names are derived from modifying the modes of a major scale. The word "altered" refers to raising or lowering the 5's and 9's of a chord or scale. This particular mode contains b9, #9, #11, and b13. In other words, all of the tensions are altered.

Here are selected modes of the tonic minor scale along with corresponding diatonic seventh chords:

FIG. 2

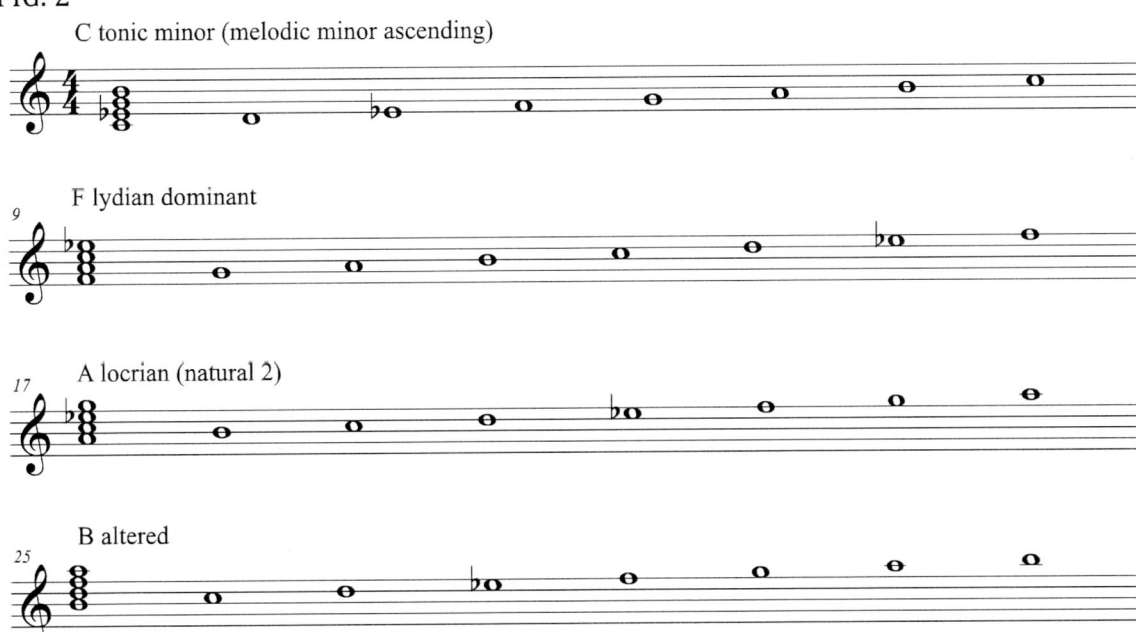

Here are some chord scale options for the chord types found in these four modes of the tonic minor scale:

m6/9: melodic minor
13(#11): lydian dominant
m7(b5): locrian natural 2
7alt: altered

The parallel modes of tonic minor starting from C described in terms of the C major scale are illustrated below. The chord symbols often associated with these scales are listed as well. Notice the chord tones (odd scale degrees) and tensions (even scale degrees) for each scale. Also, notice how the chord symbols are embedded in the corresponding scale.

FIG. 3

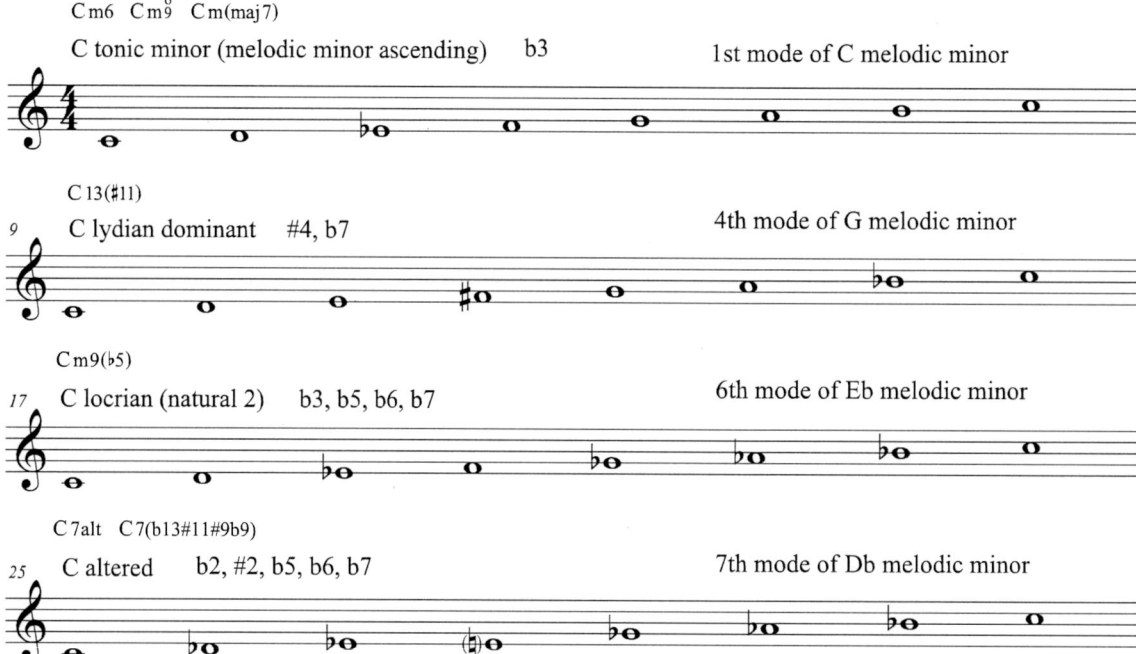

Although the altered scale can express m7b5, it is more often used to express 7b13, #11, #9, b9, or more simply put, 7alt. The dominant seventh is embedded in the altered scale, but with an altered 5th. Another difference is that two tensions (b9 and #9) are consecutive scale degrees throwing off the chord tone/tension alternation found in the other scales. **Important:** the 3rd of the altered scale is the 4th scale degree, and corresponds to the 3rd of the related 7alt. When building arpeggio-patterns later in the chapter keep this in mind.

Also, be aware that now we have two possible chord scales that can express m7b5: locrian and locrian (nat. 2). The former is derived from the major scale, the latter from melodic minor. Traditionally, locrian is used for minor ii–V's, but modern players often use locrian (nat. 2). Monk talked about playing a Cm6 with the 6th in the bass to express Am7b5. That would mean he was thinking in terms of C melodic minor to play Am7b5. Charlie Parker, on the other hand, would often use locrian (or at least a fragment of locrian) to play m7b5. Ultimately, it comes down to personal taste, and context.

Even though we won't name each mode, it is still important to practice all 7 modes of the tonic minor scale. Practice each mode in rhythm from the tonic up to the 7th scale degree and back down in eighth notes. Then, practice the parallel modes as you did in the previous section.

At this point, let's go through the four steps outlined in the previous section in order to better assimilate the tonic minor scale.

Step 1: Creating stepwise motion from anywhere in the scale.

Practice 5-note fragments up and down the scale in 3-beat phrases with a simple LH shell pattern alternating between 1–5 and 2–5.

FIG. 4

STEP 2: FREELY PLAYING DIATONIC INTERVALS FROM ANYWHERE WITHIN THE SCALE.

Below, the intervallic exercise from the last section is applied to the tonic minor scale.

Chapter 5 • B

FIG. 5

STEP 3: PLAYING CONTINUOUS DIATONIC BROKEN THIRDS, ARPEGGIATED TRIADS AND SEVENTH CHORDS WITH OR WITHOUT APPROACH TONES.

Try the following sequence of diatonic broken thirds in several keys. Notice how it's a variation of the broken third pattern from FIG. 7, Chapter 5A. For this exercise and the exercises that follow feel free to add a LH shell pattern like before.

FIG. 6

Next, add an approach tone a half step below each third and practice like this:

FIG. 7

Play the following sequence of diatonic arpeggiated triads. Experiment with changing the direction of the arpeggio i.e. playing bottom to top vs. top to bottom.

FIG. 8

Add approach tones above each triad.

FIG. 9

Play seventh chord arpeggios through the scale.

FIG. 10

Advanced students can add the syncopated LH shell patterns found in FIG. 12 of Chapter 5A to the RH patterns above.

Chapter 5 • B

STEP 4: MOVING BLOCK CHORDS THROUGH THE SCALE.

We are now ready to play block chords with a movable 7th on each scale degree up and down the scale.

FIG. 11

To create block chord patterns for im6/9, IV13(#11), vi9(b5), VII7alt, build seventh chords from the tonic and 3rd of the i tonic minor scale.

For Cm6/9, F13(#11), Am9(b5), and B7alt, build seventh chords from the tonic and 3rd of the C tonic minor scale.

Thinking in terms of the modes of melodic minor:

1. For m6/9 build 7th chords from the R or 3rd of tonic minor
2. For 13(#11) build 7th chords from the 5th or 7th of lydian dominant
3. For m9(b5) build 7th chords from the 3rd or 5th of locrian (natural 2)
4. For 7alt build 7th chords from the b9 or 3rd of altered

For each block chord pattern below (FIG. 12) practice over the root of each chord symbol listed above. This way you can hear the entire chord sound. Use the pedal to help you, and transpose to several keys.

FIG. 12

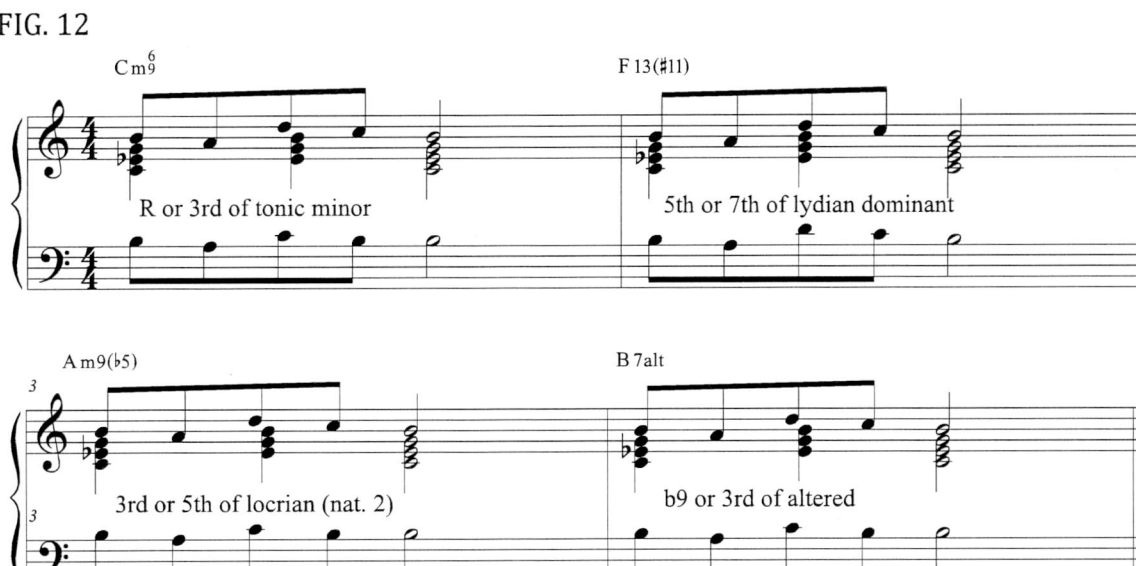

Workout 45: Playing Block Chords on the changes to Sarah Vaughan's "Lullaby of Birdland." Apply a block chord pattern to the song as you play along with the inimitable Divine One. Start after the intro. For now, concentrate on the "A" section. You may notice that the piano player plays a quick Am7–D7 right before the bridge. For our purposes, staying on Dmaj7 in the 2nd ending will work fine. Nevertheless, it's important to be aware of all of these subtleties when listening to the recording.

FIG. 13

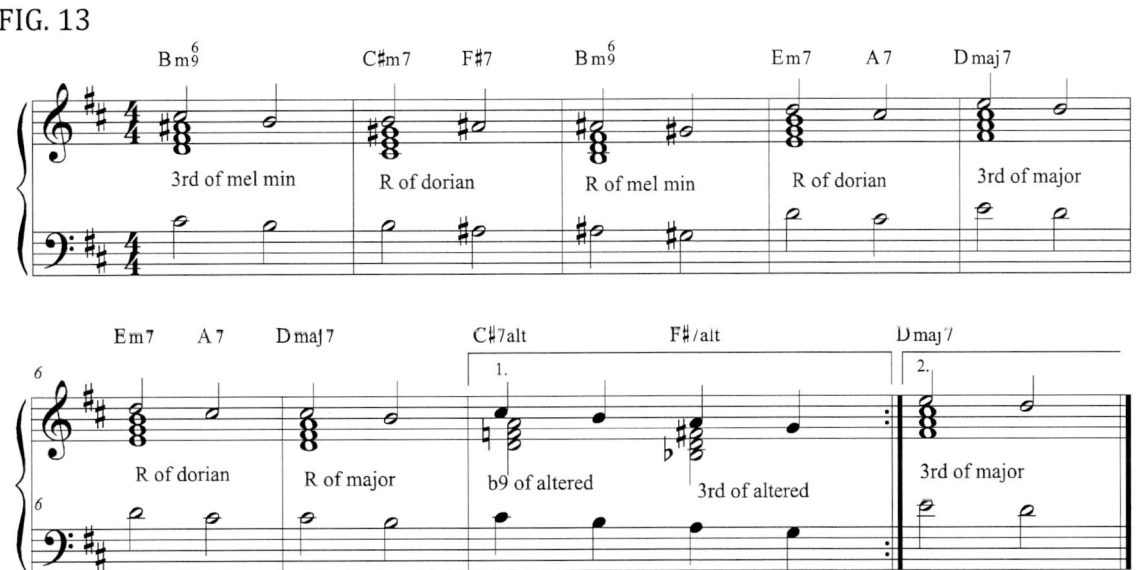

Arpeggiate the RH of the block chord pattern to create an interesting solo line. On beat 3 of m. 8, the arpeggio is a bit different than the original block chord in FIG. 13 (m. 8) in order to create a smoother melodic line. For F#7alt build the arpeggio from the 7th of the F# altered scale. Refer to **DL TRK 23-24** for a demo and play-along track. At this time, only play the "A section." On the demo, block chords are used during the 1st "A section"; arpeggiated block chords are played during the 2nd "A."

FIG. 14

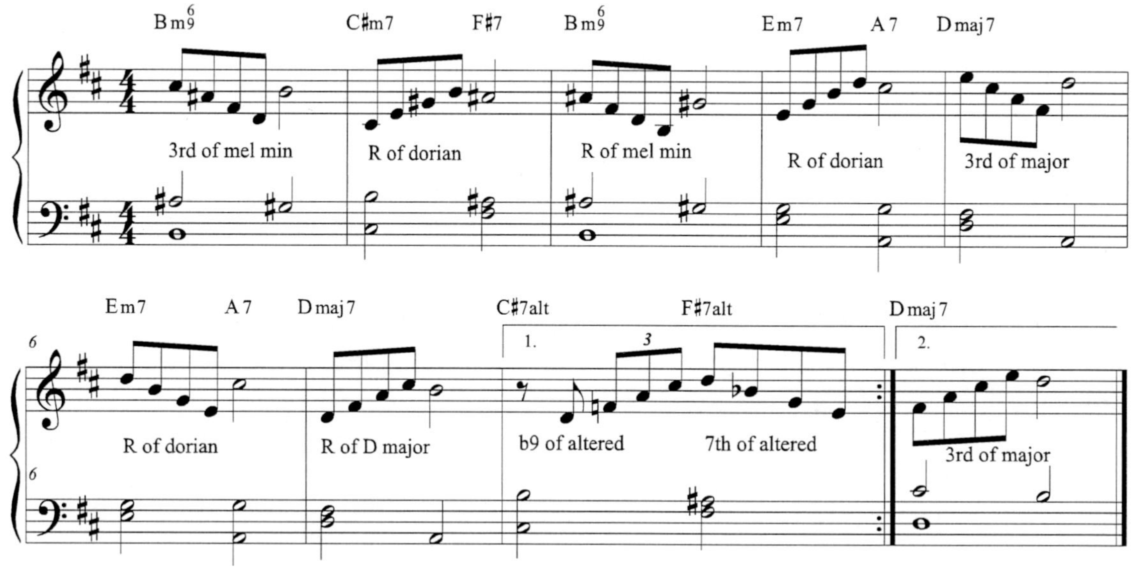

The Harmonic Minor Scale

The harmonic minor scale also has 7-notes, and is created by lowering the 3rd and 6th of the major scale. Commonly known as the 2nd type of minor scale with b3, b6, and natural 7, its intervallic pattern is: W/H/W/W/H/A2/H. The unusual augmented 2nd found in the scale between scale degrees 6 and 7 gives it an Eastern, exotic sound.

FIG. 1

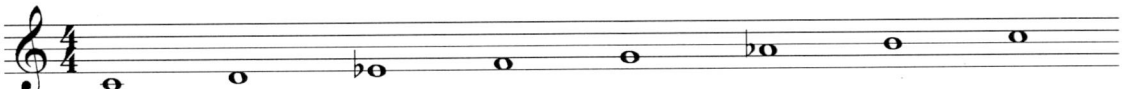

Practice the scale in rhythm up to the 7th degree and down again, like before.

We'll concentrate on four modes of the harmonic minor scale that are often used for improvisation: the first, second, fifth and seventh. Unlike the modes of the major scale and tonic minor scale, most of the modes of harmonic minor do not have commonly used names. Aside from the first mode (harmonic minor) their names are based on similar modes of the major scale that have been modified.

FIG. 2

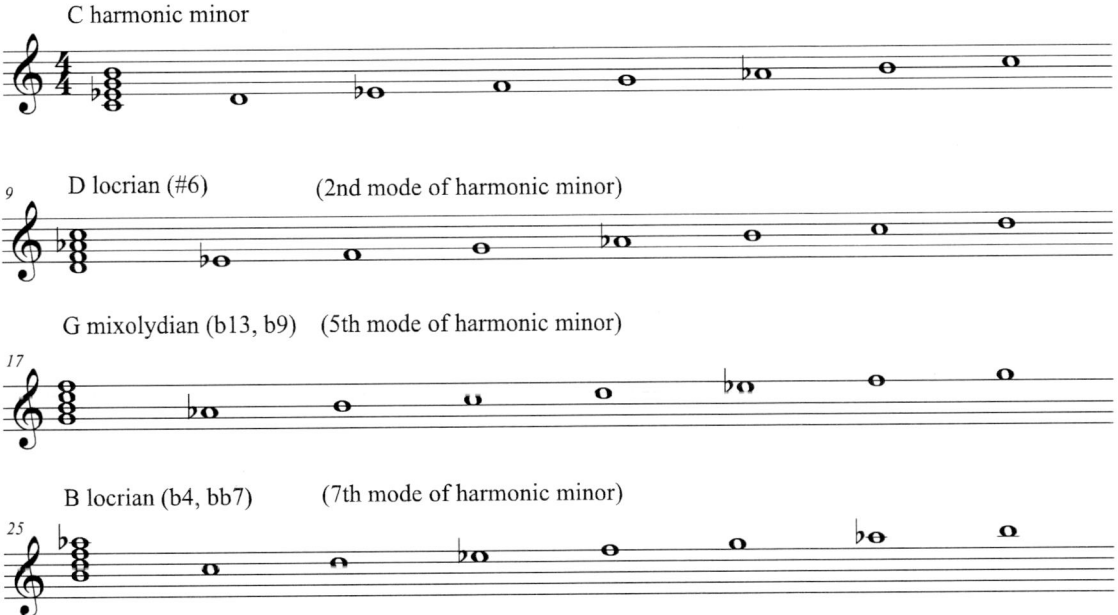

The modes of harmonic minor give us some interesting chord scale options for the following chord types:

m: harmonic minor
m7(b5): second mode of harmonic minor, AKA locrian (#6)
7(b13 b9): fifth mode of harmonic minor, AKA mixolydian (b13, b9)
o7: seventh mode of harmonic minor, AKA locrian (b4, bb7)

The modes of harmonic minor give you some beautiful options for chord scales that are not the usual choices, and are a bit off the beaten path.

Below are the parallel modes of harmonic minor starting from C with chord tones and tensions labeled.

FIG. 3

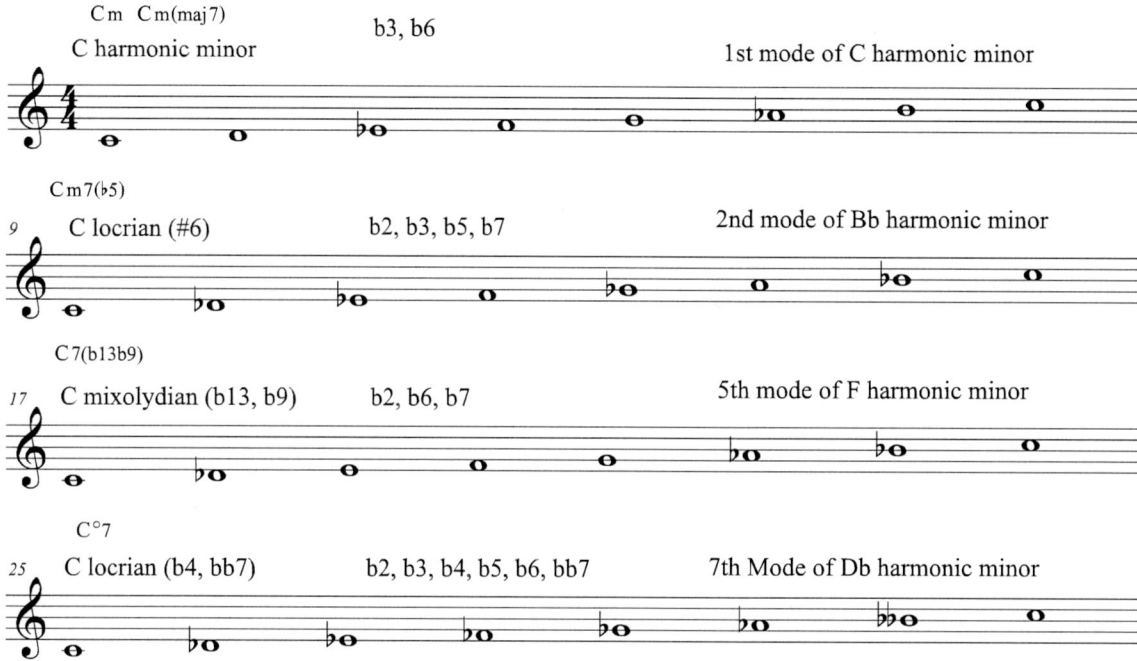

Again, even though most of the modes of the harmonic minor scale are not known by commonly-used specific names, it is worthwhile to practice all of the modes of harmonic minor in rhythm as you did with the tonic minor and major scales.

Again, we return to the four steps outlined in the previous sections in order to better assimilate the harmonic minor scale.

STEP 1: CREATING STEPWISE MOTION FROM ANYWHERE IN THE SCALE

Practice 5-note fragments up and down the scale in 3-beat phrases with a simple LH shell pattern alternating between 1–5 and 2–5.

FIG. 4

[musical notation]

STEP 2: FREELY PLAYING DIATONIC INTERVALS FROM ANYWHERE WITHIN THE SCALE

Below, the intervallic exercise from the last section is applied to the harmonic minor scale.

FIG. 5

Chapter 5 • C

STEP 3: PLAYING CONTINUOUS DIATONIC BROKEN THIRDS, ARPEGGIATED TRIADS AND SEVENTH CHORDS WITH OR WITHOUT APPROACH TONES

Try the following sequence of diatonic broken thirds in several keys. Notice how it's yet another variation of the broken third pattern from before. For this exercise and the exercises that follow feel free to add a LH shell pattern like before.

FIG. 6

Next, add an approach tone a half step below each third and practice like this:

FIG. 7

Play the following sequence of diatonic arpeggiated triads. Experiment with changing the direction of the arpeggio i.e. playing bottom to top vs. top to bottom.

FIG. 8

Add approach tones above each triad.

FIG. 9

Play seventh chord arpeggios through the scale.

FIG. 10

Advanced students can add the syncopated LH shell pattern found in FIG. 12 of Chapter 5A to the right hand patterns above.

STEP 4: MOVING BLOCK CHORDS THROUGH THE SCALE

We are now ready to play block chords with a movable 7th on each scale degree up and down the scale.

FIG. 11

To create block chord patterns for i minor build seventh chords from the 3rd or 5th of the i harmonic minor scale. For ii7b5 build seventh chords from the 2nd, 4th, or 6th (with a lowered 5th); for V7(b13b9) build seventh chords from the 2nd, 4th (with a lowered 5th), or 7th; and for viio7 build seventh chords from 4th (with a lowered 5th) or 7th. All of these block chord patterns above are derived from i harmonic minor.

So, for Cm build seventh chords from the 3rd or 5th of the C harmonic minor scale. For Dm7b5 build seventh chords from the 2nd, 4th, or 6th (with a lowered 5th) of C harmonic minor. For G7(b13b9) build seventh chords from the 2nd, 4th (with a lowered 5th), or 7th of C harmonic minor. And for Bo7 build seventh chords from the 4th (with a lowered 5th) or 7th of C harmonic minor.

Thinking in terms of the modes of harmonic minor:

1. For m, build seventh chords from the 3rd or 5th of harmonic minor
2. For m7(b5) build seventh chords from the R, 3rd, or 5th (with a lowered 5th) of locrian #6
3. For 7(b13b9), build seventh chords from the 3rd, 5th, 7th (with a lowered 5th), of mixolydian (b13b9)
4. For o7, build seventh chords from the R or the 5th (with a lowered 5th) of locrian (b4, bb7)

Note that certain seventh chords have a lowered 5th to avoid m9ths between the block chord and bass note or 3rd of the chord. Interestingly, m9ths sound good for dom7 chords, but not for m7b5 or o7. For this reason, be careful when building seventh chords from the 3rd of locrian #6. Because the dissonant note resolves right away, this block chord is allowable, especially if a sensitive bass player chooses a note other than the root when playing m7b5.

FIG. 12

Workout 46: Playing Block Chords on the changes to Sonny Clark's "Softly, as in a Morning Sunrise." Apply a block chord pattern to the song as you play along with the recording. The first eight bars of the tune are provided below. All block chords are derived from the C harmonic minor scale. On the recording, D7(♭7)–G7♭9 is used from time to time instead of Dm7(♭5)–G7(♭9) in the even measures. Listen closely to Sonny Clark's LH. Regardless, the voicing below should work.

FIG. 13

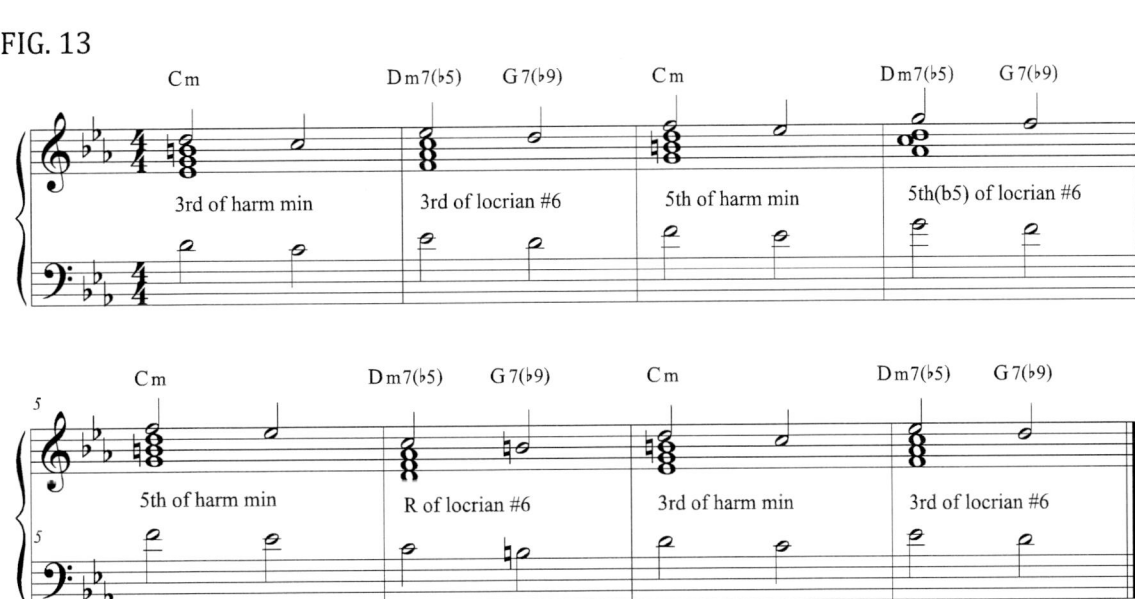

Again, we can arpeggiate the RH of the block chord pattern to create a smooth solo line. Below the bridge of "Softly" is illustrated. Refer to **DL TRK 25-26** for a demo and play-along track. On the demo, block chords are used during for the 1st half; arpeggiated block chords are played during the 2nd half.

FIG. 14

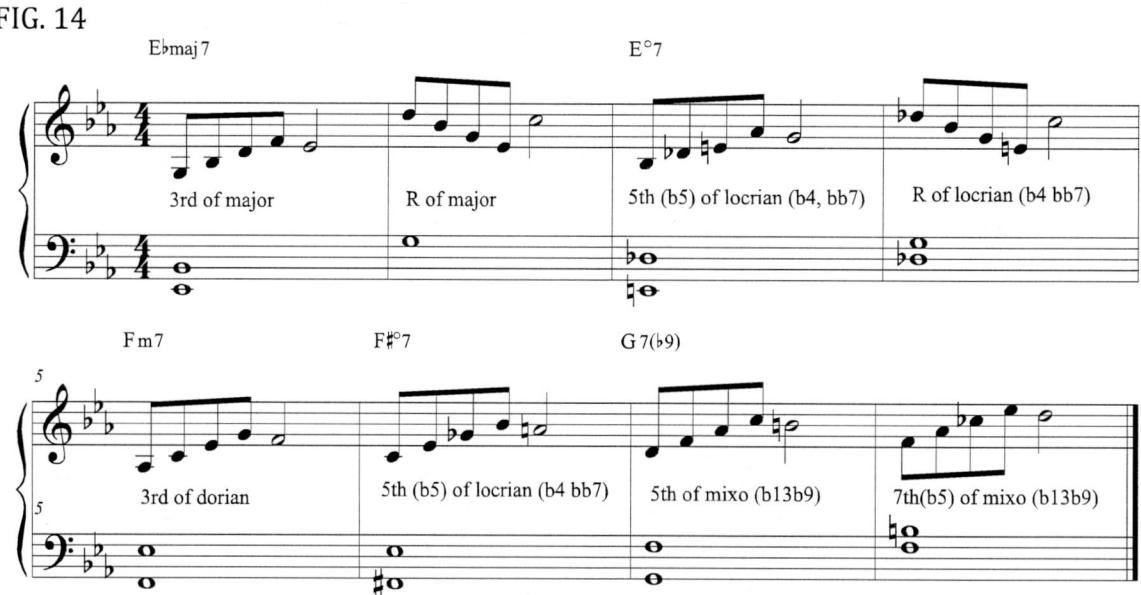

It's helpful to compare the two ways to generate block chords for creating a cadence (ii7(b5)–V7(b9)) that leads you into minor. You can either use melodic minor or harmonic minor for the parent scale. Melodic minor is possible when the natural 9 of the ii7(b5) will not clash with the melody. Harmonic minor is preferable when the melody passes through a b9 on the ii7(b5) of the minor ii-V cadence. Many standards fall under the latter category. The melody is often diatonic to the minor key destination. For example, in the bridge to "Lullaby of Birdland," the melody on the F#m7(b5) chord contains a G natural (the 3rd of E minor). For that situation, harmonic minor would be better.

Below, two possible minor ii-V cadences are illustrated below to be played through the keys, one using melodic minor, one using harmonic minor.

FIG 15

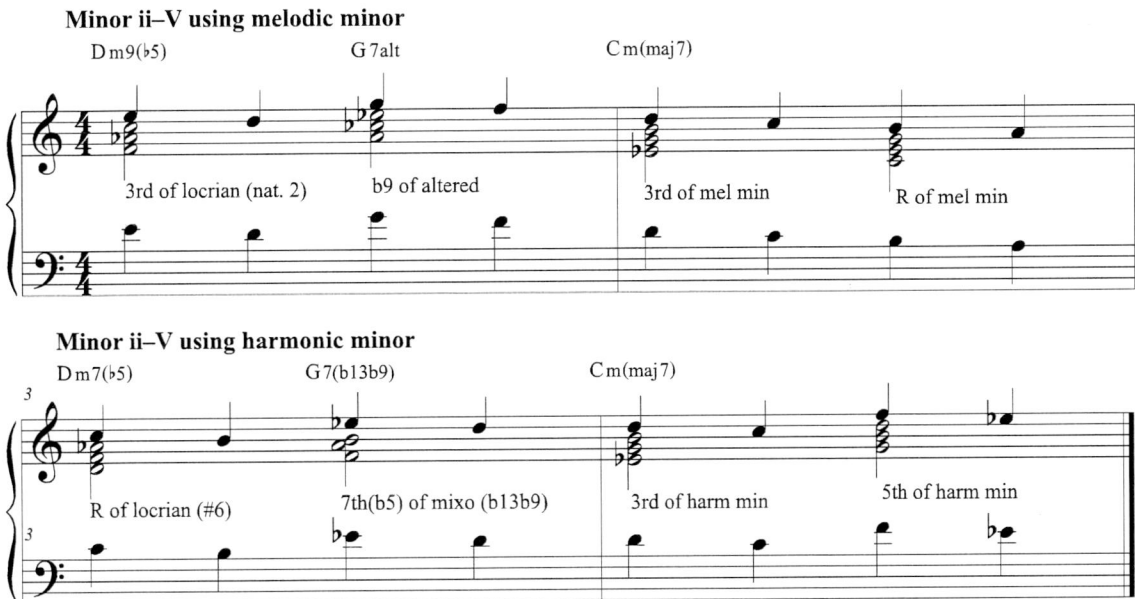

Now you can successfully play through the entire form of "Lullaby of Birdland." The basic block chords for the bridge are illustrated below. To accommodate the melody, modes of harmonic minor are used to create block chords for the minor ii-Vs. Note the two different scales used for the E minor chord in the 2nd and 6th bar. Also note that the block chord to express m7 is sometimes built off the 5th of the dorian scale. For the last "A" section take the 1st ending. Refer to **DL TRK 23-24** for a demo and play-along track. On the demo, block chords are used for the 1st "A" and the bridge; arpeggiated block chords are played during the 2nd and last "A."

FIG. 16

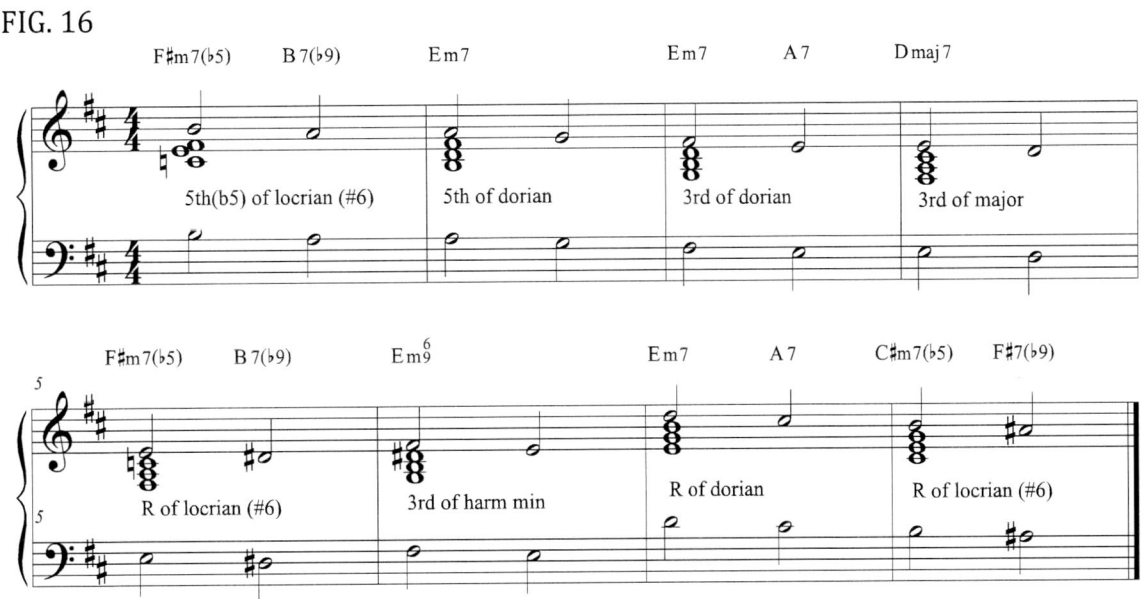

The Diminished Scale

The diminished scale consists of 8 notes, created by combining the 4 chord tones of a diminished seventh chord with their 4 leading tones. The intervallic pattern is therefore symmetrical alternating wholes steps and half steps: WHWHWHWH. This pattern makes the scale easy to work with.

FIG. 1

Practice the scale from the root to the 8th scale degree and back down.

There are only two unique modes of the diminished scale: the whole-half (alternating whole steps and half steps) and the half-whole (alternating half steps and whole steps).

FIG. 2

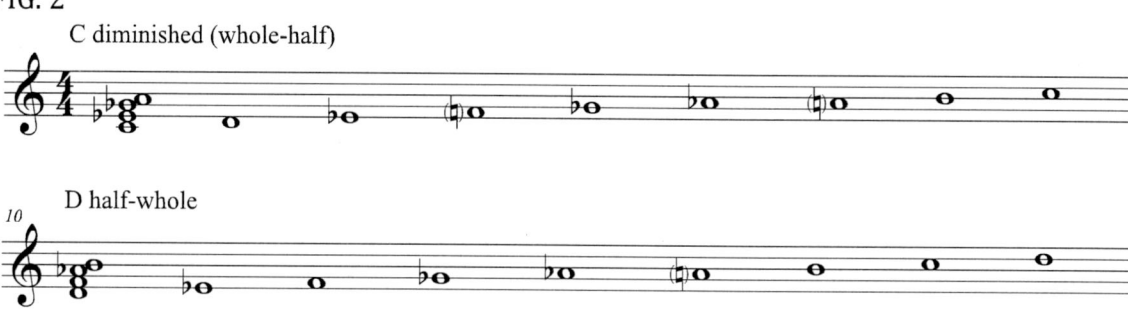

Interestingly, there are only 3 diminished scales that exist in the 12-note chromatic scale, just as there are only 3 unique diminished seventh chords. After that they repeat. Co7, Ebo7, Gbo7, and Ao7 are inversions of each other. In other words, they consist of the same notes and form a family. Therefore Family 1 would be: Co7, Ebo7, Gbo7, and Ao7. Family 2 would be: C#o7, Eo7, Go7, and Bbo7, and Family 3: Do7, Fo7, Abo7, and Bo7. That covers the entire chromatic scale.

If you lower the root of each diminished seventh chord from each family you create three families of dom7 chords sometimes called "brother and sister chords." The families of dom7 chords are related to the families of o7 chords. Each "brother and sister" chord is a minor third away from one another. Most importantly, the related chords in one family share the same diminished scale.

Family 1 (o7): Co7, E♭o7, G♭o7, Ao7	Family 1 (dom7): B7, D7, F7, A♭7
Family 2 (o7): C#o7, Eo7, Go7, B♭o7	Family 2 (dom7): C7, E♭7, G♭7, A7
Family 3 (o7): Do7, Fo7, A♭o7, Bo7	Family 3 (dom7): D♭7, E7, G7, B♭7

To find the diminished scale to express a diminished chord play the diminished scale that starts from the root of the diminished seventh chord, otherwise known as the whole-half scale. To find a diminished scale to express a dominant seventh chord play the diminished scale built on the ♭9, but start from the root of the dom7 chord. This scale is also known as the half-whole scale.

For example, to play Cdim7 play the C diminished scale starting on the root, making it the C whole-half scale. To play B7 play the C diminished scale but start on B, making it the B half-whole scale. In the end, it doesn't matter where you start or end the scale, Cdim7 and B7 both share the same chord scale: the C diminished scale. In fact, any chord in the Family 1 row can be expressed with the C diminished scale from different starting points. The numbers over the scales indicate chord tones (R, 3rd, 5th, and 7th written in bold) and tensions.

FIG. 3

Unlike the major, melodic minor, and harmonic minor modes, which have unique intervallic patterns depending on from which note you start, the diminished modes only have two: whole-half or half-whole. This makes assimilating the diminished scale easier than the other scales.

Practice the C diminished scale, eight notes up and down starting from each note of the scale. Transpose to D♭ and D.

Let's now go through the 4 steps to become better acquainted with the diminished scale.

STEP 1: CREATING STEPWISE MOTION FROM ANYWHERE IN THE SCALE

Practice 5-note fragments up and down the scale in 3-beat phrases with a simple LH shell pattern alternating between 1–5 and 2–5.

FIG. 4

STEP 2: FREELY PLAYING DIATONIC INTERVALS FROM ANYWHERE WITHIN THE SCALE.

Below, the intervallic exercise from the last section is applied to the diminished scale. Enharmonic spellings are sometimes used.

FIG. 5

Thirds

Sixths

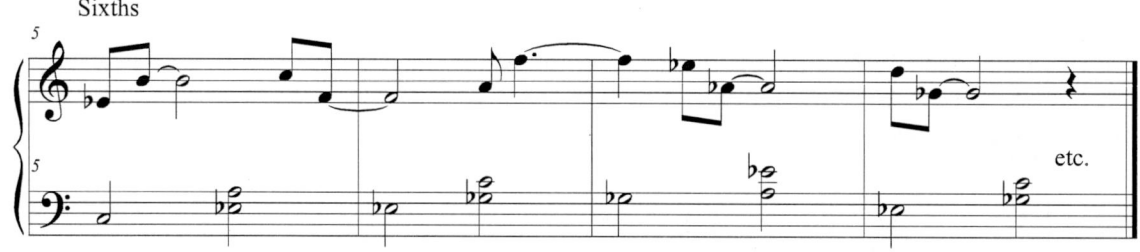

STEP 3: PLAYING CONTINUOUS DIATONIC BROKEN THIRDS, ARPEGGIATED TRIADS AND SEVENTH CHORDS WITH OR WITHOUT APPROACH TONES

Try the following sequence of diatonic broken thirds in three keys. For this exercise and the exercises that follow feel free to add a LH shell pattern like before.

FIG. 6

Next, add an approach tone a half step below each third and practice like this:

FIG. 7

Play the following sequence of diatonic arpeggiated triads. Experiment with changing the direction of the arpeggio i.e. playing bottom to top vs. top to bottom.

FIG. 8

Add approach tones above each triad.

FIG. 9

Play seventh chord arpeggios through the scale.

Chapter 5 • D

FIG. 10

Advanced students can add one of the following syncopated LH shell patterns to the RH patterns above.

FIG. 11

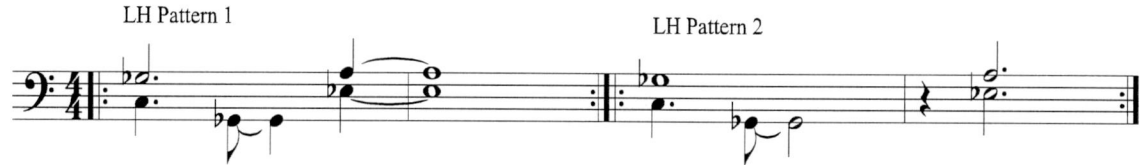

Step 4: Moving block chords through the scale

We are now ready to play block chords with a movable 7th on each scale degree up and down the scale. Start with a dim(Δ7) in the RH and move 7's down a step. Repeat this movement on each scale step. Alternate between dim(Δ7) and m7b5.

FIG. 12

To create block chord patterns for o7, build dim(Δ7) chords from the tonic, 3rd, 5th, or 7th of the whole half diminished scale. For 7(13b9) build dim(Δ7) chords from the 2nd, 4th, 6th, or 8th of the half whole diminished scale.

So, for Co7 build dim(Δ7) chords from the tonic, 3rd, 5th, or 7th of the C whole half diminished scale. For B7(13b9) build dim(Δ7) chords from the 2nd, 4th, 6th, or 8th of the B half whole diminished scale.

Another way to look at it is:

1. For o7 build dim(Δ7) from the R, b3, b5, or bb7 of the related diminished 7th chord.
2. For 7(13b9) build dim(Δ7) from the b9, 3, 5, or b7 of the related dominant 7th chord.

FIG. 13

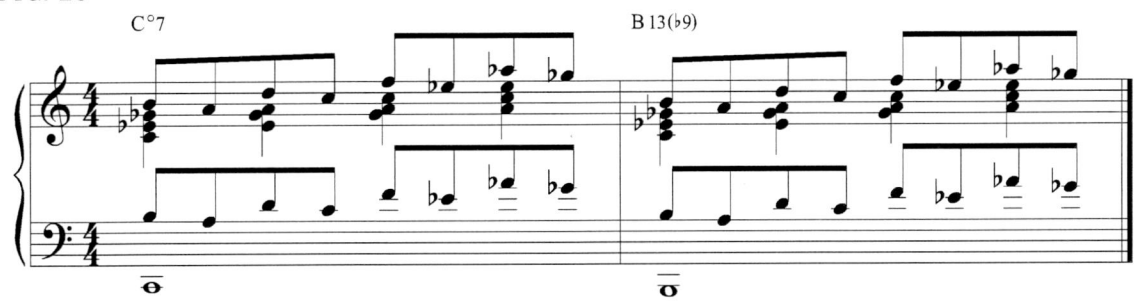

Note how the block chord pattern for Co7 and B13(b9) is nearly identical. The only difference is the bass note.

Workout 47: Playing Block Chords on the changes to "Someday My Prince Will Come." Apply block chords to the popular standard and play along with the recording. For major and dorian you may build seventh chords from the 5th as well as the tonic and 3rd. This will allow for some better melodic connections as you navigate through the chord progression. Also, note the use of the Bb major scale to generate block chords for Ebmaj7(#11). Bbmaj7/Eb is equivalent to Ebmaj7(#11) and can be used to create a lydian sound.

One possible solution for the first half of the song is offered below. See if you can find other options. Learn the second half by ear or find a chord sheet and apply chord scales/block chords.

FIG. 14

Arpeggiate block chords for the last 8 bars of the form and play over shell patterns (see below). Then practice playing along with Miles Davis. For the first half of the chorus play block chords; for the second half arpeggiate the block chords. Refer to **DL TRK 27-28** for a demo and play-along track. On the demo, block chords are used during the 1st half; arpeggiated block chords are played during the 2nd half.

FIG. 15

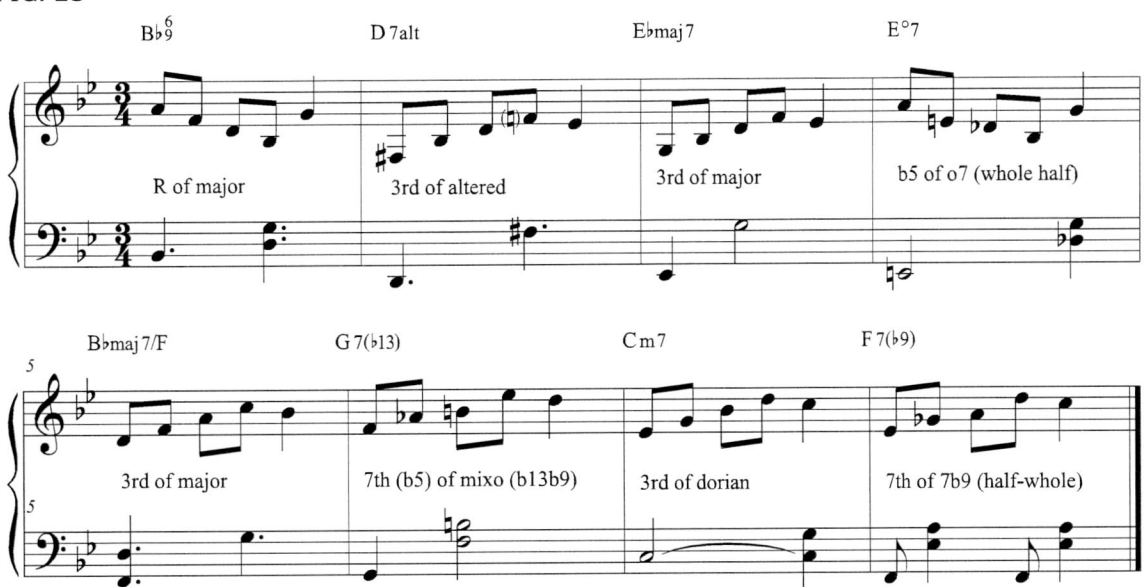

Finally let's return to "Afternoon in Paris." Now that we have a voicing for 13(b9) we can create a block chord pattern for the bridge. Practice arpeggiating block chords in the RH and playing them over LH shells as you play the whole tune along with the recording. Note that the first six measures of the bridge are over a G pedal. Refer to for a demo and play-along track. On the demo, block chords are used for the 1st "A" and the bridge; arpeggiated block chords are played during the 2nd and last "A."

FIG. 16

The Whole Tone Scale

The whole tone scale consists of 6 notes, consisting entirely of whole steps: WWWWWW.

FIG. 1

This distinctive intervallic pattern gives the scale a dreamy, ethereal quality. Because of this pattern of intervals, there are only two whole tone scales in the chromatic scale. No matter where you start, you will always be playing one of these two scales. C whole tone, D whole tone, E whole tone, F# whole tone, G# whole tone, and A# whole tone are identical scales with the same intervallic makeup, just with a different starting point. On the other side of the "whole tone coin" you have the other 6 identical whole tone scales: Db whole tone, Eb whole tone, F whole tone, G whole tone, A whole tone, and B whole tone. Practice the two whole tone scales from C to the C above; and then from Db to the Db above. Observe the fingering below.

FIG. 2

The chords most associated with the whole tone scale are the augmented triad (+) and the augmented dominant seventh (7#5). Here are the two whole tone scales along with corresponding diatonic seventh chords:

FIG. 3

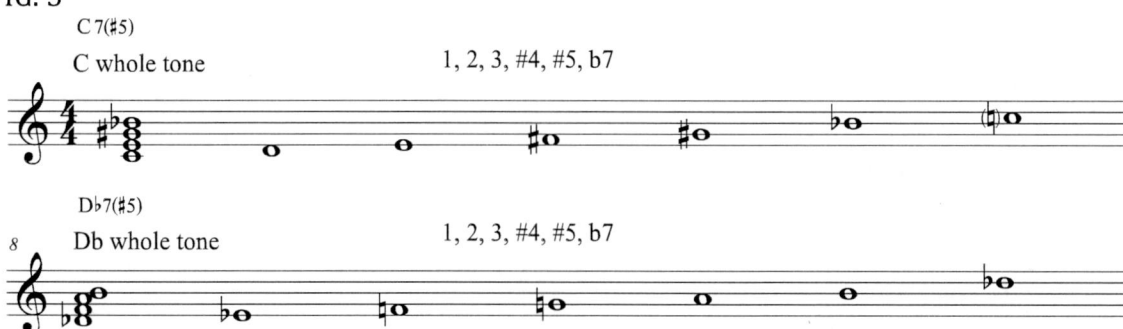

Here are the four steps to assimilate the whole tone scale.

STEP 1: CREATING STEPWISE MOTION FROM ANYWHERE IN THE SCALE

Practice 5-note fragments up and down the scale in 3-beat phrases with a simple LH shell pattern alternating between 1–5 and 2–5.

FIG. 4

STEP 2: FREELY PLAYING DIATONIC INTERVALS FROM ANYWHERE WITHIN THE SCALE

Below, the intervallic exercise from the last section is applied to the whole tone scale. Enharmonic spellings are sometimes used.

FIG. 5

Chapter 5 • E

STEP 3: PLAYING CONTINUOUS DIATONIC BROKEN THIRDS, ARPEGGIATED TRIADS AND SEVENTH CHORDS WITH OR WITHOUT APPROACH TONES

Try the following sequence of diatonic broken thirds and apply it to both whole tone scales. For this exercise and the exercises that follow feel free to add a LH shell pattern like before.

FIG. 6

Next, add an approach tone a half step below each third and practice like this:

FIG. 7

Play the following sequence of diatonic arpeggiated triads.

FIG. 8

Add approach tones above each triad.

FIG. 9

Play seventh chord arpeggios through the scale.

FIG. 10

Advanced students can add one of the following syncopated LH shell patterns to the RH patterns above.

FIG. 11

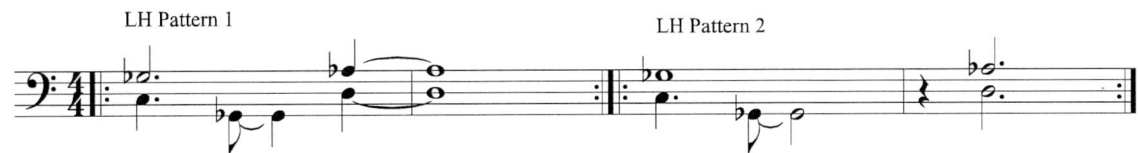

STEP 4: MOVING BLOCK CHORDS THROUGH THE SCALE

To generate block chords using the whole tone scale, start with the 3rd inversion of E7#5 in the RH. This way C is on top of the voicing: D–E–G#–C (from bottom to top). Notice how there is an augmented triad at the top of the voicing.

Instead of moving 7 to 6 in the melody voice as we did for major, minor, and diminished, move the #5 to b5.

Build 3rd inversion 7#5 chords on any scale degree. Simply double the melody in the LH and move #5–b5 of each embedded seventh voicing. Move up and down the scale. Make sure to transpose up a half step to get familiar with the other whole tone scale.

Tip: Use the augmented triad that exists at the top of the voicing to help you construct the RH shape.

FIG. 12

As an alternative, you could build 7b5 chords on each scale degree in the RH and double the melody in the LH. For the following workout, however, the 3rd inversion 7(#5) chords work very well. Because of the intervallic makeup of the scale, almost any shape that exists in the scale can be moved easily up and down. Make sure to explore the multitude of options for creating block chords using the whole tone scale.

Workout 48: Playing Block Chords on the changes to Duke Ellington's "Passion Flower." Apply block chords from all 5 scales studied in the Chapter as you play along with Duke Ellington's masterpiece from *Ella at Duke's Place.* Possible chord scales include: major, dorian, modes of melodic and harmonic minor, 7b9 half-whole (H/W), diminished whole-half (W/H), and whole tone.

Below the A section is illustrated with block chords and corresponding chord scales. Note that for the chords changing every half note, the inner seventh chord motion (7–6 or #5–b5) is omitted. The chord changes with suggested chord scales for the B section are also shown below. The song form is AABA. Refer to **DL TRK 29-30** for a demo and play-along track. On the demo, block chords are used for the 1st "A" and the bridge; arpeggiated block chords are played during the 2nd and last "A."

FIG. 13

After playing block chords, arpeggiate the RH seventh chord and play in multiple octaves to create fleeting, wisps of sound modeled after Duke's own incredible comping.

Duet 6: Working Out on the Five Important Scales. You and a partner pick one of the 5 important scales: major, tonic minor, harmonic minor, diminished, or whole tone. Choose one of the assimilation exercises for a given scale and play it together in time. For example, for tonic minor Player 1 starts playing 5-note scale fragments as Player 2 plays arpeggiated seventh chords. Don't be alarmed by points of dissonance. Listen for the overall sound of tonic minor.

Chapter 6
Melodic Building Blocks for Soloing

Now that we've practiced the five important scales from Chapter 5, and have digested the modes of each scale, we want to begin to create building blocks for use in melodic improvisation.

The ultimate goal is to be able to access classic jazz recordings, transcribe and assimilate the classic solos. While doing that, it is suggested that you learn the basics about how to clearly outline chord changes. Understanding a little bit about the inner workings of how to play on chords will help you expand upon the masters. The idea is to create your own improvisations strongly rooted in the tradition, rather than mindlessly regurgitating notes that you hear on the recordings.

In this chapter four powerful melodic building blocks and tools are offered to help jump-start your skills as a melodic improviser. These include:

1. 5-note Scale Fragments
2. Arpeggio-Patterns
3. Approaching and Surrounding Chord Tones
4. Bebop Scales and Triplets

At the conclusion of the chapter, fifteen suggested solos are listed for you to transcribe and begin to unlock the treasure trove of musical material the solos represent. One melodic phrase extracted from one of the solos will be analyzed and manipulated to show how you can add the new phrase to your already impressive repertoire of melodic building blocks. This process of transcribing and assimilation will give you a lifetime of music to study and enjoy.

5-note Scale Fragments

The first melodic building block to get under our fingers is the 5-note scale fragment. For each chord symbol encountered, assign a chord scale that elicits the sound of the chord. After that, find a simple fragment of the chord scale that you can instantly play that clearly reveals the harmony. With these manageable, largely step-wise patterns, you should be able to quickly and easily play through the chords of a song in a melodic way.

One wrinkle that quickly comes to light is the fact that chords often have more than one "parent" scale. It's not as simple as: pick a chord–plug in a scale. There are decisions to be made. For example, C7 can be found in the C mixolydian scale, but also in the C half-whole scale, the C altered scale, the C Lydian dominant scale, the C whole tone scale, and even the 5th mode of F harmonic minor. The improviser has to choose the desired shade of color before using the brush.

In this section, you will find different "shades" in the form of various 5-note fragments categorized in terms of chord quality and harmonic function.

Here is a guide on how to construct 5-note scale fragments in major and minor. The 5-note fragments in boldface refer to scale degrees. "1" is always the root of the corresponding chord. The associated chord symbol(s) and chord scale(s) are listed above each 5–note scale fragment.

Of course, there are many other options for chord scales not shown. The following is meant only to be a jumping off point to get you started when choosing a chord scale to express a particular chord.

Chapter 6

Major Key Area

I7, Imaj7, I6/9, I6, Imaj (major or mixolydian)	iim7 (dorian)	V7 (mixolydian)
1–2–3–4–5	**1–2–b3–4–5**	**5–6–b7–1–9**
I7, I6/9, I6, Imaj (major or mixolydian)	iim7b5 (locrian nat. 2)	V7 (half-whole)
5–6–1–2–1	**1–2–b3–4–b5**	**5–6–b7–1–b9**
iiim7 (phrygian)		V7alt (altered)
1–b2–b3–4–5		**b9–#9–3–#11–b13**
vim7 (aeolian)		
b3–4–5–b6–b7		

In the key of C major:

FIG. 1

Minor Key Area

im(maj7), im6/9, im6, im, (tonic minor)	iim7♭5 (locrian)	V7(♭13♭9) (mixo ♭13♭9) (5th mode of harmonic minor)
1–2–♭3–4–5	1–♭2–♭3–4–♭5	5–♭13–♭7–1–♭9
im6/9, im6, im (tonic minor)		V7alt (altered)
5–6–1–2–1		♭9–#9–3–#11–♭13
vim7♭5 (locrian nat. 2)		
♭3–4–♭5–♭6–♭7		

In the key of C minor:

FIG. 2

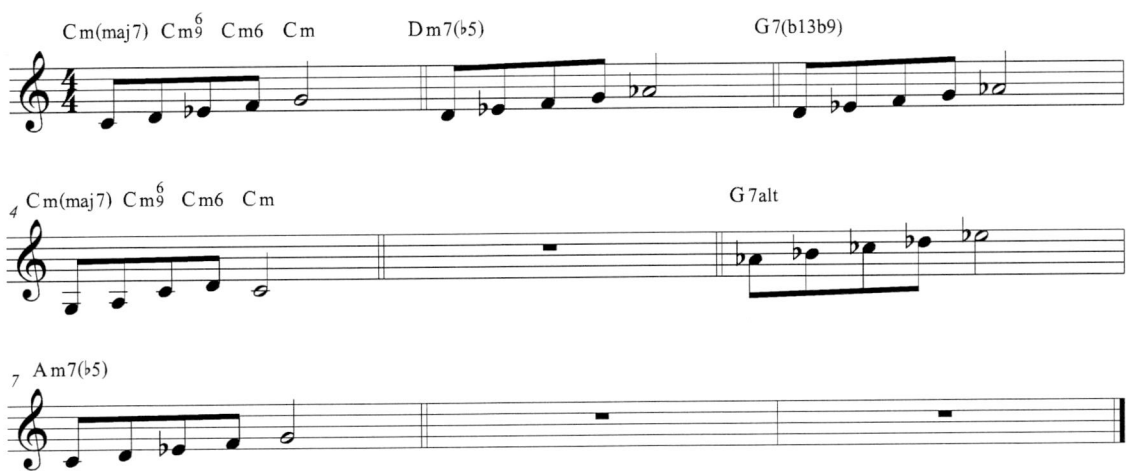

Even though these 5-note scale fragments are shown being applied to ii–V–I in major and minor, their usefulness is much broader. These patterns can be used for any major, dominant, minor, or half-diminished chord that you encounter in a song.

Apply 5-note scale fragments to a real song in real time. Go through the entire form of "Ornithology", applying the patterns to the given chord changes and suggested chord scale.

Unless otherwise notated, the chord scale and chord symbol share the same root. For example, "major" in m. 1 (FIG. 3) refers to G major. If the measure contains two chords, use the first chord to find the corresponding chord scale.

FIG. 3

Note in m. 21–m. 22 since the m7 chords move every two beats it is impossible to play the entire 5-note scale fragment. Beat 3 of m. 21 is the "5" of the Bbm7 5-note pattern.

By changing the order of notes and the rhythmic placement, you can make these rather dull scalar patterns sound more like music. For best results, choose 5-note scale fragments that are stepwise when applying motifs. Below, eight motifs are derived from the C major 5-note scale fragment.

FIG. 4

Eight Motifs

Practice the 8 motifs by applying them to ii–V–I. For each measure below choose a motif from above and apply it to the chord changes. Link each motif together like building blocks. Omit the fifth note of a motif if necessary to connect to the next desired motif. Experiment with displacing the motifs ahead or behind 2 beats. The motif number and chord scale are listed below each pattern.

Be careful not to repeat notes when connecting motifs. Transpose the following 2 and 4-measure ii–V–Is.

FIG. 5

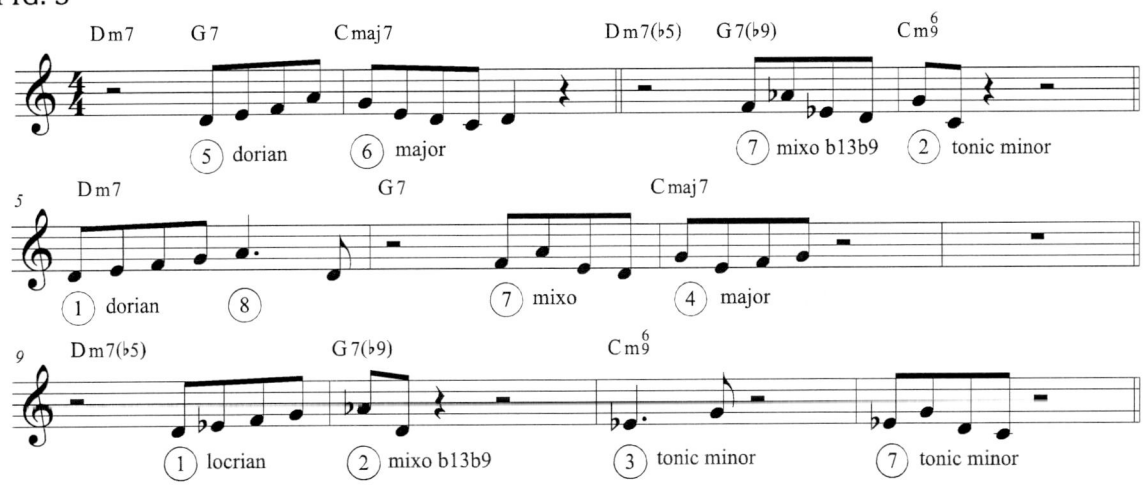

The motifs above represent what is possible when you rearrange and displace a small sample of notes. By manipulating the 5-note scale fragments, you can create music that is more compelling. Feel free to create your own motifs derived from the original 5-note fragments. The possibilities are endless.

Workout 49: 5-note Scale Fragments on the changes to Bud Powell's "Ornithology." Play along with Bud Powell from *The Amazing Bud Powell* by applying 5-note scale fragments to the well-known jazz standard. You can use FIG 3 as a guide. Use the 5-note fragments with variations. Apply the motifs above to add melodic and rhythmic interest.

Here are the first eight bars of the form. The motif number and chord scale of each manipulated 5-note fragment is listed below. LH shells, and drones from Chapter 2 are added to simulate a two-handed piano solo. Listen to how rhythmic Bud Powell is when changing directions in his melodic line. Try adding some of these accents to your own melodic patterns. Refer to **DL TRK 31-32** for a demo and play-along track. On the demo, FIG. 6 is played during the first eight bars of the first chorus.

FIG. 6

DIMINISHED 5-NOTE SCALE FRAGMENTS

Diminished seventh chords can also be expressed using 5-note scale fragments derived from either diminished or harmonic minor scales. For best results, use the scale that best reflects the chord that you are going to. Start the pattern on the third of the diminished chord.

viio7, #ivo7, biiio7, io7 (W/H diminished) b3–4–b5–b6–bb7	viio7, #ivo7,#io7, #iio7, biiio7 (7th mode of harmonic minor) b3–b4–b5–b6–bb7

If you play Bo7 going to C major (viio7–Imaj), start on the b3 of Bo7 and run up the B whole half scale (starting on D), which contains E natural, and nicely hints that you are going to C major. Note how this 5-note pattern is the same as the one starting on the 5th used to express G7(b13) derived from the G H/W scale from the last section.

If going to C minor (viio7–i), start on the b3 of Bo7 and run up the 7th mode of C harmonic minor (AKA B locrian (b4 bb7), which contains E flat, giving you more of the C minor flavor. Notice how this 5-note pattern is the same as the one starting on the 5th used to express G7(b13, b9) derived the C harmonic minor scale from the last section.

For #ivo7 you may choose, either diminished or harmonic minor. Often when playing blues or rhythm changes, the harmonic minor is a smoother choice, hinting at the dominant seventh chord coming up. For #io7–iim7 or #iio7–iiim7 harmonic minor is preferred, as it smoothly moves to the next minor chord. For biiio7 harmonic or diminished can work. For io7, the whole-half diminished scale usually works the best.

FIG. 7

Workout 50: 5-note Scale Fragments on the changes to Al Haig's "'S Wonderful"
Play along with the album, "The Al Haig Trio." This is a swinging version of this Gershwin standard. Apply 5-note scale fragments. Specifically, apply diminished 5-note patterns to m.m. 3-4. The first eight bars are illustrated below. Motifs and chord scales are labeled. Motif (0) means that the 5-note scale fragment has been varied in a new way. Remember, the 5-note patterns can be varied in countless ways. The 8 motifs are only meant to be a jumping off point.

Be aware of the following details. For Eo7, the 7th mode of harmonic minor scale a half step higher is used (F harmonic minor). At the end of m. 4, the Fm7 is anticipated with motif 2 applied to F dorian.

Refer to **DL TRK 33-34** for a demo and play-along track. On the demo, FIG. 8 is played during the first eight bars of the first chorus.

FIG. 8

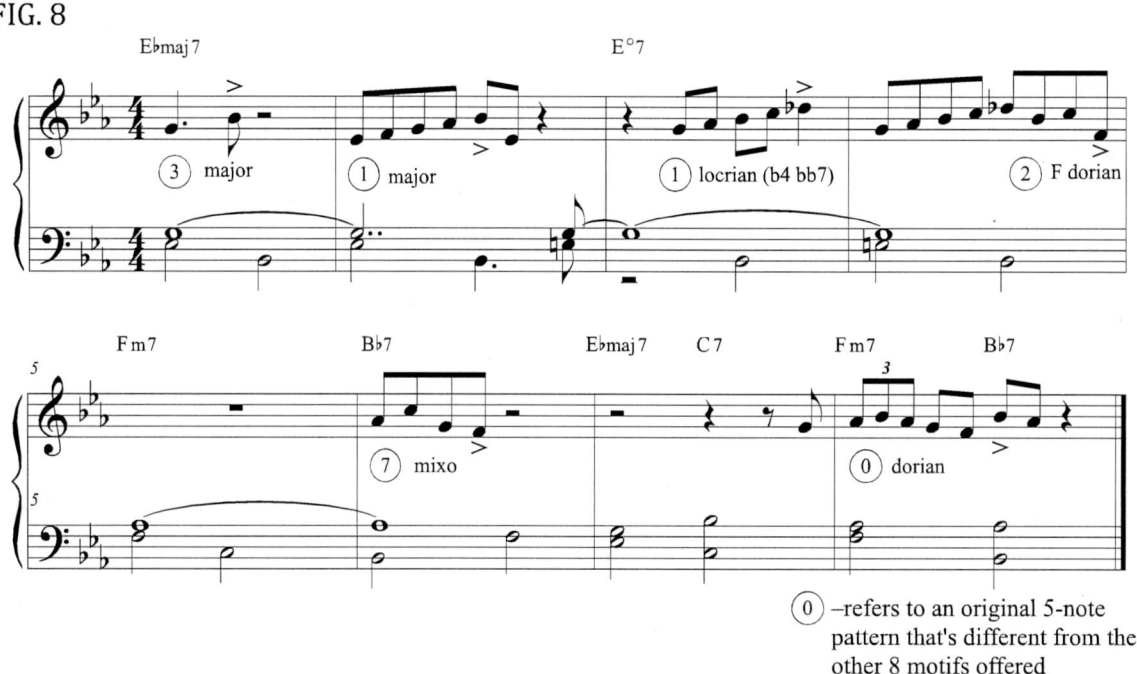

(0) –refers to an original 5-note pattern that's different from the other 8 motifs offered

Arpeggio-Patterns

Arpeggios are a crucial component of spelling the harmony. They allow you to outline the harmony in a melodic way by playing vertical structures one tone at a time. Arpeggios allow non-chordal instruments to give the impression of polyphony. They highlight the melodic beauty of a chord.

We've already practiced basic arpeggio-patterns in Chapter 5 by outlining selected block chords extracted from chord scales. In the current section we will go further; by linking arpeggio-patterns together, inverting them, and displacing them rhythmically.

Here are some commonly used arpeggio-patterns (4-note arpeggios that resolve to a fifth note) listed with corresponding chord symbol(s) and chord scale(s) built from the root, 3rd, 5th of the chord or acceptable substitution.

Major Key Area

Imaj7, I6/9, I6, Imaj (major)	iim7 (dorian)	V7 (mixolydian)
1-3-5-7-6	1-b3-5-b7-6	3-5-b7-9-1
3-5-7-9-1	b3-5-b7-9-1	5-b7-9-11-3
5-7-9-11-3	5-b3-1-b7-6	5-3-1-7-b7
5-3-7-5-6		
iiim7 (phrygian)		**V7b9 (H/W dim)**
1b3-5-b7-b6		3-5-b7-b9-1
b3-5-b7-b9-1		
vim7 (aeolian)		
b3-5-b7-9-1		
5-b7-9-11-b3		

Minor Key Area

im(maj7), im6/9, im6, im, (tonic minor)	iim7b5 (locrian #6)	V7(b13b9) (mixo b13b9)
1-b3-5-7-6	1-b3-b5-b7-6	3-5-b7-b9-1
b3-5-7-9-1	b3-b5-b7-b9-1	5-b7-b9-11-3
5-7-9-11-b3	b5-b3-1-b7-6	b13-3-1-7-b7
5-b3-7-5-9		
vim7b5 (locrian nat. 2)		
b5-b7-9-11-b3		
b3-b5-b7-9-1		

Practice long ii–V–I's by playing an arpeggio-pattern from each column starting on beat 1. Also, experiment with playing the 4-note arpeggio in reverse order. The following arpeggio-patterns are labeled in terms of chord scale and starting note.

The mixo b13b9 (arp–b13) pattern contains a passing tone (7) not in the original mixo b13b9 scale. This addition of a chromatic note to a seven-note scale is a common device used to keep chord tones on the beat. In Chapter 6D, this practice will be examined further when we study bebop scales.

FIG. 1

By omitting the last note of each arpeggio pattern or by making other minor adjustments, you can string several together. For example, mixo and mixo b13b9 arp–5/arp–b13 patterns have a long form for delaying the resolution and a short form for connecting patterns together

Long Form	Short Form
5–3–1–7–b7	5–3–1–b7
b13–3–1–7–b7	b13–3–1–b7

Below are several examples of arpeggio-patterns that are fused together to create longer phrases. Observe the melodic connections between patterns. The arpeggio patterns can be displaced ahead or behind two beats (see m. 9-10 below). Modifications can also be made to avoid repeating notes (see m. 10 below). In this case, the arp-pattern on beat one is changed from b3–b5–b7–9 to b3–b5–b7–1.

Transpose the following 2 and 4-measure ii–V–Is to several keys.

FIG. 2

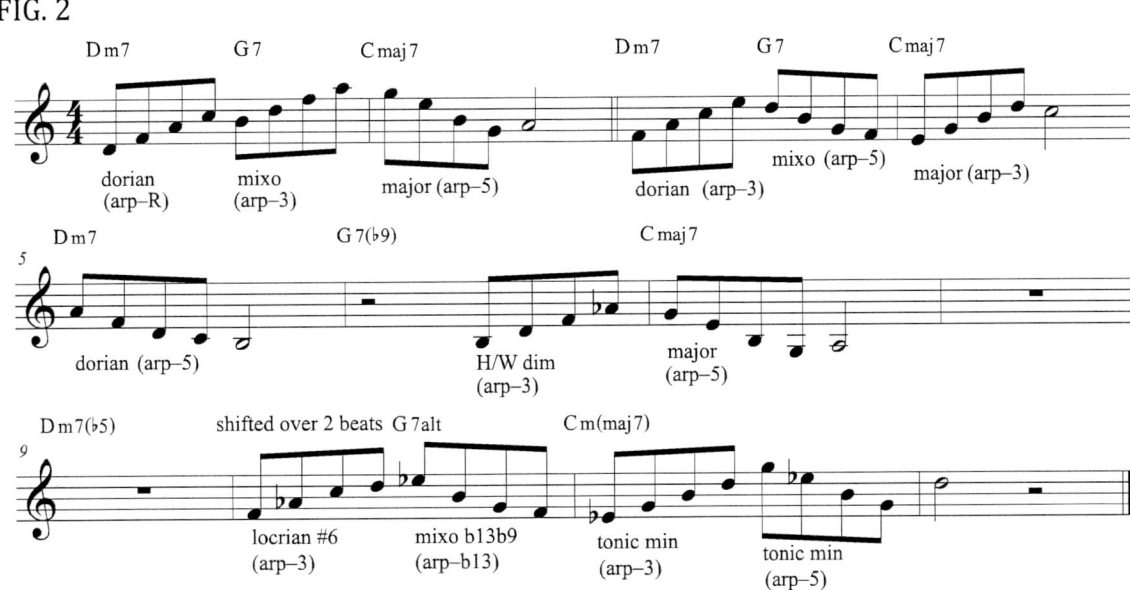

By displacing the second note of selected arpeggio-patterns up or down an octave you can create interesting melodic shapes. The change of direction in your improvised line can add melodic and rhythmic interest to your solo. This process of pivoting can also help solve range problems when soloing on other instruments. Even though the piano can handle a broad range, by limiting it you often end up with a more interesting line. Check out these cadential arpeggio-patterns that contain pivoting. Note that the 4-note arpeggio in m. 7 is left unresolved to add rhythmic interest to the line.

FIG. 3

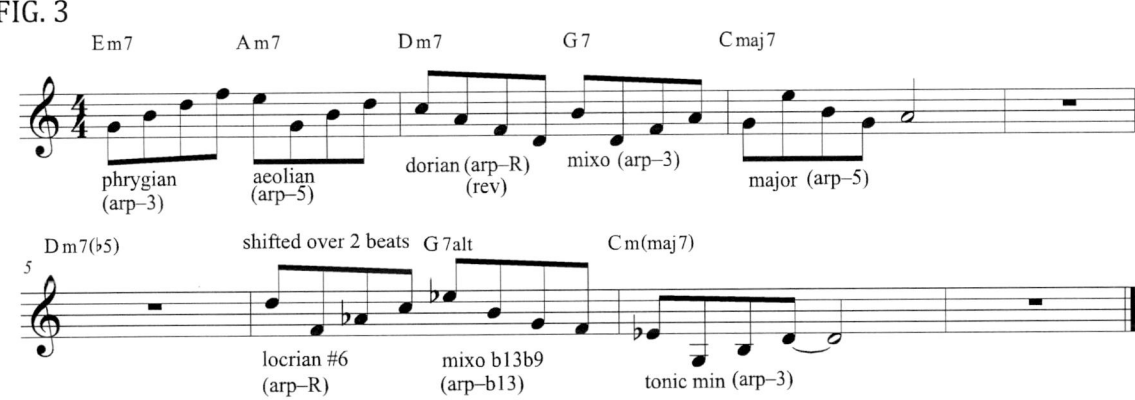

Before applying these arpeggios to "Ornithology" changes, let's add one more useful arpeggio pattern that can be used on dominant chords. The augmented triad arpeggio built on the root of the dom 7th chord provides effective connecting material. This arpeggio works for dominant chords part of major or minor ii–V–I progressions.

FIG. 4

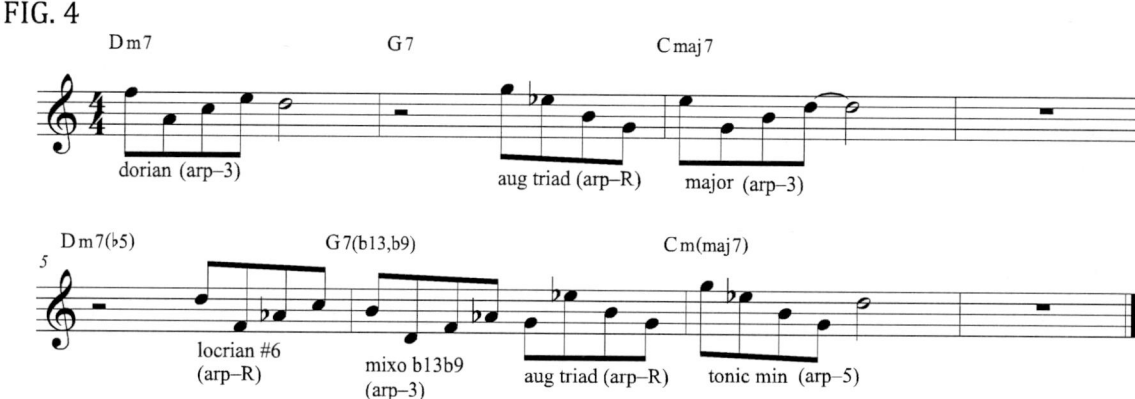

Workout 51: Arpeggio-Patterns on the changes to Bud Powell's "Ornithology."
Navigate through the changes using arpeggio-patterns as you solo along with the recording. When possible link together multiple arpeggio patterns. Include pivoting. The chord scale of each arpeggio-pattern is listed. The chord tone from which the arpeggio is built is listed next to the scale. Here are the first 8 bars. Refer to **DL TRK 31-32** for a demo and play-along track. On the demo, FIG. 5 is played during the third quarter of the first chorus.

FIG. 5

Diminished Seventh Arpeggio-Patterns

Diminished seventh chords can be spelled using diminished arpeggio-patterns drawing from two main parent chord scales: diminished and harmonic minor.

viio7, #ivo7, biiio7, io7 (W/H diminished)	viio7, #ivo7, #io7, #iio7, biiio7 (locrian b4 bb7)
1–b3–b5–bb7–b13	1–b3–b5–bb7–b13
b5–bb7–1–11–b3	b3–b5–bb7–b9–1
bb7–1–b3–b13–b5	b5–bb7–1–b4–b3

Creating arpeggio-patterns using the W/H scale is one way of spelling a diminished chord that creates a fresh, modern sound. Usually choosing the harmonic minor scale associated with the chord you are moving toward yields a more melodically satisfying sound.

Here are the arpeggio-patterns from the above chart written out in the key of C. Note that arp-patterns for Bo7 (viio7) derived from the B whole-half diminished scale can also be used for G13b9 (V13b9). Likewise, arp-patterns for Bo7 (viio7) derived from the 7th mode of C harmonic minor (7th mode of i harmonic minor) can also be used for G7(b13b9) (V7(b13b9).

FIG. 6

Chapter 6 • B

Workout 52: Arpeggios on the changes to Al Haig's " 'S Wonderful" Play along with the album, "The Al Haig Trio." Apply arpeggio-patterns. Specifically, apply diminished arpeggio patterns to express Eo7. The second eight bars of the form are illustrated below. Chord scale and starting point is labeled for each arpeggio-pattern. Refer to **DL TRK 33-34** for a demo and play-along track. On the demo, FIG. 7 is played during the second quarter of the first chorus.

FIG. 7

Approaching and Surrounding Chord Tones

A common technique used in line playing is approaching and surrounding chord tones. By preceding a chord tone with a chromatic or diatonic approach tone, or enclosing a given chord tone with note(s) above and below the targeted note, you can create richness in the line.

In this section approaching chord tones from a half step below or a diatonic step above will be discussed. Also, 2 and 3-note enclosures will be illustrated and applied to improvising on "Ornithology" changes.

First, a quick review of definitions:

Approach Tone: a note that precedes the target note (in this case a chord tone) by a diatonic or chromatic step.

Enclosure: A melodic structure made up of 2, 3, or more notes above and below a given target note (in this case a chord tone) by step that has the effect of surrounding, encircling, or enclosing the target note.

Here are some basic approach tone ideas that can be applied to a major triad derived from the major scale and minor triad derived from harmonic minor. Approach each chord tone from a diatonic step above or a chromatic step below.

To really get these patterns under your fingers, practice each one or two-measure idea separately (see double bars). Practice the pattern up and down the piano; practice starting on different beats; practice in all 12 keys.

Dia (A)= diatonic step above (chord tone)
Chr (B)= chromatic step below (chord tone)

Approach Tone Patterns

FIG. 1

FIG. 2

2-note enclosures precede each target chord tone with a diatonic scale step above and chromatic scale step below.

Practice the following 2-note enclosures applied to a major and minor triad. Note the difference between patterns that start with the diatonic step above vs. ones that start with the chromatic step below.

2-note Enclosures

Refer to the chord scale to find a diatonic step above each chord tone as you create 2-note enclosures for the dominant seventh chord. Note the two enclosure configurations: diatonic above–chromatic below vs. chromatic below–diatonic above.

FIG. 5

Apply 2-note enclosures to major and minor ii–V–I progressions.

FIG. 6

Try these typical 3-note enclosures for surrounding chord tones. Apply them to major and minor ii–V–I. Surround the root, third, and fifth of non-dominant chords and the third, fifth, and seventh of dominant chords.

Start each 3-note enclosure on the diatonic step above the targeted chord tone (refer to the chord scale). If it's a whole step higher, go a half step down then a whole step down, then resolve a half step up to the chord tone. If it's a half step higher, skip down a m3, go a half step up, then resolve another half step up to the chord tone.

3-note Enclosures

FIG. 7

FIG. 8

Workout 53: Approach Tones and Enclosures on the changes to Bud Powell's "Ornithology." Navigate through the form using only chord tones embellished with approach tones and enclosures as you solo along with the recording. Below, the second 8 bars are illustrated. Refer to **DL TRK 13-14** for a demo and play-along track. On the demo, FIG. 9 is played during the second quarter of the first chorus.

AT= Approach Tone
2n–Enc= 2-note Enclosure
3n–Enc= 3-note Enclosure

FIG. 9

DIMINISHED APPROACH TONE AND ENCLOSURE PATTERNS

Again, use the harmonic minor and diminished scales to create approach tone and enclosure patterns for use when spelling diminished seventh chords. Listen to the difference in sound between the brighter C whole-half diminished scale patterns vs. the darker Db harmonic minor patterns as you target the basic C diminished triad. Transpose to Db and D.

FIG. 10

Workout 54: Approach Tones and Enclosures on the changes to Al Haig's "'S Wonderful." Navigate through the form using only chord tones embellished with approach tones and enclosures as you solo along with the recording. For the first four measures, G major approach tone patterns are used.

Below, the bridge is illustrated. Although the first four bars of the bridge alternates between Gmaj7 and Am7–D7, the overall key area is G, and therefore approaching the chord tones of G major works for the entire four measures. Also observe how an approach tone pattern derived from the W/H diminished scale is used to spell the Gbo7 in m. 6.

Refer to **DL TRK 13-14** for a demo and play-along track. On the demo, FIG. 11 is played during the bridge of the first chorus.

FIG. 11

Bebop Scales and Intro to Triplets

Jazz lines often involve adding a chromatic note(s) to a chord scale to make it sound stronger and more accurate, harmonically. Bebop scales are scales in which chromatic notes are added or taken away to ensure that chord tones fall on the beat.

The general rule to gain a more focused sound when soloing (and less like you are meandering around) is to play chord tones on the beat. In Chapter 5 we practiced scales up and down from the root to the 7th to ensure that each chord tone would be played on the beat. Of course, experienced soloists can play non-chord tones on downbeats and make it sound good. The trick is they know how to resolve it so that it sounds right.

To begin let's play the C major scale descending from the root. Since the scale has 7 tones, the first thing to do is to add a b6 to the scale to make it 8 tones. C major scale with the Ab (b6) added is called the ***C major bebop scale.*** Notice how the root, 6th, 5th, and 3rd all occur on downbeats (beats 1, 2, 3, 4) if you start on beat 1. This scale clearly outlines C6.

FIG. 1

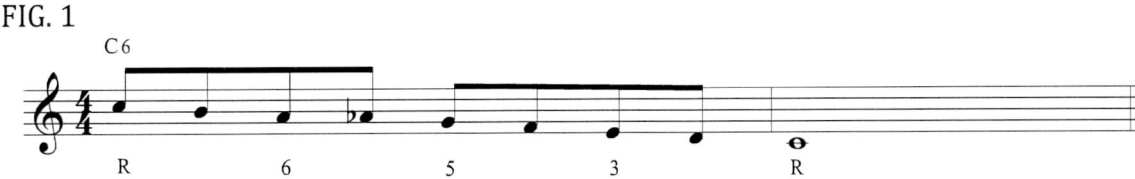

If we start on D (the 9th) we can take away the b6 and just play C major scale and the chord tones will line up. Starting on E, works the same as starting on C, remember to add b6. For now, we will skip F. Starting on the G (5th) works the same. Starting on A (6th) works fine as long as you add the b6. Finally, starting on B (7th) requires an additional chromatic tone to make the chord tones line up. Add Bb and Ab to the C major scale. In conclusion starting from the R, 3rd, 5th, 6th requires one additional chromatic tone (Ab). If you start on the 9th, take the b6 away, and just play C major. If you start on the 7th you need to add 2 chromatic tones to get back on track.

FIG. 2

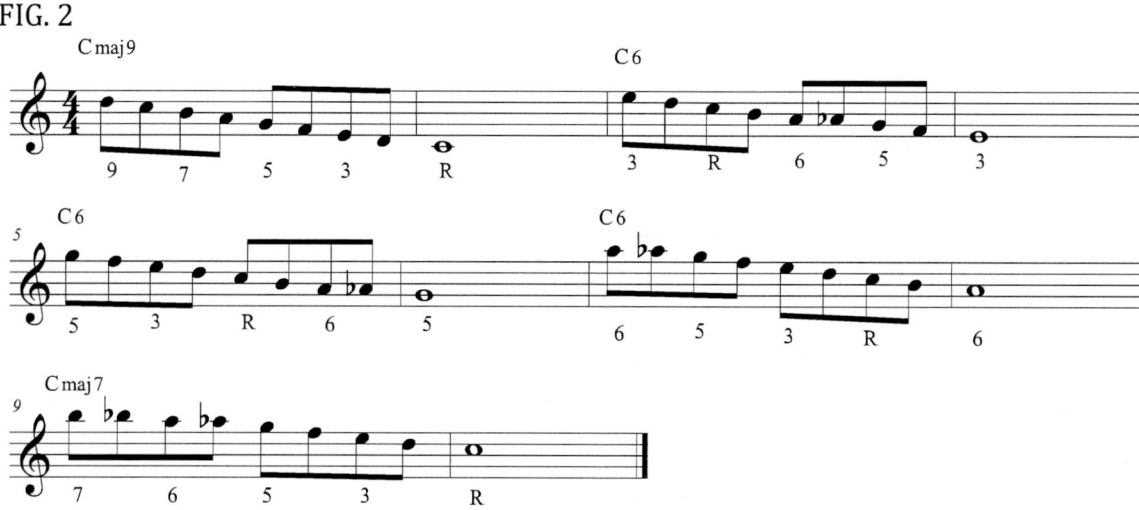

Let's now take the G mixolydian scale and play it descending from the root. To make it line up we need to add a chromatic tone (making it 8 tones). This time we add the major 7th. G mixolydian with an added F# (maj 7th) is called the **G7 bebop scale**.

FIG. 3

If we start from the 9th, we can either take the major 7th away or add another chromatic tone. For added chromatic interest, let's add the b9 and the maj7th. Starting from the 3rd is just like starting from the root (we add the maj7th). As a rich chromatic variation, we can add 3 chromatic tones (#9, b9, and maj7). Skip the 11th. Starting from the 5th is just like the root. If we begin with the 13 we need to add 2 chromatic tones to resolve (b13 and maj7). Starting from the b7 is just like starting from the root.

FIG. 4

Therefore, you need to add 1 or 3 chromatic tones to a 7-note scale to make it even if you start descending from a chord tone on the beat. If you start from a tension you can either add 0 or 2 chromatic tones. It's all about creating a scale with an even number of notes so that the chord tones line up on the beat.

Try this ii–V–I exercise using fragments of the G7 bebop and C major bebop scales. The G7 bebop scale is used in all of the odd-numbered measures–which works well over Dm7 and G7. The chord tones and tensions indicated underneath refer to G7. The C major bebop scale is used in all of the even-numbered measures. This scale can be used for C6, Cmaj7, C6/9, etc. The chord tones and tensions under these measures refer to C6.

ii–V–I Bebop Scales

FIG. 5

Bebop scales can also be created in minor. Adding a maj7th to G7 mixo (b13, b9) produces the **G7b13b9 bebop scale.** By adding the b6 to the C tonic minor scale you can create the **C minor bebop scale.**

FIG. 6

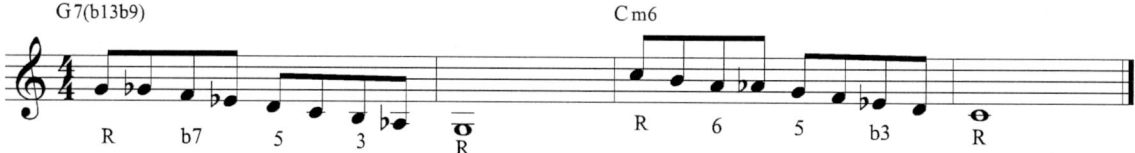

Below is a minor ii–V–I exercise employing fragments of these bebop scales. The G7b13b9 bebop scale is employed in the odd-numbered measures; the C minor bebop scale is used in all of the even-numbered measures. The chord tones and tensions listed under all of the odd-numbered measures refer to G7(b13b9); the ones under the even-numbered measures refer Cm6.

Notice how the G7(b13, b9) scale starts from a number of different starting points with chromatic tones added or taken away: from the root (with an added maj7); from the b9 (with no added chromatic tones); from the #9 (with an added natural 9); from the 11 (with an added #9 and 9); from the 5th (with an added maj7); and from the b7 (with no added chromatic notes).

The C minor bebop scale starts from chord tones except for m. 6 and m. 8 in which the scale starts from 7 and 9 respectively. In both cases, two chromatic tones (b7 and b6) are added to the scale. Notice how the chord tones mostly line up on the beat.

FIG. 7

Minor ii–V–I Bebop Scales

The use of triplets in bebop is an incredibly important subject. For our purposes we will be concentrating on just a few specific ways of incorporating 8th note triplets to add rhythmic interest to your lines.

You can use a triplet on beat 1 before beginning your descent down a bebop scale. We will start the pattern from a non-chord tone. This way we can play 8th note triplets on beat one and maintain chord tones on the beat. Check out these major and minor V7–I patterns.

FIG. 8

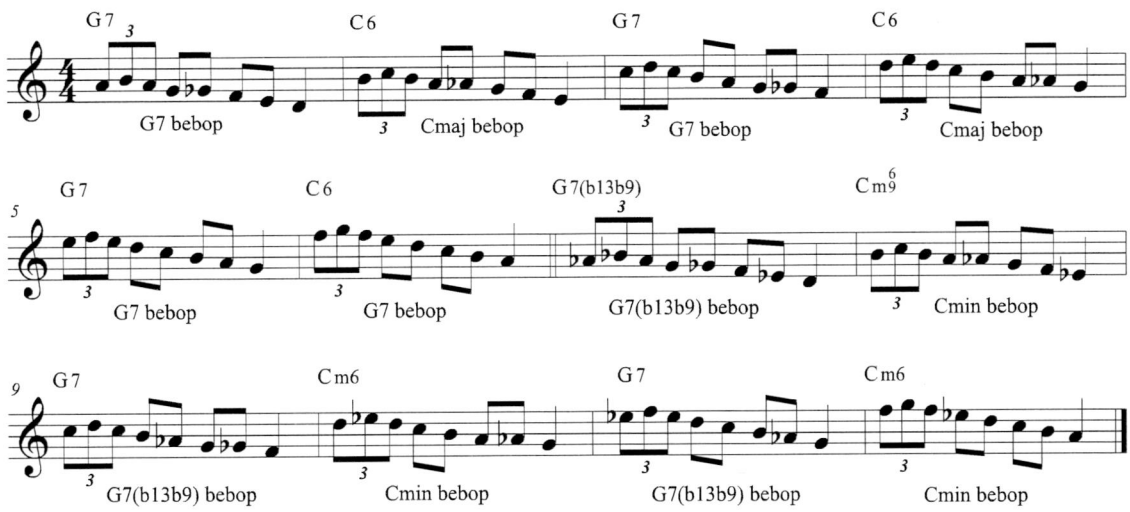

Playing an ascending triplet arpeggio on beat 2 or beat 4 (with an approach tone or chord tone on the preceding upbeat) and then descending via bebop scale on beat 3 or 1 is also a very effective use of the triplet. Here are some common examples including an ascending triplet arpeggio followed by a descending G7 bebop scale.

FIG. 9

Here are similar patterns with slight variations in minor employing the G7(b13b9) bebop scale.

FIG. 10

Workout 55: Bebop Scales and Triplets on the changes to Bud Powell's "Ornithology." Play through the last 8 bars of the form using bebop scales and triplets as you solo along with the recording. Refer to **DL TRK 31-32** for a demo and play-along track. On the demo, FIG. 11 is played during the last eight bars of the first chorus.

FIG. 11

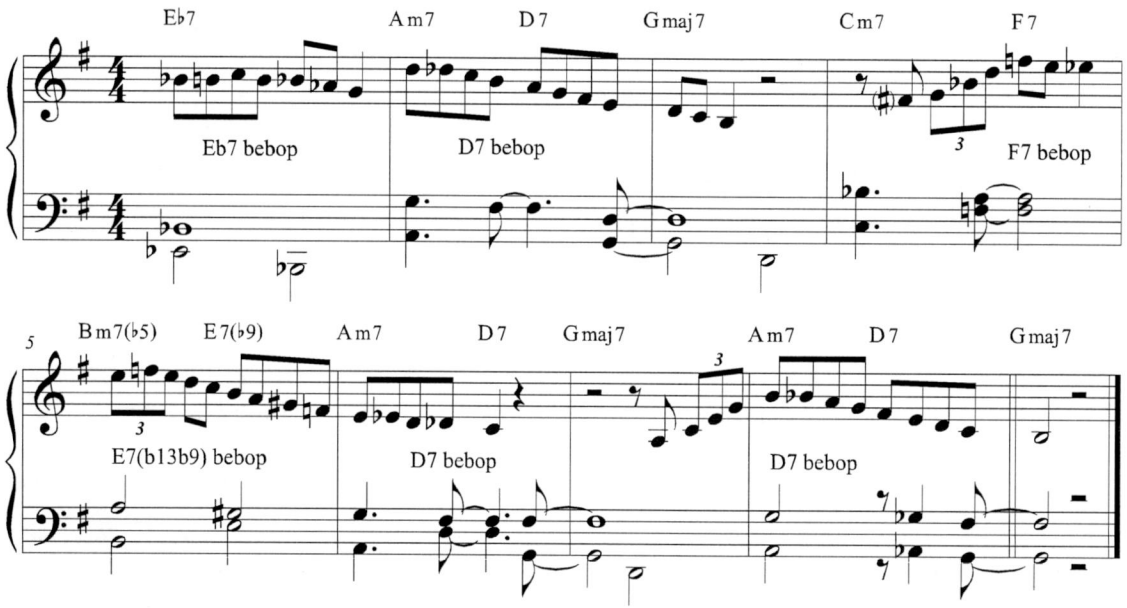

When applying bebop scales to diminished seventh chords, using harmonic minor with an added chromatic maj7th is usually the way to go. Creating a bebop scale out of the W/H diminished scale is not as common, since the scale already has 8 notes.

Workout 56: Bebop Scales and Triplets on the changes to Al Haig's "'S Wonderful." Play through the last 8 bars of the form using bebop scales and triplets. Observe the biiio7 chord in m. 3–4 and apply a bebop scale derived from harmonic minor. In this case, the chord scale associated with Gbo7 is the 7th mode of G harmonic minor. So, apply the D7(b13b9) bebop scale. Notice how Gbo7(F#o7) is nearly identical to D7(b13b9). The only real difference is the bass note. Refer to DL TRK 33-34 for a demo and play-along track. On the demo, FIG. 12 is played during the last eight bars of the first chorus.

FIG. 12

Workout 57: Combining Melodic Building Blocks. Finally, here is one complete solo chorus of "Ornithology" using a mixture of all four melodic building blocks: 5-note Patterns, Arpeggio-Patterns, Approach tones/Enclosures, and Bebop scales. Use this as a starting point, as you play along with Charlie Parker's famous recording, *One Night in Birdland*. Refer to DL TRK 31-32 for a demo and play-along track. On the demo, FIG. 13 is played during the third chorus. If some of the LH structures are too big, use your RH to play the top note of the LH voicing. Build your own solo on a tune of your choice and play along with your favorite recording.

Chapter 6 • D

FIG. 13

Combining Melodic Building Blocks
On the Changes to "Ornithology"

Transcribing Solos and Assimilating What You Transcribe

Now that you have an idea of how to create patterns from scales and construct some bebop-type phrases, it's time to actually go to the primary source and figure out what the masters are truly playing on the recordings. This is actually the first step to learning how to improvise. Once you open your eyes and ears to the treasure trove of beautiful material found on the classic jazz recordings you will have a never-ending source of musical inspiration. Transcribing what you hear is the key to unlocking this incredibly rich wellspring of jazz information.

Since the beginning, jazz musicians have learned from their elders, as apprentices, at jam sessions, from live performances, from piano rolls, from 45s, LPs, from cassette tapes, from CDs, from videos, etc. It's essentially an aural tradition.

Transcribing music is the process of transferring notes that you hear on a recording onto paper in written notation. Learning solos by ear is also very valuable, and perhaps an even more important skill to develop. Whether you write it down and then memorize it, or learn it by ear from the beginning, the important thing is to soak up the information from the recording. Unlike a transcription that is already done for you (easily found online or in a transcription book), a transcription you do yourself contains countless musical elements that exist other than the notes. These include touch, dynamics, swing feel, the overall vibe of the album, etc., crucial to developing a sound, and developing your own jazz feel.

Here are 15 accessible solos suggested to transcribe. Notice how the list includes horn solos as well. Pianists can learn so much from non-piano players especially when it comes to creating lines. Of course, there are thousands of other solos that would be just as suitable, it's just that with so much information available nowadays, having some specific direction might be helpful. Begin with transcribing just one.

SUGGESTED SOLOS TO TRANSCRIBE

1. Horace Silver's piano solo on "Funk in Deep Freeze" from Hank Mobley's album, *Hank Mobley Quintet,* Blue Note, (BLP 1550)
2. Horace Silver's piano solo on "Walkin' the Fence" from Hank Mobley's album, *Hank Mobley Quartet*, Blue Note, (BLP 5066)
3. Horace Silver's piano solo on "Home Cookin'" from Horace Silver's album, *The Stylings of Silver*, Blue Note, (BLP 1562)
4. Sonny Clark's piano solo on "Don't Get Too Hip" from Hank Mobley's album, *Curtain Call*, Blue Note (BNJ 61006)
5. Sonny Clark's piano solo on "Blue Minor" from Sonny Clark's album, Cool Struttin', Blue Note (BLP 1588)
6. Sonny Clark's piano solo on "Jubilee Shout" from Stanley Turrentine's album, *Jubilee Shout!!!*, Blue Note (BST 84122)

7. Wynton Kelly's piano solo on "Temperance" from Wynton Kelly's album, *Kelly at Midnight*, Vee-Jay
8. Wynton Kelly's piano solo on "Softly as in a Morning Sunrise" from Wynton Kelly's album, *Kelly Blue*, Riverside
9. Bud Powell's piano solo on "Celia" from Bud Powell's album, *Jazz Giant*, Norgran/Verve
10. Bud Powell's piano solo on "Bouncin' with Bud" from Bud Powell's album, *The Amazing Bud Powell Vol. 1*, Blue Note (BLP 5003)
11. Miles Davis's trumpet solo on "So What" from Miles Davis' album, *Kind of Blue*, Columbia
12. J.J. Johnson's trombone solo on "Pennies from Heaven" from J.J. Johnson's album, *The Eminent Jay Jay Johnson Vol. 2*, Blue Note (BLP 5057)
13. Hank Mobley's tenor solo on "The Best Things in Life are Free" from Hank Mobley's album, *Workout*, Blue Note (BST 84080)
14. Charlie Parker's alto solo on "Cool Blues" Master, Take C from Charlie Parker's album, *Charlie Parker on Dial*, Disc 2, Spotlite Records
15. Charlie Parker's alto solo on "Home Cooking 3 (I Got Rhythm) from Charlie Parker's album, *Charlie Parker on Dial*, Disc 1, Spotlite Records

The goal here is to memorize the solo. Begin with 2 or 4 bars. After memorizing them go to the next 2 or 4. Memorize the whole solo like this, in small digestible portions. Don't be alarmed, this process is very tedious and takes some patience. The important thing is to go through the hard work. It will pay off.

The many transcription aids available to you now can be helpful. It's important to be able to slow things down, and also to be able to fine tune things from old recordings that may be in between pitches.

Transcribing allows you to play along with your heroes. At this point it's all about imitation. When the recording melts away and you blend together with the sound of whom you are transcribing it can be a magical feeling.

Start simple. Try just the RH if you are transcribing a piano player. Figure out single lines. Eventually the sound of chords will become sounds that you recognize. The way green is green, Ab13#11 eventually is Ab13#11. But this process takes time.

Below are some transcription tips to get you started down this long road.

HELPFUL TIPS FOR TRANSCRIBING:

1. Listen to the whole solo 10 times. Sing along with the section to be transcribed.
2. Identify the form, key, and the basic chord progression.
3. Identify the style.
4. Identify the instruments. Decide on whether you are going to write it out in concert or transposed.
5. Identify the time signature.
6. Identify the tempo of the quarter note. In many cases you can simply listen to the bass player's quarter notes.
7. Sing the first phrase several times. Try playing it on your instrument without writing anything down.
8. In order to write it down, or to play it back accurately, you need to find beat 1. Does the solo start as a pick up, or after beat 1?
9. Decide on the type of notes the soloist plays to open his solo (quarters, eighths, triplets, etc.)
10. After completing the first phrase you can use it as a guide to help with subsequent phrases.
11. If you can't hear a whole phrase and sing it back, try learning it in sections. Sometimes writing noteheads only first can be helpful. After writing the noteheads, find a musical landmark by matching a musical event with a rhythmic event. For example, maybe the soloist plays a C on beat 2, and then F on beat 1 of the next measure. Usually you can fill in the missing material if you have 2 or more musical landmarks that you are sure of.
12. After transcribing a particular musician's solo or arrangement a style will begin to emerge helping you predict what might come next. Everyone has a style, or identifying characteristic that can help you figure out a tough spot. For example, ask questions such as: does the pianist have a large hand or small hand? Is it a figure or chord voicing characteristic of this pianist? Etc.

Workout 58: Playing a Transcription along with a Classic Recording. Transcribe your choice of solo(s) and play the solo for memory along with the original recording. Feel free to slow the recording down. Ultimately, strive to play it at tempo. Try to blend your solo with the recording so that it becomes one solo.

Assimilating a Solo

Taking elements from the solo and developing them into your own language is called assimilation. Besides imitating, assimilating can be crucial to your growth as a jazz musician. Rushing to this second step, however, is a mistake. Spend a week or more just playing the solo as is, savoring the nuances and all of the little details before analyzing it, taking it apart, and creating licks from it.

I believe sometimes cutting up solos into licks and transposing the licks to all 12 keys sort of destroys the essence and beauty of the original solo. On the other hand, having a solo frozen in time, stuck as is, in the transcription state, can also be largely unhelpful to your development as a jazz musician. Perhaps the worst thing is to learn a solo only by muscle memory, and then marvel at yourself as you go through the motions of playing the solo up to speed, but having no idea of the content as it flies by.

To get started, let's pretend that you have already transcribed and memorized Bud Powell's groundbreaking solo on his composition, "Celia," from *Jazz Giant*.

Below Bud Powell's famous solo break is extracted.

FIG. 1

The first step to assimilating is to make sure the material is short enough to fully digest and in a form that's easy to manipulate. The break is complex because it's too long and in double time.

Here is a more manageable portion starting from the "and" of 2 in the second bar. In the new easier variation, the pattern starts from the "and" of 4 and is written in eighth notes. This way the pattern still ends on beat 1.

Chord symbols have been written in to make the assimilation process easier. In addition, chord tones, tensions, and approach tones are labeled to show how the solo relates to the chord symbols.

FIG. 2

For this to be a living and breathing phrase that you can use in your own playing you have to be able to do these things:

1. Understand how it fits on the chord(s)/understand how it is constructed
2. Elongate it/Shorten it to fit different situations without changing its identity
3. Create small variations without changing its identity
4. Find places where you can change octaves to change the overall direction of the phrase without changing its identity
5. Rhythmically displace the whole phrase
6. Transpose It
7. Alter the modality without destroying its identity, to make major and minor ii–V–Is
8. Apply it to Standard Songs

The phrase is made up of two chromatic approach tones leading to the 5th of iim7, a descending arpeggio from 5th of iim7 to the 3rd of V7, then a 3-note enclosure of the 5th of tonic major.

Here are two other variations, one shorter than the original, one longer. Note how both the elongated and truncated variation still preserves the key points of the phrase: the 5th of iim7 moving to the 3rd of V7, and then to the 5th of tonic major.

FIG. 3

FIG. 4

By changing the direction of the approach tones so that they approach the 5th of iim7 from below, you can introduce small variations without changing the identity of the phrase.

FIG. 5

By inverting the pattern or pivoting, you can change the overall direction of the phrase while retaining the same notes.

FIG. 6

Experiment with starting the phrase on a different beat. The following two examples are displaced rhythmically.

FIG. 7

FIG. 8

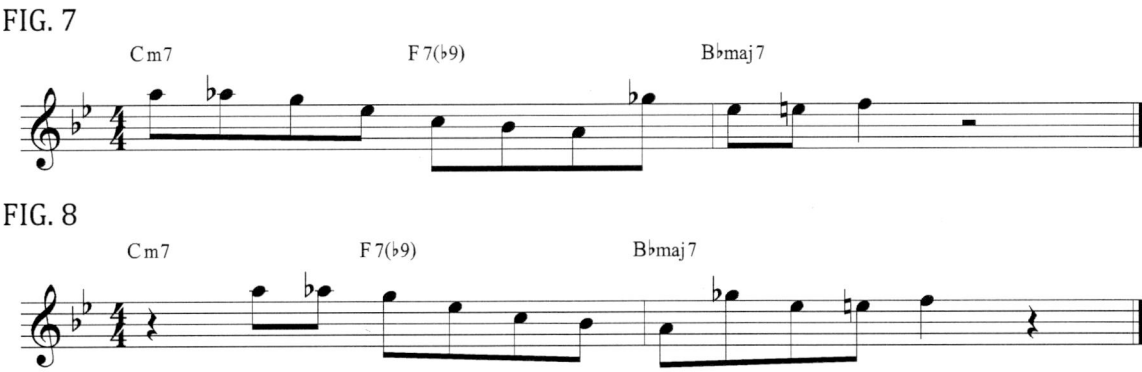

Try transposing the phrase around the circle of 4ths, up and down in half steps, in whole steps, in minor thirds, etc.

FIG. 9

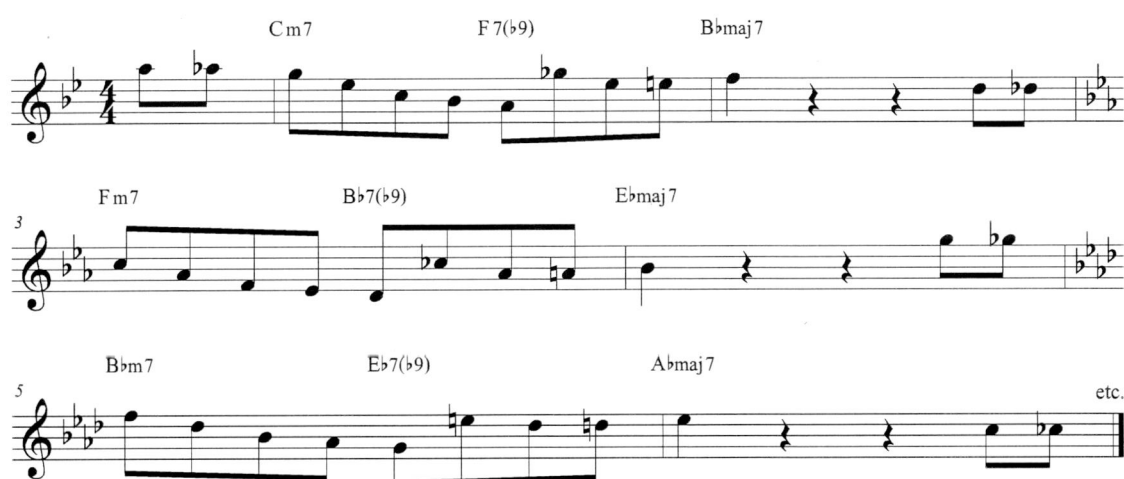

For the final step, find ways of altering a few notes so that the phrase can work in a different modality. In this case by changing the approach tones so that they target b5 from above or below, the phrase can be changed to work in minor.

FIG. 10

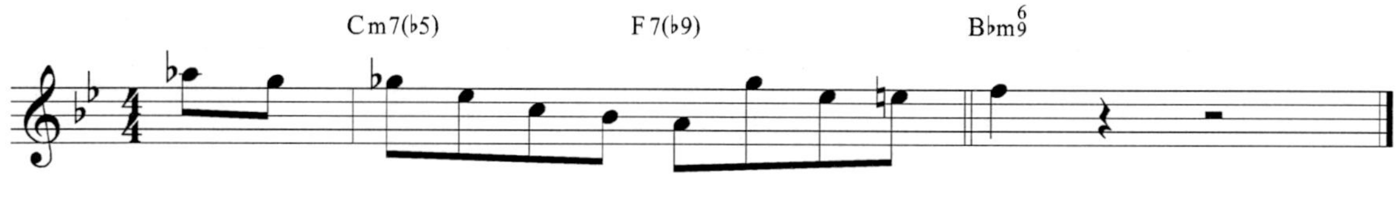

FIG. 11

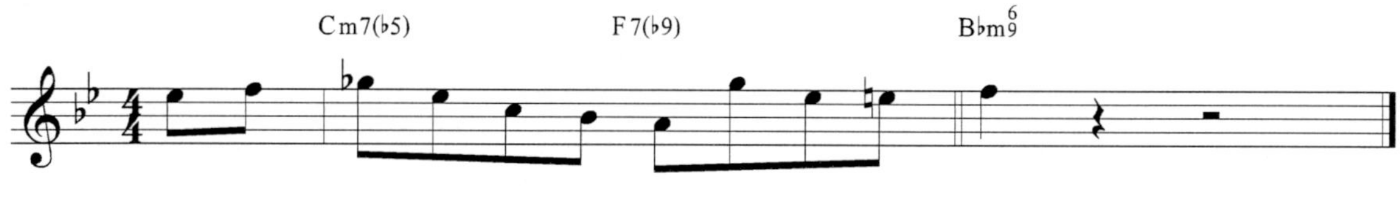

At this point, not only can you transpose the phrase easily because you understand where it starts on the chord, you can elongate it, shorten it, introduce small variations, change its direction, change the rhythmic placement, and change the modality. In other words, you know it backwards and forwards. Now is the right time to apply it to a tune. Without going through these steps, it's only a lick that you can cut and paste. After completing this assimilation process, the phrase and all of its variations become something more personal and organic.

Workout 59: Applying the Assimilated Bud Powell Phrase on the changes to John Lewis' "Afternoon in Paris." Here is one possibility for the first eight bars. Find other variations and continue through the tune as you solo along with the recording.

FIG. 12

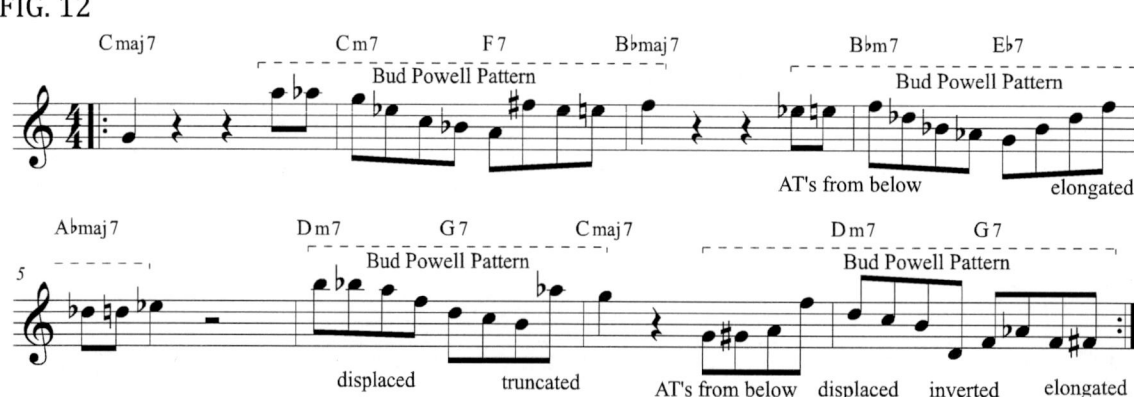

Workout 60: Applying the Assimilated Bud Powell Phrase on the changes to "Hot House" as played by Bud Powell. Here is one possibility for the first eight bars. This time some of the other devices from earlier in the chapter are incorporated. Find other variations and continue through the tune as you solo along with the recording.

FIG. 13

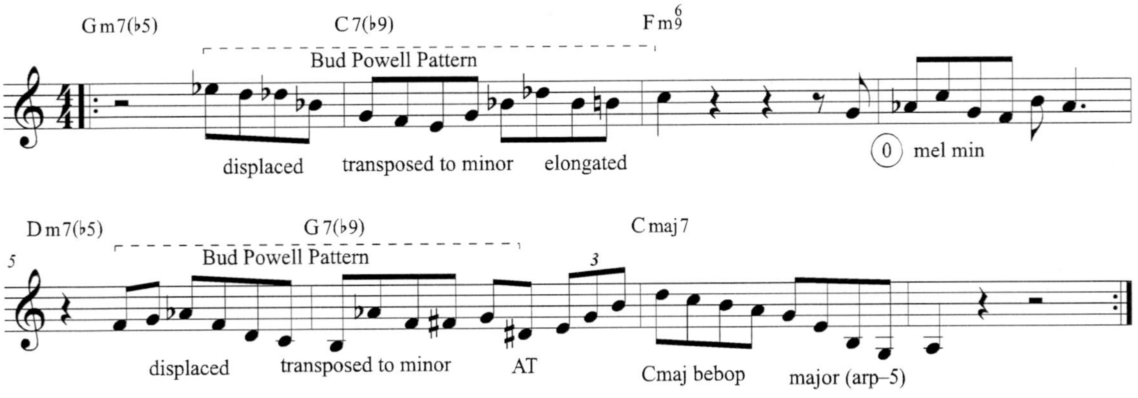

Duet 7: Soloing and Comping. Player 1 plays a RH solo over LH shells using the melodic devices and building blocks from Chapter 6. Player 2 comps using a mixture of open and closed position voicings. Practice grooving without drums or bass. Both players should internalize the quarter note pulse and be able to swing together in time.

Appendix
List of Workouts with Corresponding Discography

Workout 1: Comping with Triads on the changes to "When the Saints Go Marching In"
as performed by Louis Armstrong from *Louis Armstrong–Classics: New Orleans to New York*
Decca DL 5225(1950) 11

Workout 2: Comping with Triads and Basic Seventh Chords on the changes to "Sunday Mornin'" by Grant Green from *Sunday Mornin'*, Blue Note, BST 84099 (1961) 15

Workout 3: Comping with Triads on the changes to "Slow Freight"
by Ray Bryant from *Slow Freight*, Cadet–LPS-781 (1966) 21

Workout 4: Comping with Triads on the changes to "A Caddy for Daddy"
by Hank Mobley from *A Caddy for Daddy*, Blue Note, BST 84230 (1966)...................... 22

Workout 5: Comping with Triads on the changes to "I Wonder Who"
as performed by Ray Charles from *The Genius Sings the Blues*, Atlantic Records
SD-8052 (1961) 24

Workout 6: Comping with Triads on the changes to "Good Morning Mr. Blues"
as performed by Otis Spann from *Good Morning Mr. Blues,* Everest FS 216/Storyville SLP 157
(1963) 25

Workout 7: Playing a Single Line Melody on the changes to "Bags' Groove"
as performed by Miles Davis from *Bags' Groove*, Prestige, PRLP 7109 (1957) 28

Workout 8: Playing a Riff Blues on the changes to "Centerpiece"
by Harry "Sweets" Edison from *Sweetenings*, Roulette, SR 52023 (1958)...................... 30

Workout 9: Playing a Riff Blues on the changes to "Ev'ry Day I Have the Blues"
as performed by Joe Williams from *Count Basie Swings, Joe Williams Sings*, Clef,
MG C-678 (1955).. 32

Workout 10: Comping with Guide Tones on the changes to "Perdido"
by Duke Ellington from *The Best of the Duke Ellington Centennial Edition*, RCA Victor/RCA
09026634592 (1941-1945) 40

Workout 11: Comping with Guide Tones on the changes to "All of Me"
as performed by Sarah Vaughan from *Swingin' Easy*, EmArcy 36109 (1957)................... 42

Appendix

Workout 12: Practicing Upbeats on the changes to "Bluesville"
as performed by Sonny Red from *Out of the Blue*, Blue Note, BST 84032 (1959) 44

Workout 13: Basic Comping Rhythms on the changes to "Perdido"
by Duke Ellington (see Workout 10) 48

Workout 14: Basic Comping Rhythms on the changes to "It Could Happen To You"
as performed by Miles Davis from *Relaxin' with the Miles Davis Quintet*, Prestige,
PRLP 7129 (1958) 48

Workout 15: Playing the Melody over Shells on the changes to "All of Me"
as performed by Sarah Vaughan (see Workout 11) 53

Workout 16: Playing the Melody over Shells on the changes to "Autumn Leaves"
as performed by Cannonball Adderley from *Somethin' Else*, Blue Note, BLP 1595 (1958) 54

Workout 17: Jammin' with Sonny Clark on "Blues Blue"
from *The Sonny Clark Trio*, Time Records, T 70010 (1960) 55

Workout 18: Guide Tone Voicings with Doubled Notes on the changes to "Sippin' At Bells"
as performed by Sonny Clark from *Cool Struttin'*, Blue Note, BLP 1588 (1958) 57

**Workout 19: Guide Tone Voicings with Doubled Notes on the changes to
"For Heaven's Sake"** as performed by Kenny Barron from *Minor Blues*, Venus Records,
VHCD-78154 (2010).. 59

Workout 20: Guide Tone Voicings with Doubled Notes on the changes to "Bye Bye Blackbird"
as performed by Miles Davis from *'Round about Midnight*, [2] Columbia Records, CL 949 (1957)   60

**Workout 21: Movable Guide Tone Voicings with Double Notes on the changes to
"Autumn Leaves"** as performed by Cannonball Adderley (see Workout 16) 63

Workout 22: Compact 3-note Voicings on the changes to "Broadway"
as performed by Ahmad Jamal from *Ahmad Jamal's Alhambra*, Argo LPS-685 (1961) 68

Workout 23: Compact 3-note Voicings on the changes to "Alone Together"
as performed by Sonny Stitt from *Sonny Stitt Quartet–New York Jazz*, Verve–MG V-8219 (1957).... 70

Workout 24: Compact 3-note Voicings on the changes to "Blues Blue"
by Sonny Clark from *My Conception* (different than Sonny Clark Trio),
Blue Note–7243 5 22674 2 2 (2000) (originally recorded in 1957, 1959) 71

Appendix

Workout 25: LH Compact 3-note Voicings on the changes to "Broadway"
as performed by Ahmad Jamal (see Workout 22)..72

Workout 26: Big band-Style Voicings on the changes to "Alone Together"
as performed by Sonny Stitt (see Workout 23)...75

Workout 27: Big band-Style Voicings on the changes to "Blues Blue"
by Sonny Clark (see Workout 24)...77

Workout 28: 4-note Close A and B Position Voicings on the changes to "Stompin' at the Savoy" as performed by Clifford Brown from *Brown and Roach Inc.*,
EmArcy MG 36008 (1955)...81

Workout 29: 4-note Close A and B Position Voicings on the changes to "Sweet Pumpkin"
as performed by Blue Mitchell from *Blue's Moods*, Riverside RLP 336 (1960)..................83

Workout 30: 4-note Close A and B Position Voicings on the changes to "Woody'n You" as
performed by Miles Davis (see Workout 14)..84

Workout 31: Comping with "Little Chords" on the changes to "Lester Leaps In"
by Lester Young from *Lester Young –The Complete Aladdin Recordings*,
Blue Note–CDP 7243 8 32787 2 5 (1995) (originally recorded 1946).........................89

**Workout 32: Using "Little Chords" for Altered Dominants on the changes to
"Lester Leaps In"** as performed by Sonny Stitt from *Now!*, Impulse A-43 (1963)..............91

Workout 33: Comping with "Little Chords" on the changes to "Hot House" as performed by
the Quintet from *Jazz at Massey Hall*, Debut/OJC America (1953)..............................92

Workout 34: Comping using "Little Chords" on the changes to "These Foolish Things" as
performed by Frank Sinatra from The Voice of Frank Sinatra, Columbia
CL-6001 (33 rpm) (1945)...96

Workout 35: Creating Comping Rhythms on the changes to "Cool Struttin"
by Sonny Clark from *Cool Struttin'*, Blue Note, BLP 1588 (1958)................................98

Workout 36: Comping the Accents on the changes to "Confirmation"
by Charlie Parker from *Charlie Parker*, Clef Records, MG C-157 (1954).........................99

Workout 37: Comping the Spaces on the changes to "Confirmation"
by Charlie Parker (see Workout 36)...99

Appendix

**Workout 38: Playing Simple Open Position Chords on the changes to
"Polka Dots and Moonbeams"** as performed by Chet Baker from *Chet Baker in
New York*, Riverside Records, RLP 12-281 (1958) 109

Workout 39: Playing UST Voicings on the changes to "Polka Dots and Moonbeams"
(see Workout 38)..116

Workout 40: Playing Spread Voicings on the changes to "Polka Dots and Moonbeams"
(see Workout 38)..121

Workout 41: Playing Drop- Voicings on the changes to "Polka Dots and Moonbeams"
(see Workout 38)..125

Workout 42: Playing 4th-like Voicings on the changes to "On Green Dolphin Street"
as performed by Miles Davis from *1958 Miles*, a compilation album on Columbia released
in 1974, originally recorded in 1958 127

**Workout 43: Comping along with Red Garland during Miles Davis' Solo on the changes
to "Trane's Blues"** as performed by Miles Davis from *Workin' with the Miles Davis Quintet*,
Prestige PRLP 7166 (1959) (recorded in 1956) 128

Workout 44: Playing Block Chords on the changes to "Afternoon in Paris"
by John Lewis from *Bud Powell/Sonny Stitt/J.J. Johnson*, Prestige PRLP 7024 (1957)
(recorded 1949) 141

Workout 45: Playing Block Chords on the changes to "Lullaby of Birdland"
as performed by Sarah Vaughan from *Sarah Vaughan*, EmArcy MG-36004 (1954).............149

Workout 46: Playing Block Chords on the changes to "Softly, as in a Morning Sunrise"
as performed by Sonny Clark from *Sonny Clark Trio*, Blue Note, BLP 1579 (1959).............157

Workout 47: Playing Block Chords on the changes to "Someday My Prince Will Come"
as performed by Miles Davis from *Miles Davis Sextet–Someday My Prince Will Come*,
Columbia CS 8456 (1961) 165

Workout 48: Playing Block Chords on the changes to Duke Ellington's "Passion Flower"
by Duke Ellington as performed by Duke Ellington and Ella Fitzgerald from
Ella at Duke's Place, Verve Records V-4070 (1965) 172

Workout 49: 5-note Scale Fragments on the changes to "Ornithology"
as played by Bud Powell from *The Amazing Bud Powell*, Blue Note–1503 (1956)
(originally recorded in 1949) 180

Appendix

Workout 50: 5-note Scale Fragments on the changes to "'S Wonderful"
as performed by Al Haig from *Al Haig Trio*, Vogue Records L.D.E 092 UK (1954)...............182

Workout 51: Arpeggios on the changes to "Ornithology" by Bud Powell
(see Workout 49)..186

Workout 52: Arpeggios on the changes to " 'S Wonderful"
as performed by Al Haig (see Workout 50)...189

Workout 53: Approach Tones and Enclosures on the changes to "Ornithology"
by Bud Powell (see Workout 49)..194

Workout 54: Approach Tones and Enclosures on the changes to "'So Wonderful"
as performed by Al Haig (see Workout 50)...195

Workout 55: Bebop Scales and Triplets on the changes to "Ornithology"
by Bud Powell (see Workout 49)..202

Workout 56: Bebop Scales and Triplets on the changes to " 'S Wonderful"
as performed by Al Haig (see Workout 50)...203

Workout 57: Combining Melodic Building Blocks on the changes to "Ornithology"
by Charlie Parker from *One Night in Birdland*, Columbia JG 34808 (1977)
(originally recorded in 1950)...203

Workout 58: Playing a Transcription along with a Classic Recording....................208

**Workout 59: Applying the Assimilated Bud Powell Phrase on the changes to
"Afternoon in Paris"** by John Lewis (see Workout 44) 212

Workout 60: Applying the Assimilated Bud Powell Phrase on the changes to "Hot House"
by the Quintet (Charlie Parker, Dizzy Gillespie, Bud Powell, Charles Mingus, and Max Roach)
(see Workout 33)..213

List of Duets

Duet 1: Accompanying a Riff Blues with a Triadic Comping Pattern (Chapter 1) 33

Duet 2: Accompanying a Melody using Guide Tone Voicings (Chapter 2) 64

Duet 3: Interacting with a Soloist on the Blues, Part 1 (Chapter 3) 100

Duet 4: Interacting with a Soloist on the Blues, Part 2 (Chapter 3) 100

Duet 5: Accompanying a Soloist Using Open Position Voicings (Chapter 4) 127

Duet 6: Working Out on the 5 Important Scales (Chapter 5) 173

Duet 7: Soloing and Comping (Chapter 6) 213

Exercises

2-Handed Warm Up Exercises for Building Technique

FIG. 1

2-Handed Major Scale Exercise
Continuous Arpeggios in 10ths

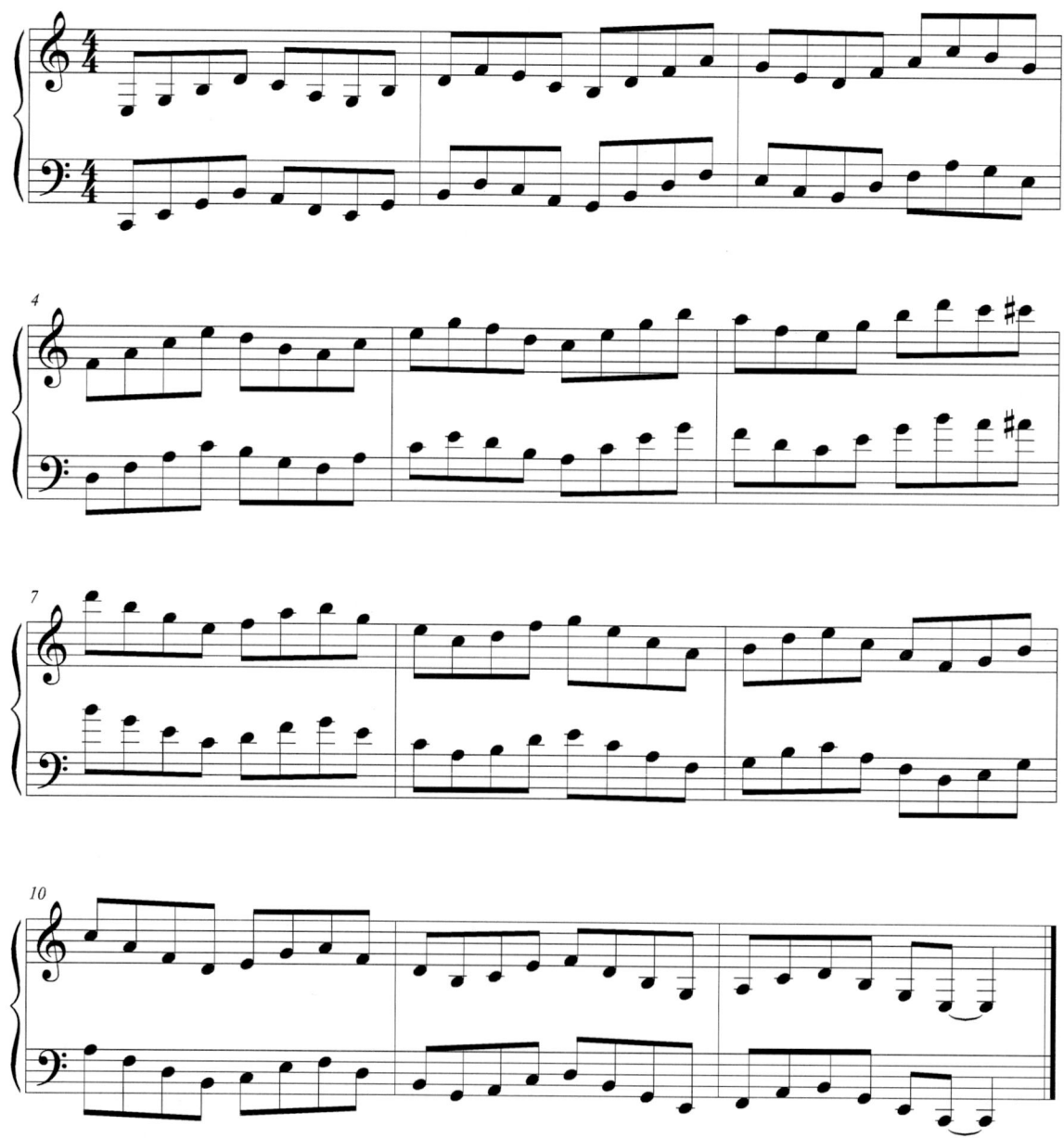

220

Exercises

FIG. 2

2-Handed Tonic Minor Scale Exercise
Continuous Arpeggios in 10ths

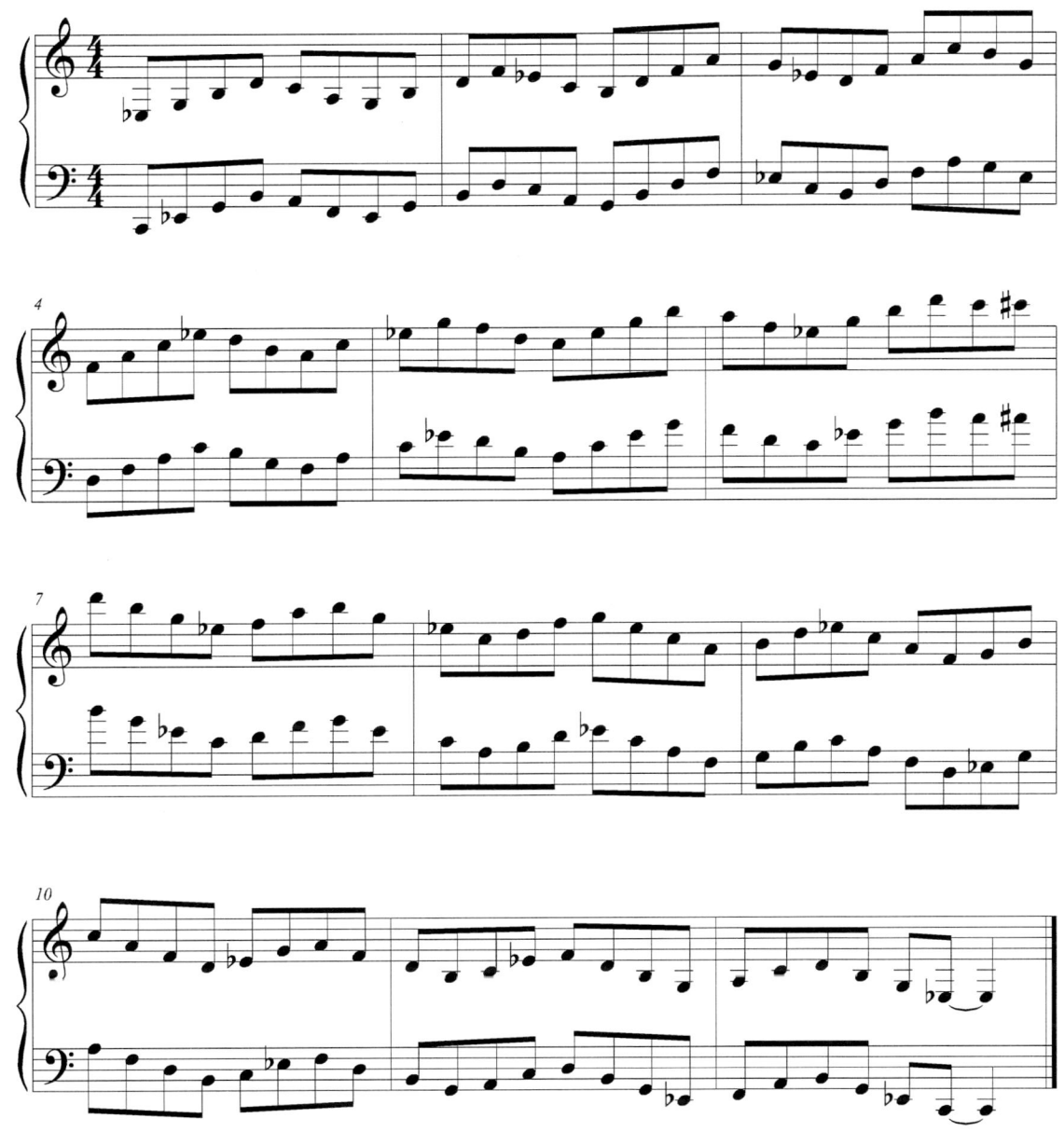

Exercises

FIG. 3

2-Handed Harmonic Minor Scale Exercise
Continuous Arpeggios in 10ths

FIG. 4

2-Handed Diminished Scale Exercise
Continuous Arpeggios in 10ths

Exercises

FIG. 5

2-Handed Whole Tone Scale Exercise
Continuous Arpeggios in 10ths

Play/Comp Along CD Information

TRACK

1 : changes to "When the Saints Go Marching In" (demo)
2 : changes to "When the Saints Go Marching In" (no piano)
3 : changes to "Sunday Mornin'" (demo)
4 : changes to "Sunday Mornin'" (no piano)
5 : changes to "I Wonder Who" (demo)
6 : changes to "I Wonder Who" (no piano)
7 : changes to "Perdido" (demo)
8 : changes to "Perdido" (no piano)
9 : changes to "Autumn Leaves" (demo)
10 : changes to "Autumn Leaves" (no piano)
11 : changes to "Alone Together" (demo)
12 : changes to "Alone Together" (no piano)
13 : F blues (demo)
14 : F blues (no piano)
15 : changes to "Sweet Pumpkin" (demo)
16 : changes to "Sweet Pumpkin" (no piano)
17 : Rhythm Changes (demo)
18 : Rhythm Changes (no piano)
19 : changes to "Polka Dots and Moonbeams" (demo)
20 : changes to "Polka Dots and Moonbeams" (no piano)
21 : changes to "Afternoon in Paris" (demo)
22 : changes to "Afternoon in Paris" (no piano)
23 : changes to "Lullaby of Birdland" (demo)
24 : changes to "Lullaby of Birdland" (no piano)
25 : changes to "Softly as in a Morning Sunrise" (demo)
26 : changes to "Softly as in a Morning Sunrise" (no piano)
27 : changes to "Someday my Prince will Come" (demo)
28 : changes to "Someday my Prince will Come" (no piano)
29 : changes to "Passion Flower" (demo)
30 : changes to "Passion Flower" (no piano)
31 : changes to "Ornithology" (demo)
32 : changes to "Ornithology" (no piano)
33 : changes to " 'S Wonderful" (demo)
34 : changes to " 'S Wonderful" (no piano)

The Sher Music Co. Catalog
visit SherMusic.com for more information and to order online.

BEST-SELLING BOOKS BY MARK LEVINE
The Jazz Theory Book
The Jazz Piano Book
Jazz Piano Masterclass: The Drop 2 Book
How To Voice Standards at the Piano

THE WORLD'S BEST FAKE BOOKS
The New Real Book - Vol. 1 - C, Bb and Eb
The New Real Book - Vol. 2 - C, Bb and Eb
The New Real Book - Vol. 3 - C, Bb, Eb & Bass Clef

The Real Easy Book - Vol. 1 - C, Bb, Eb & Bass Clef
The Real Easy Book - Vol. 2 - C, Bb, Eb & Bass Clef
The Real Easy Book - Vol. 3 - C, Bb, Eb & Bass Clef
The Latin Real Easy Book - C, Bb, Eb & Bass Clef
Drum Supplement for Real Easy Book - Vol. 1

The Standards Real Book - C, Bb and Eb
The Latin Real Book - C, Bb and Eb
The Real Cool Book - Octet charts from the 1950s
The All-Jazz Real Book - with selected audio
The European Real Book - with selected audio
The Best of Sher Music Real Books - C, Bb & Eb
The World's Greatest Fake Book - C only
Jazz Arrangements of Public Domain Songs
The Yellowjackets Songbook - separate parts

LATIN MUSIC BOOKS
Contemporary Latin Jazz Guitar - by Neff Irizarry
Decoding Afro-Cuban Jazz - by Mauleon & Valdes
The Salsa Guidebook - by Rebeca Mauleõn
101 Montunos - by Rebeca Mauleõn
The Latin Bass Book - by Oscar Stagnaro & Chuck Sher
The Latin Real Book - C, Bb, & Eb
The True Cuban Bass - by Carlos del Puerto
The Brazilian Guitar Book - by Nelson Faria
Inside the Brazilian Rhythm Section - Faria/Korman
Conga Drummer's Guidebook - by Michael Spiro
Language of the Masters - by Michael Spiro
Introduction to the Conga Drum DVD - by M. Spiro
Afro-Caribbean Grooves for Drumset - JPhi Fanfant
Afro-Peruvian Percussion Ensemble - H. Morales
Flamenco Improvisation - Vol.1-3 by Enrique Vargas
Muy Caliente! - Afro-Cuban Book & Play-Aong audio
Music of the Arará Savalú Cabildo - Galvin & Spiro

DIGITAL FAKE BOOKS
The New Real Book - Vol.1 - C, Bb & Eb
The Digital Standards Songbook - individual songs with lyrics, plus C, Bb, Eb, High Voice & Low Voice
The Digital Real Book (650 songs from all our books)

THE DIGITAL SONGBOOK SERIES
The Kenny Barron Songbook
The Carla Bley Songbook
The Tom Harrell Songbook
The Oscar Hernandez Songbook
The Alan Pasqua Songbook
The Horace Silver Songbook
The Steve Swallow Songbook
The Ralph Towner Songbook
The Wayne Wallace Songbook
The Kenner Werner Songbook
The Randy Brecker Songbook
The Larry Dunlap Songbook
The Barry Finnerty Songbook
The Benny Golson Songbook
The Steve Khan Songbook
The Doug Morton Songbook
The Andy Narell Songbook
The Enrico Pieranunzi Songbook
The Dave Tull Songbook
The Denny Zeitlin Songbook

FOR STUDENT MUSICIANS
The Real Easy Book - Vol. 1 - C, Bb, Eb & Bass Clef
The Real Easy Book - Vol. 2 - C, Bb, Eb & Bass Clef
The Real Easy Book - Vol. 3 - C, Bb, Eb & Bass Clef
The Latin Real Easy Book - C, Bb, Eb & Bass Clef
Drum Supplement for Real Easy Book - Vol. 1
The Blues Scales - C, Bb, Eb, Bass Clef & Guitar
Rhythm First! - C, Bb, Eb & Bass Clef - by Tom Kamp
Guitarist's Introduction to Jazz - by Randy Vincent
Walking Bassics - by Ed Fuqua
Foundation Exercises for Bass - by Chuck Sher

CDs
Poetry+Jazz: A Magical Marriage - by Chuck Sher
Play-Along CDs for The New Real Book - Vol.1
The Latin Real Book Sampler CD

continued on next page

Sher Music Co. JAZZ METHOD BOOKS
available in both print & digital forms

GUITAR
- **Jazz Guitar Voicings: The Drop 2 Book** - Randy Vincent
- **Three-Note Voicings and Beyond** - Randy Vincent
- **Line Games** - Randy Vincent
- **Jazz Guitar Soloing: The Cellular Approach** - Randy Vincent
- **The Guitarist's Introduction to Jazz** - Randy Vincent
- **Contemporary Latin Jazz Guitar** - Neff Irizarry

PIANO
- **The Jazz Piano Book** - Mark Levine
- **Jazz Piano Masterclass: The Drop 2 Book** - M. Levine
- **How To Voice Standards at the Piano** - Mark Levine
- **An Approach to Comping - Vol. 1** - Jeb Patton
- **An Approach to Comping - Vol. 2** - Jeb Patton
- **Introduction to Jazz Piano: A Deep Dive** - Jeb Patton
- **Playing for Singers** - Mike Greensill
- **Wisdom of the Hand** - Marius Nordal
- **The Jazz Solos of Chick Corea** - Peter Sprague

SAXOPHONE
- **The Practice Notebooks of Michael Brecker**
- **The Jazz Saxophone Book** - Tim Armacost

VOiCE
- **The Digital Standards Songbook** - individual songs with lyrics, plus C, Bb, Eb, High Voice & Low Voice
- **The Jazz Singer's Guidebook** - David Berkman

DRUMS
- **Syncopation Companion** - Bryan Bowman
- **Inner Drumming** - George Marsh
- **Drum Supplement for Real Easy Book Vol.1** - Alan Hall
- **Afro-Caribbean Grooves for Drumset** - JPhi Fanfant

TRUMPET
- **New Orleans Trumpet** - Jim Thornton
- **Modern Etudes for Solo Trumpet** - Cameron Pearce

BASS
- **The Improvisor's Bass Method** - Chuck Sher
- **Concepts for Bass Soloing** - Marc Johnson & C. Sher
- **Walking Bassics** - Ed Fuqua
- **Foundation Exercises for Bass** - Chuck Sher

JAZZ THEORY AND HARMONY
- **The Jazz Theory Book** - Mark Levine
- **The Jazz Harmony Book** - David Berkman
- **Forward Motion** - Hal Galper
- **Metaphors for the Musician** - Randy Halberstadt
- **Minor is Major!** - Dan Greenblatt
- **Rhythm Changes Guide** - Lukas Gabric
- **Jazz Scores and Analysis - Vol.1** - Richard Lawn
- **Jazz Scores and Analysis - Vol. 2** - Richard Lawn
- **The Blues Scales** - C, Bb, Eb, Bass Clef & Guitar - Dan Greenblatt

PRACTICE GUIDES
- **The Practice Notebooks of Michael Brecker**
- **Jazz Musician's Guide to Creative Practicing** - David Berkman
- **The Serious Jazz Practice Book** - Barry Finnerty
- **The Serious Jazz Book II** - Barry Finnerty
- **Building Solo Lines from Cells** - Randy Vincent

EAR TRAINING
- **The Real Easy Ear Training Book** - Roberta Radley
- **Reading, Writing and Rhythmetic** - Roberta Radley

RHYTHM SECTION GUIDES
- **Essential Grooves** - Moretti, Stagnaro & Nicholl
- **Inside the Brazilian Rhythm Section** - Nelson Faria & Cliff Korman
- **The Salsa Guidebook** - Rebeca Mauleón
- **Decoding Afro-Cuban Jazz** - Mauleón & Valdes

BILINGUAL OR LIBROS EN ESPANOL
- **101 Montunos** - Rebeca Mauleón
- **Muy Caliente!** - Afro-Cuban Book & Play-Along
- **El Libro del Jazz Piano** - Mark Levine
- **The Latin Real Book** - C, Bb and Eb

MISCELLANEOUS
- **Method for Chromatic Harmonica** - Max de Aloe
- **Jazz Songs for the Student Violinist** - Kevin Mitchell & Joanne Keefe

Sign up for our monthly discount newsletter by writing shermuse@sonic.net